CASEBOOK SERIES

JANE AUSTEN: *Emma* (Revised) David Lodge
JANE AUSTEN: *'Northanger Abbey' & 'Persuasion'* B. C. Southam
JANE AUSTEN: *'Sense and Sensibility', 'Pride and Prejudice' & 'Mansfield Park'*
  B. C. Southam
BECKETT: *Waiting for Godot* Ruby Cohn
WILLIAM BLAKE: *Songs of Innocence and Experience* Margaret Bottrall
CHARLOTTE BRONTE: *'Jane Eyre' & 'Villette'* Miriam Allott
EMILY BRONTE: *Wuthering Heights* (Revised) Miriam Allott
BROWNING: *'Men and Women' & Other Poems* J. R. Watson
CHAUCER: *The Canterbury Tales* J. J. Anderson
COLERIDGE: *'The Ancient Mariner' & Other Poems* Alun R. Jones & W. Tydeman
CONRAD: *'Heart of Darkness', 'Nostromo' & 'Under Western Eyes'* C. B. Cox
CONRAD: *The Secret Agent* Ian Watt
DICKENS: *Bleak House* A. E. Dyson
DICKENS: *'Hard Times', 'Great Expectations' & 'Our Mutual Friend'* Norman Page
DICKENS: *'Dombey and Son' & 'Little Dorrit'* Alan Shelston
DONNE: *Songs and Sonets* Julian Lovelock
GEORGE ELIOT: *Middlemarch* Patrick Swinden
GEORGE ELIOT: *'The Mill on the Floss' & 'Silas Marner'* R. P. Draper
T. S. ELIOT: *Four Quartets* Bernard Bergonzi
T. S. ELIOT: *'Prufrock', 'Gerontion' & 'Ash Wednesday'* B. C. Southam
T. S. ELIOT: *The Waste Land* C. B. Cox & Arnold P. Hinchliffe
T. S. ELIOT: *Plays* Arnold P. Hinchliffe
HENRY FIELDING: *Tom Jones* Neil Compton
E.M. FORSTER: *A Passage to India* Malcolm Bradbury
WILLIAM GOLDING: *Novels 1954–64* Norman Page
HARDY: *The Tragic Novels* (Revised) R. P. Draper
HARDY: *Poems* James Gibson & Trevor Johnson
HARDY: *Three Pastoral Novels* R. P. Draper
GERARD MANLEY HOPKINS: *Poems* Margaret Bottrall
HENRY JAMES: *'Washington Square' & 'The Portrait of a Lady'* Alan Shelton
JONSON: *Volpone* Jonas A. Barish
JONSON: *'Every Man in his Humour' & 'The Alchemist'* R. V. Holdsworth
JAMES JOYCE: *'Dubliners' & 'A Portrait of the Artist as a Young Man'* Morris Beja
KEATS: *Odes* G.S. Fraser
KEATS: *Narrative Poems* John Spencer Hill
D.H. LAWRENCE: *Sons and Lovers* Gamini Salgado
D.H. LAWRENCE: *'The Rainbow' & 'Women in Love'* Colin Clarke
LOWRY: *Under the Volcano* Gordon Bowker
MARLOWE: *Doctor Faustus* John Jump
MARLOWE: *'Tamburlaine the Great', 'Edward II' & 'The Jew of Malta'* J. R. Brown
MARLOWE: *Poems* Arthur Pollard
MAUPASSANT: *In the Hall of Mirrors* T. Harris
MILTON: *Paradise Lost* A. E. Dyson & Julian Lovelock
O'CASEY: *'Juno and the Paycock', 'The Plough and the Stars' & 'The Shadow of a
  Gunman'* Ronald Ayling
EUGENE O'NEILL: *Three Plays* Normand Berlin
JOHN OSBORNE: *Look Back in Anger* John Russell Taylor
PINTER: *'The Birthday Party' & Other Plays* Michael Scott
POPE: *The Rape of the Lock* John Dixon Hunt
SHAKESPEARE: *A Midsummer Night's Dream* Antony Price
SHAKESPEARE: *Antony and Cleopatra* (Revised) John Russell Brown
SHAKESPEARE: *Coriolanus* B. A. Brockman

Shakespeare

A Midsummer Night's Dream

A CASEBOOK

EDITED BY

ANTONY PRICE

MACMILLAN

First published 1983 by
THE MACMILLAN PRESS LTD
Houndmills, Basingstoke, Hampshire RG21 2XS
and London
Companies and representatives
throughout the world

ISBN 0–333–27013–4

A catalogue record for this book is available
from the British Library.

Printed in Hong Kong

Sixth edition 1994

CONTENTS

Part One: *Critical Comment, 1607–1927*

EDWARD SHARPHAM (1607), p. 25 – SAMUEL PEPYS (1662), p. 25 – JOHN DRYDEN (1667), p 26 – ANONYMOUS (1692), p. 26 – JOHN DOWNES (1708), p. 27 – RICHARD LEVERIDGE (1716), p. 27 – SAMUEL JOHNSON (1765, 1773), p. 28 – ANONYMOUS (1774), p. 30 – S.T. COLERIDGE (? 1811), p. 31 – WILLIAM HAZLITT (1817), p. 31 – HENRY HALLAM (1839), p. 33 – G.G. GERVINUS (1849), p. 34 – H. WOELFFEL (1852), p. 35 – HENRY MORLEY (1853, 1856), p. 36 – BJØRNSTJERNE BJØRNSON (1865), p. 39 – J.O. HALLIWELL-PHILLIPPS (1879), p. 40 – W. OECHELHÄUSER (1885), p. 40 – GEORGE BERNARD SHAW (1895), p. 41 – G.K. CHESTERTON (1904), p. 42 – FRANK SIDGWICK (1908), p. 45 – HARLEY GRANVILLE-BARKER (1914), p. 47 – SIR ARTHUR QUILLER-COUCH (1918), p. 48 – BENEDETTO CROCE (1920), p. 49 – ENID WELSFORD (1927), p. 50.

Part Two: *Modern Critical Studies*

Part Three: *Twentieth-Century Productions*

ACKNOWLEDGEMENTS

The editor's warmest thanks are due to Mr Beda Lim and the staff of the University of Malaya Library, and to Mr F Weston Fenhagen, Professor John S Hill and Mr David Ormerod.

The editor and publishers wish to thank the following who have kindly given permission for the use of copyright material:
C L Barber, extracts from *Shakespeare's Festive Comedy: A Study of Dramatic Form and its Relation to Social Custom* (1972). Copyright © 1959 by Princeton University Press reprinted by permission of the publishers; Anne Barton, extracts from 'Introduction to *A Midsummer Night's Dream*' in *The Riverside Shakespeare* (1974), edited by G Blakemore Evans, *et al.* Copyright © 1974 by Houghton Mifflin Company, reprinted by permission of the publishers; John Russell Brown, extract from *Free Shakespeare* (1967), by permission of Heinemann Educational Books Ltd.; G K Chesterton, extracts from two-part essay 'A Midsummer Night's Dream', by permission of A P Watt Ltd.; R W Dent, extracts from 'Imagination in *A Midsummer Night's Dream*' in *Shakespeare Quarterly*, Vol. XV, 1964; Stephen Fender, extract from *Shakespeare: A Midsummer Night's Dream*, No. 35, in *Studies in English Literature* (1968) by permission of Edward Arnold (Publishers) Ltd.; Harley Granville-Barker, extract from preface to *A Midsummer Night's Dream*, Savoy Theatre Acting Edition, 1914, by permission of The Society of Authors on behalf of the Harley Granville-Barker Estate; Sally Jacobs, extracts from article 'Designing the Dream: from Tantras to Tunics' in *Peter Brook's Production of William Shakespeare's 'A Midsummer Night's Dream' for the Royal Shakespeare Company: The Complete and Authorised Edition* (1974) by permission of Glen Loney, editor; Frank Kermode, extracts from essay 'The Mature Comedies' in *Early Shakespeare* edited by J Russell Brown and B Harris, Stratford-on-Avon Studies, No. 3, 1961, by permission of Edward Arnold (Publishers) Ltd.; G Wilson Knight, extracts from *The Shakespearean Tempest* (1968), by permission of Methuen & Co. Ltd.; Jan Kott, extracts from *Shakespeare our Contemporary*, (1964) translated by Boleslaw Taborski, by permission

of Methuen & Co. Ltd.; Minor White Latham, extracts from The Elizabethan Fairies, (1930) by permission of Columbia University Press; Alexander Leggatt, extracts from *Shakespeare's Comedy of Love*, (1974) by permission of Methuen & Co. Ltd.; George C D Odell, extracts from *Shakespeare from Betterton to Irving* (1920), by permission of Charles Scribner's Sons; Paul A Olson, extracts from essay 'A Midsummer Night's Dream and the Meaning of Court Marriage' in *ELH, A Journal of English Literacy*, Vol. 24, 1957, by permission of the author and The Johns Hopkins University Press; Noel Purdon, extracts from *The Words of Mercury, Shakespeare and English Mythography of the Renaissance* (1974), by permission of the author; William Rossky, extracts from essay 'Imagination in the English Renaissance, Psychology and Poetic' in *Studies in the Renaissance*, V, 1958 by permission of the author and The Renaissance Society of America; Ernest Schanzer, extracts from essay 'The Moon and the Fairies in *A Midsummer Night's Dream*' in *University of Toronto Quarterly*, Vol. 24, 1955, by permission of University of Toronto Press; G Bernard Shaw, extract from *Our Theatres in the Nineties*, by permission of The Society of Authors on behalf of the Bernard Shaw Estate; Frank Sidgwick, extracts from *The Sources and Analogues of Midsummer Night's Dream* (1908) by permission of Chatto and Windus Ltd.; Robert Speaight, extracts from *Shakespeare on the Stage: an Illustrated History of Shakespearean Performance* (1973) by permission of The Rainbird Publishing Group Ltd.; Andrew D Weiner, extracts from article 'Multiformitie Uniforme: A Midsummer Night's Dream' in *ELH: A Journal of English Literacy*, Vol. 38, No. 3, 1971, published by The Johns Hopkins University Press, by permission of the author; Harcourt Williams, extracts from *Old Vic Saga* (1949), by permission of John Sterling Williams; David P Young, extract from 'The Art of *A Midsummer Night's Dream*' in *Something of a Great Constancy* (1966) by permission of Yale University Press.

The typing of the manuscript was made possible by a grant from the University of Malaya, which the editor gratefully acknowledges.

Every effort has been made to trace all the copyright holders but if any have been inadvertently overlooked the publishers will be pleased to make the necessary arrangements at the first opportunity.

GENERAL EDITOR'S PREFACE

The Casebook series, launched in 1968, has become a well-regarded library of critical studies. The central concern of the series remains the 'single-author' volume, but suggestions from the academic community have led to an extension of the original plan, to include occasional volumes on such general themes as literary 'schools' and genres.

Each volume in the central category deals either with one well-known and influential work by an individual author, or with closely related works by one writer. The main section consists of critical readings, mostly modern, collected from books and journals. A selection of reviews and comments by the author's contemporaries is also included, and sometimes comment from the author himself. The Editor's introduction charts the reputation of the work or works from the first appearance to the present time.

Volumes in the 'general themes' category are variable in structure but follow the basic purpose of the series in presenting an integrated selection of readings, with an Introduction which explores the theme and discusses the literary and critical issues involved.

A single volume can represent no more than a small selection of critical opinions. Some critics are excluded for reasons of space, and it is hoped that readers will pursue the suggestions for further reading in the Select Bibliography. Other contributions are severed from their original context, to which some readers may wish to turn. Indeed, if they take a hint from the critics represented here, they certainly will.

A. E. DYSON

TEXTUAL NOTE

In all cases where contributors have quoted from a modernised text, the Act, scene and line references have been regularised to those of the New Penguin Shakespeare (ed. Stanley Wells, 1967) for the convenience of the reader.

In the few cases where contributors have quoted from the quartos (Q1 1600, Q2 1619 but falsely dated 1600) or First Folio (1623) the lineation has been left unchanged.

Where they have merely referred to a passage without quoting it the lineation of the New Penguin has been used.

A. P.

INTRODUCTION

In 1662 Samuel Pepys confided to his Diary that *A Midsummer Night's Dream* 'is the most insipid ridiculous play that ever I saw in my life', yet just under three hundred years later Frank Kermode declared, 'I should myself be prepared to maintain that [it] is Shakespeare's best comedy'.*

How has such a change in taste come about? Was Pepys undervaluing and Kermode vastly overvaluing the play? The easiest answer is to blame the waning belief in fairies, their relegation to the nursery; but that, surely, would have made it more difficult for Kermode than for Pepys to accept the play. The real answer is that, even by 1662, the play had lost much of its original meaning, and has continued to lose it, since each age is trapped by its own semantics: the 'rational' in the eighteenth century, the 'Ideal' in the nineteenth (see Coleridge and Hazlitt in Part One below), and that only in the twentieth are we far enough away from Shakespeare to have to make a conscious (but enjoyable) effort to recover as much as possible of that original meaning.

Valuable pioneering work has been done by Frank Sidgwick, in his investigations into the ancestry of Oberon and Titania; by Minor White Latham in enquiring more deeply into the size and appearance of fairies and, by demonstrating that Puck is neither a fairy nor a midget, showing how far the theatrical traditions of the previous hundred and fifty years have distorted the author's intentions; by G. Wilson Knight, in drawing attention to the image-patterns and the oppositions between birds and beasts, music and tempest; and by William Rossky, whose investigation of the Renaissance concepts of 'fancy' and 'imagination' has cleared away the critical confusion surrounding these terms created by the Romantic poets. R. W. Dent, by relating these concepts to the play as a whole, has demonstrated

---

* The absence of a numbered source–reference for a critical comment or study mentioned in this Introduction signifies that it forms part of the ensuing selection. The references pertaining to other material will be found in the Notes at the end of the Introduction.

the central thematic importance of 'Pyramus and Thisbe'. In this he has been followed, in different ways, by a number of recent critics, most notably by Noel Purdon. Similarly, Cesar L. Barber's seminal work – from which it is possible to include only an excerpt in this selection – has solved many of the difficulties encountered by earlier critics (Johnson in Part One below, Farmer, Steevens, Malone, and almost all the German critics of the nineteenth century, whose views are discussed in the Preface to the *New Variorum*), and has analysed the play's imagery in a different way from Wilson Knight.

One obvious result of recent scholarly and critical interest has been that the earlier view that Titania's reference to the disruption of the seasons as a result of her quarrel with Oberon [II i 81–117] refers to the wet summer of 1594 or '95 (conjectured by Steevens in 1773, and debated throughout the nineteenth century) has given place to a very different interpretation, dependent on Elizabethan ideas about 'order' and 'degree', and thus more closely related to what we know of Shakespeare's thought elsewhere: see the essays of Wilson Knight, Schanzer, Olson and Fender in Part Two below.

Similarly, the frequent eighteenth- and nineteenth-century allegorical interpretations of Oberon's lines about the 'fair vestal throned by the west' [II i 148–68], whereby the 'vestal' stands for Queen Elizabeth I, the 'mermaid' for Mary, Queen of Scots, 'young Cupid' for the Earl of Leicester, the 'little western flower' for Lettice, Countess of Essex, and the 'certain stars' for the Earls of Northumberland and Westmorland and the Duke of Norfolk – comment on which occupies sixteen and a half pages of notes in the *New Variorum* – are no longer taken seriously. The most persuasive of the new interpretations is surely that of Purdon.

The most influential recent criticism has been concerned with Theseus and Hippolyta; with the double setting in the rational world of Athens, ruled by Theseus, and the irrational world of the wood, ruled by Oberon (Olson, Fender, Leggatt); with the important contrast between the earlier love-affairs of Theseus and Hippolyta and their balanced, mature love as shown in the play (Knight, Olson, Hunter, Dent, Barton); with the contrast between their marriage and that of Oberon and Titania (Knight, Schanzer, Olson); and with the lovers, who now, for the first time, are seen to be comic (Knight, Schanzer, Hunter, Dent, Barton, Leggatt).

Recent criticism has also sought to examine the play's intellectual structure, its central 'contrast between reasonable and unreasonable love . . . celestial and earthly love' (Olson), the psychomachia between Diana and Cupid (Purdon), to relate the thought of the play to Elizabethan ideas about imagination (Dent), about love and marriage (Olson, Weiner), and to relate the play (and particularly Oberon and Titania) to a wider literary tradition than was recognised by earlier critics. Thus there is now widespread recognition that Bottom's speech on waking from his dream [IV i 199–216] is a parody of St Paul [I Corinthians ii 7–14]: see Olson, Kermode, Dent, and Weiner. As a result of modern scholarship and criticism, it is not too much to say that we are now in a better position to understand Shakespeare's meaning than anyone since the middle of the seventeenth century.

This by no means indicates that there is a wide body of opinions accepted by every critic. Indeed no. Most have agreed that the play's central argument about reasonable and unreasonable love depends on a contrast between 'doting' (caused by the eyes), and true love (a product of the mind), although there has been some dispute about one of the key speeches. Helena's soliloquy at the end of the opening scene tells us:

> Love looks not with the eyes, but with the mind,
> And therefore is winged Cupid painted blind.
> Nor hath love's mind of any judgement taste;
> Wings and no eyes figure unheedy haste.   [I i 234–7]

These lines appear to contradict neo-Platonist doctrine, until we recognise that she is speaking in the first line of true love, and then shifting her attention to mere infatuation. R. A. Zimbardo, however, suggests

Helena is led to consider love . . . not as a power which is elicited from the lover by a beautiful object, but rather as a projection by the lover of an imagined beauty upon the object. . . . Love then is the projection upon 'reality' of fantasy, or imagined reality. It does not have to do with the eyes, those organs that transmit the external inward. Rather it is the working of the 'minde' or imagination, which, in lovers, being 'all compact', does not differentiate between subject and object, but rather invests the object with the subject's own feeling and thereby *makes* it beautiful[1]

Fender, on the other hand, thinks: 'The "mind" with which love "looks" is not, of course, the rational faculty; this "mind" is without balanced judgement, and would correspond more to emotional impulses, or "the will" in Shakespeare's terminology.'

There are wider disagreements about the fairies, though modern writers in general take them seriously. Here there are four main schools of thought. Those who have applied the traditional folklore to the play tell us that the fairies are evil, or at any rate amoral, creatures. This notion is especially prevalent among critics who have presumably read the text in translation, and who are more familiar with European than with English folklore. Thus the allegations of G. G. Gervinus that 'they tempt mortals to be unfaithful' and 'with the mental torture of the lovers they have not a jot of sympathy' can be disproved merely by quotation from the text [e.g., II i 245–6, 260–6; II ii 82–5; III ii 94–9, 356–69]. The most celebrated interpretation of this sort is that of Jan Kott, whose views have had a disproportionate influence on recent productions. At Stratford Ontario, in 1968, John Hirsch explained that the minor fairies in his production

are extensions of Oberon and Titania – those two alone are morally conscious, their followers have the innocence, passion and cruelty of animals. They must create the possibility of imminent physical battle. The fairy kingdom is on the verge of chaos.[2]

Such a view also seems to rely on a one-sided reading of the disorder speech [II i 81–117], and to ignore the actual behaviour of the fairies in the play. One might also enquire why, if they are to be seen as 'downright malevolent' (Fender, speaking of Oberon's relations with Titania) they should bless the bridal couples at the end. Fender also states that 'Oberon and Puck, though capable of restoring order in the wood, also do their best to disrupt it'; but this surely contradicts their behaviour towards the lovers throughout the play (except in the minor matter of Puck's accidentally mistaking Lysander for Demetrius) and overlooks the facts that they *do* wipe out this mistake, *do* prevent a duel between the rival suitors, and *do* eventually restore order.

The opposite view is held by G. K. Hunter, who tells us that Oberon and Titania 'are concerned not with mischief, as traditionally, but with *order* in a quasi-human fashion'. In this he is supported by Latham, by Katherine Briggs's observation that the fairies

show an active kindness. Puck, indeed, is glad to do a certain amount of mischief, but that is almost by accident, and it is from no spite to mortals, for he is equally ready to play a prank on his own Queen. Titania feels concern at the hardships which their quarrels are inflicting on the human mortals. Oberon intervenes to set the lovers' affairs to rights, they both go to bless Theseus' marriage-bed. Even Titania's child-theft has an affectionate motive . . . she took the child because of her love for its dead mother,[3]

and by Schanzer's view that Oberon and Titania are 'the counterpart in the spirit-world of Theseus and Hippolyta, like them full of stateliness and dignity, though more ceremonious and distant'.

This view is also supported indirectly by Lou Agnes Reynolds and Paul Sawyer, who, quoting contemporary herbals, argue that Midsummer Night is 'the time most favorable for gathering medicinal products', and that Titania's four attendants (whom Kott sees in quite a different manner) are given names which clearly relate to such products: 'cobwebs were placed on a cut to staunch the flow of blood'; if a lover 'were jilted, the pain of the lost love was eased by rubbing the whole body with the hay of the pea plant'; mustardseed had two common uses: 'in a plaster or poultice to ease a sore back or aching muscles and its table use as a condiment to be served on beef'; and the moth 'because of its caustic properties . . . was made into a plaster to treat old sores and was also used to prepare a diuretic for kidney and bladder ailments'.[4]

The third view is that of Walter F. Staton, Jnr[5] who argues that Oberon, Titania and Puck bear a striking resemblance to Jupiter, Juno and Mercury in many Ovidian tales: 'the philandering king who is trying to get away with something, the jealous and watchful queen, and the cunning agent of the king'; and that Titania's wooing of Bottom, 'the theme of a nymph wooing a reluctant boy', occurs frequently in Ovid and in Elizabethan Ovidian romances, most notably in Shakespeare's own *Venus and Adonis*. Staton notes seven points of similarity:

(1) Both love-scenes take place on flowery beds. (2) Both women forcibly detain somewhat reluctant lovers. (3) Both women boast of supernatural

power. . . . (4) Both women promise their lovers rewards. . . . (5) Both love
actions are similar: Titania 'coys' Bottom's cheeks and kisses his ears, while
Venus strokes Adonis's cheeks and kisses his brow, his cheek, his chin;
Titania enrings Bottom as the ivy does the elm, while Venus entangles
Adonis in her arms like a bird in a net. (6) Both reluctant lovers are
compared to animals: Bottom has an ass's head; [Adonis's] horse knows
more about love than Adonis. . . . (7) Bottom's hairiness is emphasised,
while Adonis's hairless face is several times alluded to.

The fourth, and surely the most acceptable, interpretation is that of
Noel Purdon, who equates Titania with Diana (quoting the precedent
of Ovid), and Puck with Cupid: see Part Two below.

Similarly, the ass's head has provoked divergent interpretations
which contradict each other. Olson sees it as 'a symbol for stupidity
and sensuality, for the carnal man as opposed to the spiritual'. Many
others detect in it an oblique reference to *The Golden Ass*, sometimes to
the adventures of Lucius (Kermode), sometimes to the interpolated
story of Cupid and Psyche (Sister M. Generosa,[6] James A. S.
McPeek[7]). Some solemn American critics, supposing that
Shakespeare came from Stratford, Connecticut, equate an 'ass' with
an 'arse' (a word not to be found in his works) and conclude this is an
appropriate designation for Bottom: their work has not been included
in this collection. Kott altogether denies the ass's stupidity, even
though every time Shakespeare used the word metaphorically he
clearly meant to refer to stupidity (see Bartlett's *Concordance*), and
attributes to Bottom 'the longest and hardest phallus of all
quadrupeds'. Fender compares him with Priapus. David Ormerod,
on the other hand, argues more cogently that he is an 'image of the
ass-headed Minotaur in the labyrinthine Athenian wood', and that
his ass's head is 'an image of the dominant motif in Shakespeare's
comic world – moral mischoice'.[8]

Few critics have paid much attention to the echo in the play's title
of 'midsummer madness', which Olivia mentions in *Twelfth Night*;
but Ernest Schanzer[9] analyses the play's treatment of 'love madness'
as its main theme, pointing out that love of this kind is 'a creature of
"seething brains" ', stemming from the imagination rather than the
eyes, and is prompted by the application of Oberon's flower.

Older writers paid little attention to a theme which is coming to
concern modern critics more and more: that of the dislocation of the
senses, particularly in Bottom's part, as when he says in his echo of St

Paul: 'The eye of man hath not heard, the ear of man hath not seen, man's hand is not able to taste, his tongue to conceive, nor his heart to report what my dream was!' [IV i 208–11] and the misplaced epithets in 'Pyramus and Thisbe'. These are commented on by Leggatt in Part Two below, and by Stanley Wells in the Introduction to the New Penguin edition, where he notes that they are clearly related to such other reversals as 'Apollo flies, and Daphne holds the chase' [II i 231], the reconciliation of opposites in the play's various situations (the maturity of Theseus and Hippolyta contrasted with 'the youthful silliness of the younger lovers', the 'ethereal Titania' coupled with the 'asinine Bottom'[10]), and the mixture of verse forms.

☆

Most scholars, noting that the play was mentioned by Francis Meres in his *Palladis Tamia* (1598) agree on a date of composition of 1595–6. Many critics also assume, from what they regard as internal evidence, that it was written for performance at an aristocratic wedding celebration – without, perhaps, fully realising that this notion originated as a tentative conjecture by the German Romantic poet Ludwig Tieck, in his notes following Schlegel's translation of 1830, and that it was much disputed in his own country and century. The principal difficulty is that it has never been possible to decide which particular wedding (Southampton's in 1598? Essex's in 1590? Derby's in 1595?) the play was designed to celebrate.[11] Nevertheless, the majority of recent critics concludes that, although it is impossible, now, to determine which wedding was involved, the play certainly owes its genesis to some such courtly occasion.

A variant of this theory, first proposed by Fleay in 1876, and modified in 1891, is that the play as originally composed for the courtly wedding ended when all the fairies had left the stage in the final scene, and that Puck's final speech was tacked on as an 'epilogue' when the play was performed in the public theatre. He asserted that the present text thus provides two alternative endings. This opinion was endorsed by the editors of the New Shakespeare in 1924 and by the editor of the New Arden in 1979, but is no longer widely accepted.

The first view, and by implication the second, has been disputed by

Stanley Wells,[12] and Alfred Harbage, on the grounds of the complete lack of evidence that *any* play was written for a special private performance before 1614, and that the costs, time and effort involved in writing, rehearsing and performing a new play exclusively for such an audience would not have been worth the company's while.[13]

The theory also overlooks the fact that *A Midsummer Night's Dream* is innocent of the verbal arabesques, the satire of false pedantry, and the jokes against the communication-gap between the common man and the sophisticate that characterise *Love's Labour's Lost*. Whatever may have been the intention of that play, it is clear that *A Midsummer Night's Dream* was aimed at the regular, paying, public playhouse audiences, and had to appeal to them in order to survive commercially.

We know that it did survive. The title-page of the first quarto (1600, set from Shakespeare's 'foul papers') tells us that, by that time, it had been 'Sundry times publickely acted'. It is also clear that it remained in the public repertoire until at least 1607, since Edward Sharpham's comment in *The Fleire* would have had little point if his audience could not have been relied on to recognise a reference to a current joke. In 1619 it was printed again, in a quarto bearing the false date '1600', set up from the earlier text: another fact which argues the play's continuing popularity. By the time of the First Folio (1623) a number of new stage directions, presumably taken from the promptbook, had infiltrated the text. For example, at the end of Act III we read, of the lovers, that 'They sleepe all the Act'   – meaning that by this time it had become the practice to observe intervals, filled out with music, between the acts. At precisely what date after 1600 this innovation occurred we cannot, of course, be sure, though a reference to 'the not-received custom of music in our theatre' in Webster's Induction to Marston's *The Malcontent*, played by Shakespeare's company in 1604, suggests that it must have been later, perhaps considerably later, than that. The existence of a stage direction ('In the act-time De Flores hides a naked rapier') at the start of Act III of Middleton and Rowley's *The Changeling* (1622 or '23, and performed by a different adult company) suggests that a year or more before the First Folio was printed act-intervals and music had been borrowed from the 'private' playhouses and had now become customary in the 'public' theatres, even though, in the case of *A Midsummer Night's Dream*, they disturb the continuity of the action.

After Shakespeare's death the play went through a variety of metamorphoses. Between 1661 and 1816 there were nine published 'improvements' on this text, some omitting the lovers entirely, some omitting Bottom and his fellows, and one interpolating the performance of 'Pyramus and Thisbe' into *As You Like It,* immediately before the masque of Hymen. Many were musical adaptations: a stage direction from the first of these, *The Fairy-Queen, An Opera* (1692), and an interpolated song from another, *The Comick Masque of Pyramus and Thisbe* (1716) are reproduced in Part One below. Most of the subsequent versions introduced songs by various composers to words by a variety of poets later than Shakespeare.[14]

The original text was restored to the London stage in 1840, by Charles Matthews and Mme Vestris, who herself *sang* the part of Oberon. This was a shortened version, without interpolations from other authors, and the first production of the play on a picture-frame stage.

That fact, and the new lighting and stage machinery now available, to say nothing of Mendelssohn's music, introduced a new kind of distortion into later Victorian productions (the work of Phelps, Kean, Daly and Benson is discussed by Morley and Shaw in Part One and by Harcourt Williams in Part Three below), since they afforded irresistible opportunities for spectacle, usually in the form of pageants and long ballet-sequences, as Hazlitt makes clear. These in turn demanded ballet-costumes for the fairies, to which were added wands and transparent wings, both unknown to Elizabethan fairies: see Minor White Latham. The new lighting (originally gas, towards the end of the century electricity) made 'moonlight' and dawn effects available, and even made it possible for the moon to traverse the backcloth, for stars to twinkle on it, and for fireflies to glimmer elsewhere. Layers of shadowy gauze curtains, lit from the front, could now be used to create the fog in which Demetrius and Lysander got lost, though Shakespeare, we should remember, relied only on words and on what David P. Young calls 'panorama', to create the wood, the moon, the fog, the dawn, and the night at the end of the play, in broad daylight on an empty stage.

Literal-minded Naturalism took things even further. Sir Herbert Beerbohm Tree, in 1900, is said to have populated his wood with real oaks, live deer, pigeons, rabbits, squirrels, and even hares. There is an old theatrical legend that, although the audiences seem to have approved of this, the actors objected bitterly to being upstaged, by amateurs, who were mere vermin!

Inevitably there has been controversy, particularly over the scenery and the music. Five later productions are discussed in Part Three below.

There have also been other kinds of vulgar distortion. Bottom is usually played as a corpulent, middle-aged, or even elderly, low comedian, yet that this was not always the case may perhaps be inferred from Titania's address in *The Fairy-Queen*:

> Come, lovely Youth, sit on this flowry Bed
> While I thy amiable looks survey

(which adds 'lovely Youth' to Shakespeare's line), and from the frontispiece to Bell's edition (1774) where he is a tall, slim, handsome young man, with a handsome ass's face, with whom it is credible that Titania might fall in love. That it need not be the case is suggested by Glynne Wickham's opinion that he is a 'good looking young work-man whose tastes and conversation are as brutish and banal as his physique is striking,'[15] and also by the view of Ronald Watkins and Jeremy Lemmon that 'There is no reason why Pyramus should be presented as a military man; he is a lover ("more condoling"), not a tyrant, and Peter Quince's introduction of him as a "sweet youth and tall" suggests, rather, a familiar miniature by Nicholas Hilliard: Pyramus should be a mockery, not of Theseus, but of Romeo, or at least Demetrius.'[16]

In recent years the Royal Shakespeare Company has introduced its own distortion. Charles Laughton in 1959 reduced the ass's head to a pair of furry ears and hooves, which certainly allowed the audiences to see his face, but made him look less like an ass than a rabbit. He was in part followed by David Waller in Peter Brook's production in 1970: this time Bottom's face was bare apart from a black rubber nose and points on his ears, which gave him the appearance, not of an ass, but of a circus clown; yet even this has been defended: see Sally Jacobs's comments in Part Three below.

What remains to be done in the study is that critics need to go back to a more detailed examination of the text of the play, and to test their theories against it. What remains to be done on the stage is that producers should learn to respect that text rather than to invent new interpretations of their own, which are commercially viable only because they have, quite rightly, never been thought of before.

NOTES

1. 'Regeneration and Reconciliation in *A Midsummer Night's Dream*', *Shakespeare Studies*, VI (1970), p. 45.

2. 'Notes on *A Midsummer Night's Dream*', in Peter Raby (ed.), *The Stratford Scene, 1958–1968* (Toronto, 1968), p. 176.

3. *The Anatomy of Puck: An Examination of Fairy Beliefs among Shakespeare's Contemporaries and Successors* (London, 1959), p. 46.

4. 'Folk Medicine and the Four Fairies of *A Midsummer Night's Dream*', *Shakespeare Quarterly*, X (1959), pp. 513–21.

5. 'Ovidian Elements in *A Midsummer Night's Dream*', *Huntington Library Quarterly*, XXVI (1963), pp. 165–78.

6. 'Apuleius and *A Midsummer Night's Dream*: Analogue or Source, Which?' *Studies in Philology*, 42 (1945), pp. 198–204.

7. 'The Psyche Myth and *A Midsummer Night's Dream*', *Shakespeare Quarterly*, XXIII (1972), pp. 69–79.

8. '*A Midsummer Night's Dream*: The Monster in the Labyrinth', *Shakespeare Studies*, XI (1978), pp. 39–52.

9. 'The Central Theme of *A Midsummer Night's Dream*', *University of Toronto Quarterly*, XX (1951), pp. 233–8.

10. *Op. cit.*, p. 28.

11. The various conjectures are fully discussed in H. H. Furness (ed.), *A New Variorum Edition of Shakespeare: A Midsummer Night's Dream* (New York, 1895, reprinted 1963), pp. 255–64.

12. Introduction to the New Penguin edition (Harmondsworth, 1967), p. 14, and 'Shakespeare without Sources' in *Shakespearian Comedy*, ed. David Palmer and Malcolm Bradbury (Stratford-upon-Avon Studies, 14), (London, 1972), pp. 67–8.

13. '*Shakespeare without Words' and Other Essays,* (Cambridge, Mass. 1972), pp. 119, 120–1.

14. These versions have been reprinted by the Cornmarket Press, and some by David Paradine Publications Limited.

15. *Shakespeare's Dramatic Heritage* (London, 1969), p. 187.

16. *A Midsummer Night's Dream* ('In Shakespeare's Playhouse'), (Newton Abbot, 1974), p. 126.

PART ONE

Critical Comment
1607–1927

Edward Sharpham   (1607)

> *Knight.* And how lives he with 'em?
> *Fleire.* Faith, like Thisbe in the play, 'a has
> almost killed himself with the scabbard.

SOURCE: extract from *The Fleire* (1607). This comedy, acted by the Queen's Revels company in 1606, appears to record stage 'business' practised during Shakespeare's working life. [Ed.]

Samuel Pepys   (1662)

29. [September 1662] *Michaelmas day.* This day my oaths for drinking of wine and going to plays are out, and so I do resolve to take a liberty today and then to fall to them again. . . . I sent for some dinner . . . (Mrs Margt Pen being by. to whom I had spoke to go along with us to a play this afternoon) and then to the King's Theatre, where we saw *Midsummer nights dreame*, which I had never seen before, nor shall ever again, for it is the most insipid ridiculous play that ever I saw in my life. I saw, I confess, some good dancing and some handsome women, which was all my pleasure. . . .

SOURCE: extract from *The Diary of Samuel Pepys*, ed. Robert Latham and William Matthews (London, 1970), pp. 207–8.

NOTE

John Middleton Murry commented: 'Each of the three main elements of the play – the love, the fairy, and the clowning – was too naive for Pepys's sophistication, and the combination of them too subtle for his naivety.' – *Shakespeare* (1936), p. 217. [Ed.]

John Dryden   (1677)

. . . poets may be allowed the . . . liberty for describing things which really exist not, if they are founded on popular belief. Of this nature are fairies, pigmies, and the extraordinary effects of magic; for 'tis still an imitation, though of other men's fancies: and thus are Shakespeare's *Tempest*, his *Midsummer Night's Dream*, and Ben Jonson's *Masque of Witches* [i.e., the *Masque of Queens*] to be defended.

SOURCE: extract from 'The Author's Apology for Heroic Poetry and Poetic Licence', prefixed to *The State of Innocence: An Opera.*

Anonymous   (1692)

> *Robin.* So, when thou wak'st with thine own Fools Eyes,
> Peep.
> [*He takes off the Ass's Head.*]
> *Oberon. Titania,* call for Musick.
> *Titania.* Let us have all Variety of Musick,
> All that should welcome up the rising Sun.

The Scene changes to a Garden of Fountains. A Sonata plays while the Sun rises, it appears red through the Mist, as it ascends it dissipates the Vapours, and is seen in its full Lustre; then the Scene is perfectly discovered, the Fountains enrich'd with gilding, and adorn'd with Statues: The view is terminated by a Walk of Cypress Trees which lead to a delightful Bower. Before the Trees stand rows of Marble Columns, which support many Walks which rise by Stairs to the top of the House; the Stairs are adorn'd with Figures on Pedestals, and Rails; and Balasters on each side of 'em. Near the top, vast Quantities of Water break out of the Hills, and fall in mighty Cascade's to the bottom of the Scene, to feed the Fountains which are on each side. In the middle of the Stage is a very large Fountain, where the Water rises about twelve Foot.

Then the 4 Seasons enter, with their several Attendants.

   One of the Attendants begin . . .

   Two others sing in Parts . . .

A Machine appears, the Clouds break from before it, and Phoebus *appears in a Chariot drawn by four Horses: and Sings . . .*

SOURCE: extract from *The Fairy Queen, an Opera* (1692), Act IV.

John Downes   (1708)

The Fairy Queen, made into an Opera, from a Comedy of Mr *Shakespeare's.* This in Ornaments was Superior to the other two [*Macbeth* and *The Tempest, or the Inchanted Island*], especially in Cloaths, for all the Singers and Dancers, Scenes, Machines and Decorations, all most profusely set off and excellently perform'd, chiefly the Instrumental and Vocal part Compos'd by the said *Mr Purcell,* and Dances by Mr *Priest.* The Court and Town were wonderfully satisfy'd with it; but the Expences in setting it out being so great, the Company got very little by it.

SOURCE: extract from *Roscius Anglicanus, or an Historical Review of the Stage from 1660 to 1706* (1708), pp. 42–3.

Richard Leveridge   (1716)

Lion (sings)   Ladies don't fright you,
        I will delight you.
            With gentle Roar.
        Let not a Creature,
        Tho' fierce in Nature,

Change any Feature,
I do implore.
Who can say fy on
So Tame a Lion,
So full of Breeding,
So far exceeding
Lions before.

SOURCE: extract from *The Comick Masque of Pyramus and Thisbe* (1716).

Samuel Johnson   (1765, 1773)

Notes on the Play   (1765)

[I ii]   In this scene *Shakespear** takes advantage of his knowledge of the theatre to ridicule the prejudices and competitions of the players. *Bottom*, who is generally acknowledged the principal actor, declares his inclination to be for a tyrant, for a part of fury, tumult, and noise, such as every young man pants to perform when he first steps upon the stage. The same *Bottom*, who seems bred in a tiring room, has another histrionic passion. He is for engrossing every part and would exclude his inferiors from all possibility of distinction. He is therefore desirous to play Pyramus, Thisbe, and the Lion at the same time.

[I ii 43]   FLUTE   Nay, faith, let not me play a woman – I have a beard coming.
QUINCE   That's all one: you shall play it in a mask, and you may speak as small as you will.

---

* Here, and elsewhere in Part One, the form 'Shakespear' is retained if so appearing in the original. [Ed.]

This passage shows how the want of women on the old stage was supplied. If they had not a young man who could perform the part with a face that might pass for feminine, the character was acted in a mask, which was at that time a part of a lady's dress so much in use that it did not give any unusual appearance to the scene; and he that could modulate his voice in a female tone might play the woman very successfully. It is observed in Downes's *Memoirs of the Playhouse* that one of these counterfeit heroines moved the passions more strongly than the women that have since been brought upon the stage. Some of the catastrophes of the old comedies, which make lovers marry the wrong women, are, by recollection of the common use of masks, brought nearer to probability.

[III i]   In the time of *Shakespear* there were many companies of players, sometimes five at the same time, contending for the favour of the publick. Of these some were undoubtedly very unskilful and very poor, and it is probable that the design of this Scene was to ridicule their ignorance, and the odd expedients to which they might be driven by want of proper decorations. *Bottom* was perhaps the head of a rival house, and is therefore honoured with an Ass's head.

[III i 173]   *the fiery glow-worm's eyes.*   I know not how *Shakespear,* who commonly derived his knowledge of nature from his own observation, happened to place the glow-worm's light in his eyes, which is only in his tail.

[III ii 367]   *this virtuous property.*   Salutiferous. So he calls, in The Tempest, *Poisonous dew,* wicked dew.

[IV i 108]   I know not why *Shakespear* calls this play a *Midsummer-Night's Dream,* when he so carefully informs us that it happened on the night preceding *May* day.[1]

Later Comment   (1773)

General Observation. . . . . Wild and fantastical as this play is, all the parts in their various modes are well written and give the kind of pleasure which the author designed. Fairies in his time were much in fashion; common tradition had made them familiar, and *Spenser*'s poem had made them great.

SOURCE: extracts from 'Notes on the Plays' in Johnson's 1765 edition of *The Plays of William Shakespear*, and in his 1773 edition.

NOTE

1. This is answered by C. L. Barber and by Noel Purdon: see Part Two below. [Ed.]

Anonymous   (1774)

In the piece before us *Shakespeare* had evidently two great and very material points in view; Novelty and Originality; the sure road, if attained, to permanency and fame: to these favourite objects, he paid such attention as sometimes to forget probability, though he always preserved character. The following piece has great poetical and dramatic merit, considered in general; but a puerile plot, an odd mixture of incidents, and a forced connexion of various stiles, throw a kind of shade over that blaze of merit many passages would otherwise have possessed. There is no character strongly marked, yet the whole shews a very great master dallying with his own genius and imagination in a wonderful and delightful manner.

SOURCE: extract from the 'Introduction' to this play in Bell's edition: *The Dramatic Censor* (1774), by various authors.

Samuel Taylor Coleridge   (? 1811)

I am convinced that Shakespeare availed himself of the title of this play in his own mind [as] a *dream* throughout, but especially (and perhaps unpleasingly) in this broad determination of ungrateful treachery in Helena, so undisguisedly avowed to herself, and this too after the witty cool philosophizing that precedes. The act is very natural; the resolve so to act is, I fear, likewise too true a picture of the lax hold that principles have on the female heart, when opposed to, or even separated from, passion and inclination. For women are less hypocrites to their own minds than men, because they feel less abhorrence of moral evil in itself and more for its outward consequences, as detection, loss of character, etc., their natures being almost wholly extroitive. But still, however just, the representation is not poetical; we shrink from it and cannot harmonize it with the ideal.

SOURCE: manuscript note, conjecturally dated December 1811, referring to I i 246–51 in a copy of the play; reprinted in *Coleridge's Shakespearian Criticism*, ed. T. M. Raysor, 2nd edn (1960), vol. I, p. 90.

William Hazlitt   (1817)

Bottom the Weaver is a character that has not had justice done him. He is the most romantic of mechanics. . . . It has been observed that Shakespear's characters are constructed upon deep physiological principles; and there is something in this play which looks very like it. Bottom the Weaver . . . follows a sedentary trade, and he is accordingly represented as conceited, serious, and fantastical. He is ready to undertake any thing and every thing, as if it was as much a matter of course as the motion of his loom and shuttle. . . . Snug the

Joiner is the moral man of the piece, who proceeds by measurement and discretion in all things. You see him with his rule and compasses in his hand. 'Have you the lion's part written? Pray you, if it be, give it me, for I am slow of study.' . . . Starveling the Tailor keeps the peace, and objects to the lion and the drawn sword. 'I believe we must leave the killing out when all's done.' Starveling, however, does not start the objections himself, but seconds them when made by others, as if he had not spirit to express his fears without encouragement. It is too much to suppose all this intentional: but it very luckily falls out so. . . .

It is astonishing that Shakespear should be considered, not only by foreigners, but by many of our own critics, as a gloomy and heavy writer, who painted nothing but 'gorgons and hydras, and chimeras dire'. His subtlety exceeds that of all other dramatic writers. . . . His delicacy and sportive gaiety are infinite. In the *Midsummer Night's Dream* alone, we should imagine, there is more sweetness and beauty of description than in the whole range of French poetry put together. What we mean is this, that we will produce out of that single play ten passages, to which we do not think any ten passages in the works of the French poets can be opposed, displaying equal fancy and imagery. Shall we mention the remonstrance of Helena to Hermia, or Titania's description of her fairy train, or her disputes with Oberon about the Indian boy, or Puck's account of himself and his employments, or the Fairy Queen's exhortation to the elves to pay due attendance upon her favourite, Bottom; or Hippolita's description of a chace, or Theseus's answer? The two last are as heroical and spirited as the others are full of luscious tenderness. The reading of this play is like wandering in a grove by moonlight: the descriptions breathe a sweetness like odours thrown from beds of flowers. . . .

It had been suggested to us, that the *Midsummer Night's Dream* would do admirably to get up as a Christmas after-piece. . . . What an opportunity for processions, for the sound of trumpets and glittering of spears! What a fluttering of urchins' painted wings; what a delightful profusion of gauze clouds and airy spirits floating on them!

Alas the experiment has been tried, and has failed. . . . The *Midsummer Night's Dream*, when acted, is converted from a delightful fiction into a dull pantomime. All that is finest in the play is lost in the representation. The spectacle was grand: but the spirit was evaporated, the genius was fled. – Poetry and the stage do not agree well together. The attempt to reconcile them in this instance fails not only of effect, but of decorum. The *ideal* can have no place upon the stage, which is a picture without perspective; everything there is in the fore-ground. That which was merely an airy shape, a dream, a passing thought, immediately becomes an unmanageable reality. Where all is left to the imagination (as is the case in reading) every circumstance, near or remote, has an equal chance of being kept in mind, and tells according to the mixed impression of all that has been suggested. But the imagination cannot sufficiently qualify the actual impressions of the senses. Any offence given to the eye is not to be got rid of by explanation. Thus Bottom's head in the play is a fantastic illusion, produced by magic spells: on the stage it is an ass's head, and nothing more; certainly a very strange costume for a gentleman to appear in. Fancy cannot be embodied any more than a simile can be painted; and it is as idle to attempt it as to personate *Wall* or *Moonshine*. Fairies are not incredible, but fairies six feet high are so. Monsters are not shocking, if they are seen at a proper distance. When ghosts appear at mid-day, when apparitions walk along Cheapside, then may the *Midsummer Night's Dream* be represented without injury at Covent Garden or at Drury Lane. The boards of a theatre and the regions of fancy are not the same thing.

SOURCE: extracts from *Characters of Shakespear's Plays* (1817). The latter half of this item appeared originally (as a review of Frederick Reynolds's Covent Garden adaptation on 17 January 1816) in the *Examiner* of 21 January of that year. [Ed.]

Henry Hallam (1839)

. . . without reviving the debated question of Shakespeare's learning, I must venture to think that he possessed rather more acquaintance with the Latin language than many believe. The phrases, unintelligible and improper, except in the sense of their primitive roots, which occur so copiously in his plays, seem to be unaccountable on the supposition of absolute ignorance. In the *Midsummer Night's Dream* these are much less frequent than in his later dramas. But here we find several instances. Thus, 'things base and vile, holding no *quantity*', for value; rivers, that 'have overborne their *continents*', the *continente ripa* of Horace; '*compact* of imagination', 'something of great *constancy*', for consistency; 'sweet Pyramus *translated* there'; the law of Athens, 'which by no means we may *extenuate*'. I have considerable doubts whether any of these expressions would be found in the contemporary prose of Elizabeth's reign, which was less overrun by pedantry than that of her successor; but, could authority be produced for Latinisms so forced, it is still not very likely that one, who did not understand their proper meaning, would have introduced them into poetry.

SOURCE: extract from *Literature of Europe* (1839), II, p. 387.

G. G. Gervinus   (1849)

Shakespeare depicts [the fairies] as creatures devoid of refined feelings and of morality; just as we too in dreams meet with no check to our tender emotions and are freed from moral impulse and responsibility. Careless and unprincipled themselves, they tempt mortals to be unfaithful. The effects of the confusion which they have set on foot make no impression on them; with the mental torture of the lovers they have no jot of sympathy; but over their blunders they rejoice, and at their fondness they wonder. Furthermore, the poet depicts his fairies as creatures devoid of high intellectuality. If their speeches are attentively read, it will be noted that nowhere is there a thoughtful reflection ascribed to them. On one solitary occasion Puck makes a sententious observation on the infidelity of man, and whoever has penetrated the nature of these things will instantly feel that the observation is out of harmony. . . . Titania has no inner, spiritual relations to her friend, the mother of the little Indian boy, but merely pleasure in her shape, her grace, and gifts of mimicry.

SOURCE: extract from *Shakespeare* (Leipzig, 1849), I, p. 246.

H. Woelffel   (1852)

If we gather, as it were, into one focus all the separate, distinguishing traits of [Lysander and Demetrius], if we seek to read the secret of their nature in their eyes, we shall unquestionably find it to be this, viz. in Lysander the poet wished to represent a noble magnanimous nature sensitive to the charms of the loveliness of soul and of spiritual beauty; but in Demetrius he has given us a nature fundamentally less noble; in its final analysis, even unlovely, and sensitive only to the impression of physical beauty. If there could be any doubt that these two characters are the opposites of each other, the poet has in a noteworthy way decided the question. The effect of the same magic juice on the two men is that Demetrius is rendered faithful, Lysander unfaithful – an incontrovertible sign that their natures, like their affections, are diametrically opposite.

SOURCE: extract from *Album des literarischen Vereins in Nürnberg für 1852*, p. 126.

Henry Morley   (1853, 1856)

Samuel Phelps's Production (1853)

. . . Mr Phelps has never for a minute lost sight of the main idea which governs the whole play. . . . He knew that he was to present merely shadows; that spectators . . . are to think they have slumbered on their seats, and that what happened before them are visions. Everything has been subdued as far as possible at Sadler's Wells to this ruling idea. . . . There is no ordinary scene-shifting; but, as in dreams, one scene is made to glide insensibly into another. We follow the lovers and the fairies through the wood from glade to glade, now among trees, now with a broad view of the sea and Athens in the distance. . . . And not only do the scenes melt dream-like one into another, but over all the fairy portion of the play there is a haze thrown by a curtain of green gauze placed between the actors and the audience, and maintained there during the whole of the second, third, and fourth acts. This gauze curtain is so well spread that there are very few parts of the house from which its presence can be detected, but its influence is everywhere felt; it subdues the flesh and blood of the actors into something more nearly resembling dream-figures, and incorporates more completely the actors with the scenes, throwing the same green fairy tinge, and the same mist over all. . . .

Of Miss Cooper's Helena we cannot honestly say very much. In that as in most of the other characters the spirit of the play was missed, because the arguing and quarrelling and blundering that should have been playful, dreamlike, and poetical, was much too loud and real. The men and women could not fancy themselves shadows. Were it possible so far to subdue the energy of the whole body of actors as to soften the tones of the scenes between Theseus, Hippolyta, Lysander, Demetrius, Hermia, and Helena, the latter character even on the stage might surely have something of the effect intended by the poem. It is an exquisite abstraction, a pitiful and moving picture of a gentle maid forlorn, playfully developed as beseems the fantastic texture of the poem, but not at all meant to excite mirth; and there was a very great mistake made when the dream was so worked out into hard literalness as to create constant laughter during those scenes in which Helena, bewildered by the change of mood among the lovers, shrinks and complains, 'Wherefore was I to this keen mockery born?' . . .

It remains for us only to speak of the success of Mr Phelps as Bottom, whom he presented from the first with remarkable subtlety and spirit, as a man seen in a dream. In his first scene, before we know what his conception is, or in what spirit he means the whole play to be received, we are puzzled by it. We miss the humour, and get a strange, elaborate, and uncouth dream figure, a clown restless with vanity, marked by a score of little movements, and speaking ponderously with the uncouth gesticulation of an unreal thing, a grotesque nightmare character. But that, we find, is precisely what the actor had intended to present, and we soon perceive that he was right. Throughout the fairy scenes there is a mist thrown over Bottom by the actor's art. The violent gesticulation becomes stillness, and the hands are fixed on the breast. They are busy with the unperceived business of managing the movements of the ass's head, but it is not for that reason they are perfectly still. The change of manner is a part of the conception. The dream-figure is dreaming, there is dream within dream, Bottom is quiet, his humour becomes more unctuous, but Bottom is translated. He accepts all that happens, quietly as dreamers do; and the ass's head we also accept quietly, for we too are in the middle of our dream, and it does not create surprise. . . . Quite masterly was the delivery by Mr Phelps of the speech of Bottom on awakening. He was still a man subdued, but subdued by the sudden plunge into a state of unfathomable wonder. His dream clings about him, he cannot sever the real from the unreal, and still we are made to feel that his reality itself is but a fiction. The preoccupation continues to be manifest during his next scene with the players, and his parting, 'No more words; away; go away', was in the tone of a man who had lived with spirits and was not yet perfectly returned into the flesh. Nor did the refinement of this conception, if we except the first scene, abate a jot of the laughter that the character of Bottom was intended to excite. The mock-play at the end was intensely ludicrous in the presentment, yet nowhere farcical. It was the dream. Bottom as Pyramus was more perfectly a dream-figure than ever. The contrast between the shadowy actor and his part, between Bottom and

Pyramus, was marked intensely; and the result was as quaint a phantom as could easily be figured by real flesh.

Charles Kean's Production (1856)

. . . Shakespeare's direction for the opening scene . . . is: 'Athens, a Room in the Palace of Theseus.' For this is read, at the Princess's Theatre: 'A Terrace adjoining the Palace of Theseus, overlooking the City of Athens'; and there is presented an elaborate and undoubtedly most beautiful bird's-eye view of Athens as it was in the time of Pericles. A great scenic effect is obtained, but it is, as far as it goes, damaging to the poem. Shakespeare took for his mortals people of heroic times, Duke Theseus and Hippolyta, and it suited his romance to call them Athenians; but the feeling of the play is marred when out of this suggestion of the antique mingled with the fairy-world the scene-painter finds opportunity to bring into hard and jarring contrast the Athens of Pericles and our own world of Robin Goodfellow and all the woodland elves . . . the poetry was missed entirely by the painting of the scene, beautiful as it is. . . .

In the second act there is a dream-like moving of the wood, beautifully managed, and spoilt in effect by a trifling mistake easily corrected. Oberon stands before the scene waving his wand, as if he were exhibitor of the diorama, or a fairy conjurer causing the rocks and trees to move. Nobody, I believe, ever attributed to fairies any power of that sort. Oberon should either be off the stage or on it still as death, and it should be left for the spectators to feel the dreamy influence of wood and water slipping by their eyes unhindered and undistracted. This change leads to the disclosure of a fairy ring, a beautiful scenic effect, and what is called in large letters upon the play-bills, 'Titania's Shadow Dance'. Of all things in the world, a shadow dance of fairies! If anything in the way of an effect of light was especially desirable, it would have been such an arrangement as would have made the fairies appear to be dancing in a light so managed as to cast no shadow, and give them true spiritual attributes. Elaborately to produce and present, as an especial attraction, fairies of large size, casting shadows made as black and distinct and possible, and offering in dance to pick them up, as if even they also were solid, is as great a sacrifice of Shakespeare to the purposes of the ballet-master, as the view of Athens in its glory was a sacrifice of poetry to the scene-painter. . . .

SOURCE: extracts from *Journal of a London Playgoer* (1866). The review of the Phelps production was first published in the *Examiner* (15 Oct. 1853).

Bjørnstjerne Bjørnson   (1865)

. . . [Mendelssohn-Bartholdy's] music has respect for the dialogue of the play. The fairies' speeches are not even melodramas (with the exception of the short formulas for exorcism). He allows the music to follow the play merely as a new fairy who sprinkles several tunes over the scene as a form of consecration prior to the entry of the spiritual procession, giving it wings upon which it can fly away. Only when the dialogue with all of its dramatis personae have receded into the background does the music hover over the forest as a sort of mist of recollection, in which our fantasy again assembles the picture of what has just taken place. For the fairies' dance . . . he only has several bars of music. Why? Because they are part of the plot, the dialogue, the situation; because the fairies' dance does not require more, the music needs only to suggest. The farmers' dance is also very short. . . .

SOURCE: extract from an article in *Aftenbladet* (28 April, 1865); trans. Edward C. Thaden; reprinted in Oswald LeWinter (ed.), *Shakespeare in Europe* (New York, 1963), pp. 290–1. It is part of a defence of Bjørnson's Christiania production, which had used Mendelssohn's music, against newspaper attacks. [Ed.]

J. O. Halliwell-Phillipps (1879)

. . . What is absurdly termed aesthetic criticism is more out of place on this comedy than on any other of Shakespeare's plays. It deadens the 'native woodnotes wild' that every reader of taste would desire to be left to their own influences. The *Midsummer Night's Dream* is too exquisite a composition to be dulled by the infliction of philosophical analysis.

SOURCE: extract from *Memoranda on the Midsummer Night's Dream* (Brighton, 1879), p. 13.

W. Oechelhäuser (1885)

. . . In the word *parody* is the key to the only true comprehension and representation of the *Summernight's Dream*; but observe, there must be no attempt at a mere comic representation of love, least of all at a representation of true, genuine love, but at a *parody of love*. Above all, there is *nothing* in the whole play which is to be taken seriously; *every* action and situation in it is a parody, and *all persons, without exception, heroes as well as lovers, fairies as well as clowns, are exponents of this parody*.

In the midst of fairies and clowns there is no place for a serious main action. But if this be granted, then (and this it is which I now urge) let the true colouring be given to the main action when put upon the stage, and let it not, as has been hitherto the case, vaguely fluctuate between jest and earnest. . . .

An exaggeration . . . is required for the Amazonian queen Hippolyta. Here the contrast between classicality and an appearance in Comedy is more striking [than in the case of Theseus]; moreover there are various indications in the play which lead directly to the conclusion that the poet intended to give this role a palpably comic tone. The jealous Titania speaks of her derisively as 'the bouncing Amazon, Your buskin'd mistress and your warrior love'. The roles of

Theseus and Hippolyta acquire the genuine and befitting shade of comicality, when they are represented as a stout middle-aged pair of lovers, past their maturity, for such was unquestionably the design of the poet, and was in harmony with their active past life. The words of Titania, just quoted, refer to that corporeal superabundance which is wont to accompany mature years. But Theseus always speaks with the sedateness of ripe age. . . .

Utterly different from this must the tendency to parody be expressed in the acts and words of the pairs of youthful lovers. First of all, every actor must rid himself of any preconceived notion that he is here dealing with ideal characters, or with ordinary, lofty personages of deep and warm feelings. Here there is nought but the jesting parody of love's passion. . . . One of Hermia's characteristics is lack of respect for her father, who complains of her 'stubborn harshness'; as also her pert questions and answers to the Duke, whose threats of death or enduring spinsterhood she treats with open levity, and behind the Duke's back snaps her fingers at both of them. . . .

SOURCE: extracts from *Einführungen in Shakespeares Bühnen-Dramen*, 2nd edn (1885), II, pp. 277, 279.

George Bernard Shaw   (1895)

. . . Mr [Augustin] Daly is in great form. In my last article I was rash enough to hint that he had not quite realized what could be done with electric lighting on the stage. He triumphantly answers me by fitting up all his fairies with portable batteries and incandescent lights, which they switch on and off from time to time, like children with a new toy. . . . Miss Lillian Swain in the part of Puck . . . announces her ability to girdle the earth in forty minutes in the attitude of a professional skater, and then begins the journey awkwardly in a swing, which takes her in the opposite direction to that in which she indicated her intention of going. . . . Another stroke of his is to make Oberon a woman. It must not be supposed that he does this solely because it is wrong, though there is no other reason apparent. He does it partly because he was brought up to do such things, and partly because they seem to him to be a tribute to Shakespeare's greatness, which, being uncommon, ought not to be interpreted according to the dictates of common sense. A female Oberon and a Puck who behaves like a page-boy earnestly training himself for the post of footman recommend themselves to him because they totally destroy the naturalness of the presentation, and so accord with his conception of the Shakespearean dramas as the most artificial of all forms of stage entertainment. . . . He swings Puck away on a clumsy trapeze with a ridiculous clash of the cymbals in the orchestra, in the fullest belief that he is thereby completing instead of destroying the effect of Puck's lines. His 'panoramic illusion of the passage of Theseus's barge to Athens' is more absurd than anything that occurs in the tragedy of Pyramus and Thisbe in the last act. . . . Theseus has to enter from his barge down a bank, picking his way through the sleeping Lysander and Hermia, Demetrius and Helena. The four lions in Trafalgar Square are not more conspicuous and unoverlookable than these four figures are. Yet Theseus has to make all his hunting speeches in an impossible unconsciousness of them, and then to look at them amazedly and exclaim, 'But soft, what nymphs are these?' as if he could in any extremity of absence of mind have missed seeing them all along. . . .

SOURCE: extract from article in the *Saturday Review* (13 July 1895), reprinted in Edwin Wilson (ed.), *Shaw on Shakespeare* (Harmondsworth, 1969), pp. 146–8.

G. K. Chesterton   (1904)

The greatest of Shakespeare's comedies is also, from a certain point of view, the greatest of his plays. No one would maintain that it occupied this position in the matter of psychological study, if by psychological study we mean the study of individual characters in a play. No one would maintain that Puck was a character in the sense that Falstaff is a character, or that the critic stood awed before the psychology of Peaseblossom. But there is a sense in which the play is perhaps a greater triumph of psychology than *Hamlet* itself. It may well be questioned whether in any other literary work in the world is so vividly rendered a social and spiritual atmosphere. There is an atmosphere in *Hamlet*, for instance, a somewhat murky and even melodramatic one, but it is subordinate to the great character, and morally inferior to him; the darkness is only a background for the isolated star of intellect. But *A Midsummer Night's Dream* is a psychological study, not of a solitary man, but of a spirit that unites mankind. The six men may sit talking in an inn; they may not know each other's names or see each other's faces before or after, but night or wine or great stories, or some rich and branching discussion may make them all at one, if not absolutely with each other, at least with that invisible seventh man who is the harmony of them all. That seventh man is the hero of *A Midsummer Night's Dream*. . . .

The sentiment of such a play, so far as it can be summed up at all, can be summed up in one sentence. It is the mysticism of happiness. That is to say, it is the conception that as man lives upon a borderland he may find himself in the spiritual or supernatural atmosphere, not only through being profoundly sad or meditative, but by being extravagantly happy. The soul might be rapt out of the body in an agony of sorrow, or a trance of ecstasy; but it might also be rapt out of the body in a paroxysm of laughter. Sorrow we know can go beyond itself; so, according to Shakespeare, can pleasure go beyond itself and become something dangerous and unknown. . . . The whole question which is balanced, and balanced nobly and fairly, in *A Midsummer Night's Dream*, is whether the life of waking, or the life of the vision, is the real life, the *sine qua non* of man. . . .

In pure poetry and the intoxication of words, Shakespeare never rose higher than he rises in this play. But in spite of this fact the supreme literary merit of *A Midsummer Night's Dream* is a merit of design. The amazing symmetry, the amazing artistic and moral beauty of that design, can be stated very briefly. The story opens in the sane and common world with the pleasant seriousness of very young lovers and very young friends. Then, as the figures advance into the tangled wood of young troubles and stolen happiness, a change and bewilderment begins to fall on them. They lose their way and their wits for they are in the very heart of fairyland. Their words, their hungers, their very figures grow more and more dim and fantastic, like dreams within dreams, in the supernatural mist of Puck. Then the dream-fumes begin to clear, and characters and spectators begin to awaken together to the noise of horns and dogs and the clean and bracing morning. Theseus, the incarnation of a happy and generous rationalism, expounds in hackneyed and superb lines the sane view of such psychic experiences, pointing out with a reverent and sympathetic scepticism that all those fairies and spells are themselves but the emanations, the unconscious masterpieces, of man himself. The whole company falls back into a splendid human laughter. There is a rush for banqueting and private theatricals, and over all these things ripples one of those frivolous and inspired conversations in which every good saying seems to die in giving birth to another. If ever the son of man in his wanderings was at home and drinking by the fireside, he is at home in the house of Theseus. All the dreams have been forgotten in the human certainty of any other triumphant evening party; and so the play seems naturally ended. It began on the earth and it ends on the earth. Thus to round off the whole midsummer night's dream in an eclipse of daylight is an effect of genius. But of this comedy . . . the mark is that genius goes beyond itself; and one touch is added which makes the play colossal. Theseus and his train retire with a crashing finale, full of honour and wisdom and things set right, and silence falls on the house. Then there comes a faint sound of little feet, and for a moment, as it were, the elves look into the house, asking which is the reality. 'Suppose we are the reality and they the shadows.' If that ending were acted properly any modern man would feel shaken to his marrow if he had to walk home from the theatre through a country lane.

It is a trite matter, of course, though in a general criticism a more or less indispensable one, to comment upon another point of artistic perfection, the extraordinarily human and accurate manner in which the play catches the atmosphere of a dream. The chase and tangle and frustration of the incidents and personalities are well known to everyone who has dreamt of perpetually falling over precipices or perpetually missing trains. While following out clearly and legally the necessary narrative of the drama, the author contrives to include every one of the main peculiarities of the exasperating dream. Here is the pursuit of the man we cannot catch, the flight from the man we cannot see; here is the perpetual returning to the same place, here is the crazy alteration in the very objects of our desire, the substitution of one face for another face, the putting of wrong souls in the wrong bodies, the fantastic disloyalties of the night, all this is as obvious as it is important. It is perhaps somewhat more worth remarking that there is about this confusion of comedy yet another essential characteristic of dreams. A dream can commonly be described as possessing an utter discordance of incident combined with a curious unity of mood; everything changes but the dreamer. It may begin with anything, but if the dreamer is sad at the end he will be sad as if by prescience at the beginning; if he is cheerful at the beginning he will be cheerful if the stars fall. *A Midsummer Night's Dream* has in a most singular degree effected this difficult, this almost desperate subtlety. The events in the wandering wood are in themselves, and regarded as in broad daylight, not merely melancholy but bitterly cruel and ignominious. But yet by the spreading of an atmosphere as magic as the fog of Puck, Shakespeare contrives to make the whole matter mysteriously hilarious while it is palpably tragic, and mysteriously charitable, while it is in itself cynical. He contrives somehow to rob tragedy and treachery of their full sharpness, just as a toothache or a deadly danger from a tiger, or a precipice, is robbed of its sharpness in a pleasant dream. The creation of a brooding sentiment like this, a sentiment not merely independent of but actually opposed to the events, is a much greater triumph of art than the creation of the character of Othello. . . .

SOURCE: extracts from '*A Midsummer Night's Dream*, I and II', in *Good Words* (Sept. and Oct. 1904).

Frank Sidgwick   (1908)

A Midsummer-Night's Dream is more of a masque than a drama – an entertainment rather than a play. The characters are mostly puppets, and scarcely any except Bottom has the least psychological interest for the reader. Probability is thrown to the winds; anachronism is rampant; classical figures are mixed with fairies and sixteenth-century Warwickshire peasants. The main plot is sentimental, the secondary plot is sheer buffoonery; while the story of Titania's jealousy and Oberon's method of curing it can scarcely be dignified by the title of plot at all. The threads which bind together these three tales, however ingeniously fastened, are fragile. . . .

It is perhaps a permissible fancy to convert Theseus' words, 'the lunatic, the lover, and the poet', to illustrate the triple appeal made by the three ingredients – the grotesque, the sentimental, and the fantastic. Each part, of course, is coloured by the poet's genius, and the whole is devoted to the comic aspect of love, to eternal youth and endless caprice, laughing at laws and laughed at by the secure. 'What fools these mortals be!' is the comment of the immortal; the corollary, left unspoken by those outside the pale, being 'What fools these lovers be!' . . .

Bottom takes his name from the wooden reel or spool on which thread is wound; 'bottom' simply meaning the base or foundation of the reel. . . .

Oberon is the English transliteration of the French Auberon in the romance of *Huon of Bordeaux*, and Auberon is probably merely the French counterpart of Alberich or Albrich, a dwarf occurring in the German *Niebelungenlied* and other works. Etymologically Alberich is composed of *alb* = elf and *rich* = king. The name Oberon appears first in English literature in Lord Berners' translation of *Huon of Bordeaux* (c. 1534), and afterwards in Spenser's *Faerie Queene* [II i 6; II x 75] and in Robert Greene's play *James IV*, which was acted in 1589. But the king of the fairies in Chaucer's *The Marchantes Tale* [983 (Skeat, E. 2227)] is Pluto, and the queen Proserpine. . . .

Proserpine is the wife of Pluto (in Greek form, Persephone, wife of Dis). In Elizabethan times, Campion's charming poem, 'Hark, all you ladies that do sleep' keeps the name of 'the fairy-queen Proserpina'. Shakespeare appears to have taken the name Titania from Ovid's *Metamorphoses*, [III 173], who uses it as an epithet of Diana, as being the sister of Sol or Helios, the Sun-God, a Titan. Scot, in his *Discovery of Witchcraft*, gives Diana as one of the names of the 'lady of the fairies'; and James I, in his *Demonology* (1597) refers to a 'fourth kind of sprites, which by the Gentiles was called Diana and her wandering court, and amongst us called the Phairie'.

Curiously enough, in Shakespeare's most famous description of the

Fairy Queen she is called Queen Mab; this is said to be of Celtic derivation. Mercutio's catalogue of Mab's attributes and functions corresponds closely with the description of Robin Goodfellow. . . .

The main characteristics of Shakespeare's fairies . . . may be summarised shortly. They are commonly under a king and queen, who hold a court; they are very small, light, swift, elemental; they share in the life of nature; they are fond of dancing and singing; they are invisible and immortal; they prefer night, and midnight is their favourite hour; they fall in love with mortals, steal babies and leave changelings, and usurp the function of Hymen in blessing the marriage-bed. Oberon, 'king of shadows', can apparently see things hidden from Puck. [See II i 155] . . .

The fairy of folk-lore in Shakespeare's day is nearly everything that the fairies of *A Midsummer-Night's Dream* are; we may possibly except their exiguity, their relations in love with mortals, and their hymeneal functions. His conception of their size as infinitesimal at least differs from that of the popular stories, where (as far as can be ascertained) they are shown to be about the size of mortal children.

SOURCE: extracts from *The Sources and Analogues of 'A Midsummer-Night's Dream'* (London, and New York, 1908), pp. 2, 3, 35–6, 36–7, 64, 65.

Harley Granville-Barker   (1914)

. . . So recklessly happy in writing such verse does Shakespeare grow that even the quarrel of the four lovers is stayed by a charming speech of Helena's thirty-seven lines long. It is true that at the end of it, Hermia, her author allowing her to recollect the quarrel, says she is amazed at these passionate words, but that the passage beginning, 'We Hermia, like two artificial gods', is meant by Shakespeare to be spoken otherwise than with a meticulous regard to its every beauty is hard to believe. And its every beauty will hardly shine through throbbing passion. No, his heart was in these passages of verse, and so the heart of the play is in them.

SOURCE: extract from his Preface to *A Midsummer Night's Dream*, Savoy Theatre Acting Edition (London, 1914), pp. *vii–viii*.

Sir Arthur Quiller-Couch   (1918)

. . . A friend of mine – an old squire of Devon – used to demonstrate to me at great length that when Shakespeare wrote . . . of the moon looking 'with a watery eye' –

> And when she weeps, weeps every little flower,
> Lamenting some enforced chastity

– he anticipated our modern knowledge of plant-fertilisation. Good man, he took 'enforced' to mean 'compulsory'; and I never dared to dash his enthusiasm by hinting that, as Shakespeare would use the word 'enforced', an 'enforced chastity' meant a chastity violated.[1]

SOURCE: extract from *Shakespeare's Workmanship* (Cambridge, 1931), p. 66; the essay was first published in 1918.

NOTE

1. A failure to understand the meaning of this phrase vitiates the arguments of Jan Kott in Part Two below and of many other recent critics. The same point is made in M. R. Ridley's British Academy lecture, 'On Reading Shakespeare' (1940) [Ed.].

Benedetto Croce   (1920)

. . . The quintessence of all these comedies (as we may say of *Hamlet* in respect of the great tragedies) is the *Midsummer Night's Dream.* Here the quick ardours, the inconstancies, the caprices, the illusions, the delusions, every sort of love folly, become embodied and weave a world of their own, as living and as real as that of those who are visited by these affections, tormented or rendered ecstatic, raised on high or hurled downward by them, in such a way that everything is equally real or equally fantastic, as you may please to call it. The sense of dream, of a dream-reality persists and prevents our feeling the chilly sense of allegory or of apology. The little drama seems born of a smile, so delicate, refined and ethereal it is. Graceful and delicate to a degree is also the setting of the dream, the celebration of the wedding of Theseus and Hippolyta and the theatrical performance of the artisans, for these are not merely ridiculous in their clumsiness, they are also childlike and ingenuous, arousing a sort of gay pity: we do not laugh at them: we smile. Oberon and Titania are at variance owing to reciprocal wrongs, and trouble has often arisen in the world. Puck obeys the command of Oberon and sets to work, teasing, punishing and correcting. But in performing this duty of punishing and correcting, he too makes mistakes, and the love intrigue becomes more complicated and active. Here we find a resemblance to the rapid passage into opposite states and the strange complications that arose in Italian knightly romances, as the result of drinking the water from one of two opposite fountains whereof one filled the heart with amorous desires, the other turned first ardours to ice.

SOURCE: extract from *Ariosto, Shakespeare, and Corneille,* trans. Douglas Ainslie.

Enid Welsford   (1927)

. . . *A Midsummer Night's Dream* is more nearly related to the genuine masque than is *Comus*. In *Comus* . . . , though dances occur, they are merely incidental, and the play would be scarcely altered by their omission. In *A Midsummer Night's Dream* most – not all – of the dances are vitally connected with the plot. For instance, Titania's awakening in IV i is an important point in the play, for it is the point where the ravel begins to be untangled, and the occasion is celebrated by a dance of reunion between Fairy King and Fairy Queen: [quotes IV i 84–91].

The rhythm of the poetry is a dance rhythm, the lines rock and sway with the movement of the fairies. Even more closely in the last scene does the verse echo the light pattering steps of the elves. There is nothing like this in *Comus*. The lyrics there are exquisite, melodious, but they are not dance-songs. Even the entry of Comus is poetry of the *Il Penseroso* order, imaginative, intellectual, reminiscent, while Shakespeare's lines are alive with movement, and suggest the repeat and turn and rhythmic beat of dancing. In a word, in *Comus* we have thought turned to poetry, while in *A Midsummer Night's Dream* we have sound and movement turned to poetry.

The influence of the dance has affected not merely isolated songs and speeches, but the whole structure. . . . The difference in style between *Comus* and *A Midsummer Night's Dream* depends upon a difference of spirit. *Comus* is a criticism of life, it springs from an abstract idea: *A Midsummer Night's Dream* is a dance, a movement of bodies. The plot is a pattern, a figure, rather than a series of events occasioned by human character and passion, and this pattern, especially in the moonlit parts of the play, is the pattern of a dance.

Enter a Fairie at one doore, and Robin Goodfellow at another. . . . Enter the King of Fairies, at one doore, with his traine; and the Queene, at another with hers.

The apearance and disappearance and reappearance of the various lovers, the will-o'-the-wisp movement of the elusive Puck, form a kind of figured ballet. The lovers quarrel in a dance pattern: first, there are two men to one woman and the other woman alone, then for a brief space a circular movement, each one pursuing and pursued, then a return to the first figure with the position of the women reversed, then a cross-movement, man quarrelling with man and woman with woman, and then, as finale, a general setting to partners, including not only lovers but fairies and royal personages as well.

This dance-like structure makes it inevitable that the lovers should be all almost as devoid of character as masquers or masque-presenters. The harmony and grace of the action would have been spoilt by convincing passion.

SOURCE: extract from *The Court Masque: A Study in the Relationship between Poetry and Revels* (1927; reprinted 1962), pp. 330–2.

PART TWO

Modern Critical Studies

Minor White Latham (1930)   The Elizabethan Fairies

. . . There is ample evidence of the belief in the reality and actual being of the fairies in the recognised existence in Elizabethan life of the changeling, a visible and material being and a member of the fairy race, and in the recognition by English law, and more especially by Scottish law, of mortals made witches by fairies who appeared to them and invested them with their powers.

The seuerall notorious and lewd Cousonages of John West and Alice West, falsely called the King and Queene of Fayries, practised very lately both in this citie and many places neere adjoyning: to the impouerishing of many simple people, as well as many women, and the arraignment and conviction, on the 14th of January, 1613, of the two imposters whose crime consisted in impersonating the king and queen of fairies, furnishes a significant illustration of the belief in visible and actual fairies at the beginning of the seventeenth century. . . .

Falstaff . . . , in *The Merry Wives of Windsor,* suffers under no illusion that the fairies who dance around him in Windsor Forest are mythical beings or creatures invented in old wives' tales. To him, if his fear or his actions are at all indicative, the fairies are real and fearful spirits who appear to mortals and who must not be spoken to under pain of death. The lawyer's clerk of *The Alchemist* does not consider an interview with the queen of the fairies an impossible feat, or her appearance to him, after due ceremonies, an extraordinary occurrence. . . .

In England . . . only adult men and women seem to have taken the part of fairy rulers [on the stage]. Doll Common, full-grown, played the Fairy Queen in *The Alchemist,* as did a man the Fairy Queen in the *Valiant Welshman.* An adult actor boasted to Greene that he 'was famous for Delphrigus, and the king of Fairies as ever was any of my time',[1] and Dame Quickly in the quarto, and Anne Page in the folio, represented the Fairy Queen in *The Merry Wives of Windsor.* It is especially noticeable, also, that Titania in *A Midsummer Night's Dream,* surrounded by an infinitesimal court in the diminutive rendition of fairyland, was represented as large enough to wind the figure of Bottom in her arms [IV i]. . . .

In *Huon of Bordeaux*, Oberon is described as three feet high. His smallness is noticed and explained as the result of enchantment. The other fairies in the romance are represented as of the size of men. . . .

With such general evidence of the beauty imputed to the fairies, it is significant to find that masks and vizards were required for the actors who represented them. In the disguise of spirits in *The Bugbears*, the actors who played the role of spirits had on 'visars like develes', and possibly a number of other kinds of visors, since it is noted that they went 'a sprityng . . . with thys face and that face and you goodman good face' or 'lyke bugbeares with vysardes to make old sootes dyssardes'. The use of the customary masks is stressed in *The Merry Wives of Windsor* where the troupe of fairies 'must all be mask'd and vizarded'. And the omission of masks in the representation of the fairies at Norwich is so unusual that it requires a statement from the devisor. (Nichols, *Prog. of Eliz.*, vol. II, p. 199.)

Such visors, for use both in the devices of fairies and in other disguisings, like those of the fourteenth and fifteenth centuries, were 'well and handsomely made', being 'peyntid visers, diffourmyd or colourid visages in eny wise'. And handsome and ugly visors must have been kept in stock and were readily obtained, to judge from the ease with which Master Ford bought them for his fairies, and from the custom recorded by Lavater:

It is a common costume in many places, that at a certaine time of the yeare, one with a nette or visarde on his face maketh Children afrayde, to the ende that ever after they should laboure and be obedient to their Parents: afterward they tel them that those which they saw, were Bugs, Witches, and Hagges, which thing they verily believe, and are commonly miserablie afrayde.

The necessity for a mask or vizard is explicable, when it is taken into account that the fairies of the sixteenth century were of different complexions – black, gray, green, white, red, and sometimes blue.

In the play of *The Bugbears*, assigned to the years 1564–1565, the 'white and red fearye' was included among the spirits of the time. The examination of John Walsh, tried for witchcraft in 1566, contained the statement that 'ther be iii. kindes of Feries, white, greene, and black'. According to *The Discovery of Witchcraft*, there were 'white spirits and black spirits, gray spirits and red spirits', and in *Macbeth* beings with the same varied complexions were invoked. . . .

Perhaps one of the best authorities for the colors of the fairies' complexions is *Merry Wives of Windsor*. Here, after great verbal and material pains have been taken to dress the fairies in white and green costumes, they are summoned by the fairy crier:

> Fairies, black, grey, green, and white,
> You moon-shine revellers, and shades of night.

This apostrophe made to the company of boys and Mistress Anne Page must have taken into account the colors of the visors which had been bought for them which were well illuminated by the round of waxen tapers on the heads of the wearers. There is little possibility that the terms, black and grey, could have been applied to the actors' costumes. These, if words could make them so, were green and white, and it was in these two colors and these only, that Anne Page could be dressed, and in these two colors that the boys were mistaken for Anne Page. . . .

The green and white of the Windsor fairies were the colors of the costumes usually affected by all Elizabethan fairies. White they used many times, so many times that they and their relatives were called 'White Nymphs' (Heywood, *Hierarchie*, p. 507). But green was their favorite color and silk their only wearing, if the ballad maker or citizen had his way, which is not to be wondered at, considering the romantic glamor which haunts both color and fabric to this present day. 'There were with King Oberon a many fayries, all attyred in greene silke', the author of *Robin Goodfellow; his mad prankes, and merry Jests*, insisted; ' . . . like Men, and Women, Souldiers, Kings, and Ladyes Children, and Horse-men clothed in green' was the comment on the fairy costumes in 1665. . . . So much given to green were they that in 1696, when Anne Jefferies saw them, they appeared as 'six small People, all in Green Clothes', and as late as 1726 Waldron recounts their materialisation in the Isle of Man 'all drest in green, and gallantly mounted'.[2]. . .

An idea of the fairies' dress can be gained also from the apparel of the characters who were mistaken for fairies in the plays of the period. Imogen in *Cymbeline* was in page's clothes when she was likened to a fairy [III vi], as was Alathe in *The Night-Walker* [Fletcher, I i]. Marina in *Pericles* was dressed in the usual costume of a gentlewoman when she was identified with the fairy race [V i], and Thomas in *Monsieur Thomas* was masquerading in his sister's clothes when he was given the role of a fairy or spirit [Fletcher, IV vi]. From these instances, it would seem that the fairies at times wore the usual male and female attire of the country. . . .

No one needed to be ill who was in their favor, since the race to which the fairies belonged could 'cause and cure most diseases' and knew 'the virtues of herbs, plants, stones, minerals, &c. of all creatures, birds, beasts, the four elements, stars, planets' and could 'aptly apply and make use of them'.[3]

Oberon, Titania, and the fairy train . . . were not acting, therefore, under the inspiration of a poetic imagination when they made use of herbs to cause love and to satisfy it. They were following a traditional characteristic of their race which every mortal knew and some favoured ones could vouch for, from actual experience. Alesoun Peirsoun, for instance, who had seen 'the guid nychtbouris mak thair sawis, with panis and fyris' and knew 'that they gadderit thair herbis, before the sone rysing, as scho did'[4] when Shakespeare was but new to poetry. . . .

On first acquaintance, there seems but little difference between the fairies of *A Midsummer Night's Dream* and those of native tradition, and of Shakespeare's other plays. . . .

On closer study, however, the fairies . . . are seen to be what Oberon calls them, 'spirits of another sort' [III ii 388]. Whatever is homely or substantial or dangerous has been removed from the picture of them, which Shakespeare repaints, and only their rulers are still invested with formidable powers and uncertain tempers. . . .

Instead of appearing as an active and powerful commonwealth with their traditional ruler, the fairies are given the role of innocuous and almost negligible attendants upon two literary or mythological sovereigns, Oberon and Titania.

Oberon, already familiar on the stage as the king of the fairies through *James the Fourth* of Greene and the *Entertainment at Elvetham*, seems to have been taken by Shakespeare directly from *Huon of Bordeaux*. With his quick and violent temper, his piety, his devotion to those mortals to whom he took a fancy, his angelic visage, his dwarfed stature, his splendid dress and his powers of enchantment – all characteristics of Oberon, the 'dwarfe kynge of the fayrey' in the romance – he was admirably adapted to play one of the leading parts in the imaginary and poetic fairy kingdom of a romantic comedy.

The name *Titania* Shakespeare appears to have taken from Ovid's *Metamorphoses* [Book III], where it occurs as one of the synonyms of Diana. The precedent for Diana's sovereignty over the fairies is to be found in R. Scot's *Discovery of Witchcraft* [1651 ed., III xvii 52], in Golding's translation of Ovid's *Metamorphoses* [IV 304], in *The Faerie Queene* ['A Letter of the Authors'], and in Lyly's *Endymion* [IV iii]. But the character of the picturesque and romantic queen who rules over the fairies of *A Midsummer Night's Dream* and the plot in which she is involved are Shakespeare's own creation.

The powers which were attributed to Diana and to Oberon, both in their own persons and in that of the king and queen of the fairies, are still exercised by the fairy rulers of Shakespeare. Their connection with mortals, however, is revealed as unfailingly beneficent and altruistic, an attitude vastly different from that of Diana, 'the goddesse of the Pagans', associated with witches in *The Discovery of Witchcraft*, and from the Oberon of whom Gerames and Huon stood in much fear in *Huon of Bordeaux*.

For the first time the fairies themselves are made consistently good. No longer do they function as the mischievous and dangerous beings they were believed to be, with occasional and erratic lapses into beneficence and the bestowal of good fortune; instead they become, in actuality, the Good Neighbours which, in flattery and in fear, they had been dubbed by mortals trembling before the idea of their advent. Every aspect of their wickedness and every sign of their devilish connection is omitted from their portrait [III ii 388], and the period of their earthly materialization is devoted to making the world happier and more beautiful [V i 389–90], without any of the usual impositions of taboos and without any of the usual demand for worship or payment.

They do not appear from underground or from hell to inspire fear. They travel from the farthest steppe of India [II i 69] to insure for the king of Athens and his bride joy and prosperity, a future of faithful love and fortunate issue. . . .

Notwithstanding their past spitefulness and malicious meddling, they cannot now bear the slightest disturbance of the peace, but, at the sound of vituperation between Oberon and Titania,

> all their elves, for fear
> Creep into acorn cups, and hide them there;   [II i 30–1]

while mortal combat so disturbs the soul of Oberon that he overcasts the night when a fight is impending, and takes steps to separate the 'testy rivals', 'As one come not within another's way' [III ii 358–9].

The fairies' passion for stealing human children from their cradles and their known practice of disfiguring them with withered arms and elvish marks is changed into an excessive solicitude about the welfare of babies [II i 21–7; V i 393–404]. Even the changeling in the fairy kingdom . . . has not been obtained by violence and human woe. He has been adopted by Titania out of friendship for his mother, who 'being mortal, of that boy did die' [II i 135].

In spite, too, of a lifetime devoted to pinchings and kidnappings, both the fairies and their sovereigns refuse to allow any hurt or discomfort to come to the mortals whom they encounter. . . . Bottom the Weaver who, it must be noticed, is changed into an ass and is brought into the fairy world through an individual prank of Robin Goodfellow, and not from any effort of the fairies nor at the command or cognizance of their rulers, is given fairies to 'attend' upon him, to fetch him 'jewels from the deep', and to 'fan the moon-beams from his sleeping eyes' [III i 148, 149, 168]. He is put to sleep on pressed flowers, and sustains no more injury than a diet of

> apricocks and dewberries,
> With purple grapes, green figs, and mulberries.   [III i 161–2]

Neither is he returned to human existence deprived of his reason and one of 'his members', as was the way of fairies with mortals. He is restored to earth at the exact minute and in the exact place where it is necessary for him to be, able to 'discourse wonders', with no other marks of his sojourn with the fairies than the remembrance of a dream [IV ii 26; IV i 203–11].

The fairy queen steps out of a tradition of infernal connections and

dark deeds to deplore the fact that the dissensions between her and
Oberon have resulted in floods and loss of crops [quotes II i 94–8].
She is much disturbed over unseasonable temperatures, and
'rheumatick diseases' that abound [II i 105]. She is distressed that
'human mortals want their winter here' [II i 101] and that 'No night
is now with hymn or carol blest' [II i 102]. . . .

Especially is the change in the character of the fairies emphasised
by Shakespeare in his introduction in the fairy kingdom of Robin
Goodfellow, who is employed, instead of the fairies, to frighten and
mislead mortals, to bewitch Bottom and carry him away into
fairyland, to clean the palace of Theseus, and to call attention to the
evil reputation and connections of the fairies of tradition.

The difference between these fairies and those of [the play] is again
made apparent in the extravagant attachment for flowers which
Shakespeare attributes to his fairies. They had always been connected
with hills and wells and green meadows, with now and then a garden
in which they had danced and sung, as in 'The Marchantes Tale' of
Chaucer, and in the *Entertainment at Elvetham*. They had been
associated, too, with flowers in Golding's translation of Ovid's
Metamorphoses [IX 337], and in *The Queene's Majestie's Entertainment at
Woodstocke*, where a handmaid of the Fayry Queene presented
Elizabeth and her ladies with 'many excellente and fine smelling
Nosegayes made of all cullers'. And in the *Entertainment at Elvetham*,
again, the fairy queen had introduced herself to Elizabeth as one

> That every night in rings of painted flowers
> Turne round, and carrell our Elisaes name.

But in *A Midsummer Night's Dream*, the fairies are completely
identified with buds and blossoms, dew-drops and butterflies. Their
similes are floral; their favors, the gold spots of cowslips; their scent
bottles, its freckles [II i 11–3]. Their preoccupations, for the most
part, consist in watering the fairy ring, hanging dewdrops in each
cowslip's ear [II i 9, 15], in killing canker in the musk-rose buds, in
putting spells upon beetles and worms, snails and spiders [II ii 3, 20–
3], and in blessing mortal rooms with 'field-dew consecrate' [V i 405].
Their names are Cobweb, Mustardseed, Moth, and Pease-blossom.
Their changeling and their victim are crowned with flowers [II i 27;

IV i 51], and their charms effected by means of 'a little western flower' [II i 166].

The fairy queen who, as Diana, rode over the kingdoms of the earth followed by a multitude of wicked women, now sleeps on

a bank where the wild thyme blows . . .   [II i 249–56]

and shows her love by sticking musk-roses in Bottom's 'sleek smooth head' [IV i 3]. And Oberon, whose anger in *Huon of Bordeaux* caused

reyne and wynde/hayle/and snowe/and . . . meruelous tempestes/with thonder and lyghtenynges/so that it shall seme to you that all the worlde sholde pereshe,

[EETS ed., I, i, 84]

is melted by the mournful sight of the dew [IV i 52–5). . . .

When *A Midsummer Night's Dream* was put upon the stage, there appeared among the fairies Robin Goodfellow, who was given, in the play, two other names also – Hobgoblin and Puck. The 'merry wanderer of the night', as he called himself, might well have uttered a protest, had he been able to speak in his real and accepted capacity, both against the company in which he was put and against the names, especially that of Puck, which were bestowed upon him. He was no fairy, if the records of his history before 1594 be true, and this was his first inclusion in fairyland. And the term *Puck* or *pouke* was a generic term applied to a class of demons or devils and to the devil himself, with whom, before *A Midsummer Night's Dream*, he had never been classified. . . .

[His] figure and person, if nothing else, would have marked him as a country spirit, or would have kept him one. He was both tall and broad, of the size of a full grown man or bigger, with nothing ethereal or graceful about his proportions. His bigness particularly set him apart from other terrestrial spirits, as Robert Burton noted when he classified him as a 'bigger kind' of terrestrial devil[5], and as Ben Jonson knew when he represented him in *Love Restored* as saying: 'I am none of those subtle ones, that can creep through at a key-hole, or the cracked pane of a window. I must come in at a door.'

So much were his shape and making different from the fairies of *A*

Midsummer Night's Dream that he was identified there by his figure, and so well known were his measurements that in *The Merry Wives of Windsor* his role was not entrusted to any of the Windsor children, not even to one of the boys who was big enough and tall enough to be mistaken for Mistress Anne Page, but was played by Pistol. . . .

However Robin Goodfellow's clothes might vary, one item of his costume never changed. This was the broom or threshing flail which he habitually carried. Find him in whatever company you may, his broom especially is in easy reach. In Jonson's *Love Restored* he 'e'en went back, and stuck to this shape . . . of mine own, with my broom and my candles, and came in confidently'. In *Grim, the Collier of Croydon* [IV i], and in Milton's *L'Allegro* [line 108], he carries a flail. One of his chief occupations, according to Jonson (*Love Restored*), Scot (*Discovery of Witchcraft*), and Tyndale ('Obed. of a Chr. Man' in *Doctrinal Treatises*), was sweeping. And Shakespeare . . . , though placing Robin Goodfellow in a poetic and etherealised fairy court, as messenger and jester of Oberon, does not take away his broom. In [V i], he . . . calls public attention to it . . . [quotes V i 379–80] . . .

There were two conditions upon which, in addition to his fee, Robin Goodfellow's domestic services were given. He required of the mistress or maid whom he served that she did not, as he put it, 'sluttish lie'; nor would he lend his aid to men or women unless they conformed to his standard of morality in regard to love. If they were true lovers, he took a tremendous interest in their affairs, in which he meddled, until he brought about a happy consummation. So well known were his match-making instincts and his devotion to the cause of true love that his endeavours in this regard were recognized as one of his functions.

In the masque of *Love Restored*, he was chosen to throw out 'that imposter Plutus, the god of money, who has stolen Love's ensigns, and in his belied figure rules the world', and to restore true love, 'in despight of this insolent and barbarous Mammon'.

In *Grim, the Collier of Croydon*, he took a great hand in furthering the cause of love:

> I like this country-girl's condition well;
> She's faithful, and a lover but to one;
> Robin stands here to right both Grim and her   [IV i]

and in punishing attempts against virtue:

> What, priest, still at your lechery?
> *Robin beats the priest.*
> I'll thresh you for your knavery;
> If any ask who beat them so,
> Tell them 'twas Robin Goodfellow.   [IV i]

In *Nimphidia* he endeavoured to restore the erring Mab to her husband; while in *A Midsummer Night's Dream* he lamented the fortunes of the love-lorn Hermia, and the knavishness of Cupid 'Thus to make poor females mad' [III ii 441). . . .

Among the diminutive and ethereal fairies of *A Midsummer Night's Dream*, Robin Goodfellow's uncouth shape and figure are stressed [II i], and the rusticity of his affections and his devotion to his broom [V i] are emphasised. He is unable to see things which Oberon can see [II i], and in contradistinction to the fairies, at least in this play, he is in terror lest daylight find him on earth [III ii]. In addition, he is reduced to the position of jester and messenger of Oberon whose commands he must obey. Although, in this situation, he is able to carry out any mad pranks which come into his head, he is forced to explain his mistakes and to suffer a sharp reproof from Oberon because of his jokes [III ii].

SOURCE: extracts from *The Elizabethan Fairies: The Fairies of Folklore and the Fairies of Shakespeare* (New York, 1930; reprinted 1972), pp. 29, 30–1, 78, 80, 82–8, 137–8, 179–84, 185–7, 219, 240, 245–6, 249–50, 254–5.

NOTES

[Reorganised and renumbered from the original – Ed.]

1. Greene, *Groatsworth of Wit*, ed. Rev. A. B. Grosart (Edinburgh, 1881–1886), XII, 131.

2. Waldron, *A Description of the Isle of Man* (1726), p. 33.

3. Burton, *Anatomy of Melancholy*, ed. A. R. Shilleto (London, 1896) I, 212.

4. *Criminal Cases in Scotland*, ed. Robert Pitcairn (Edinburgh, 1833), I, 163.

5. Burton, *op. cit.*, I, 220.

G. Wilson Knight (1932) 'Dissension in Fairyland'

. . . The action depends largely on Oberon's quarrel with Titania. Dissension has entered fairyland itself, due to these spirits' desire for human love, just as later human beings are caused trouble by their contact with the fairies: [quotes II i 68–73]. Oberon parries Titania's speech with reciprocal jealousy. Now this dissension makes 'tempests' in nature, untuning the melodic procession of the seasons: [quotes II i 81–117]. Unruly floods, disorder in the seasons, storm and mud and all natural confusion result from this dissension in fairyland. And this tempest is at the heart of the play, sending ripples outward through the plot, vitalizing the whole middle action. Hence our dissensions and mistakes, our comedy; in fact, our drama: most of the action is related to the Oberon-Titania quarrel.

Fairyland is set against mortality. Close to her tempest speech Titania has a lovely passage on the fairies' Indian home: [quotes II i 121–34]. Note the 'spiced air' and also the 'yellow sands', reminding us of Venus' promise to dance, like a nymph, on the sands, 'and yet no footing seen'; and also the ship and 'merchandise' imagery; and the thought of Titania and her Indian 'votaress' amused at 'the traders on the flood'. India, we must remember, is fairyland itself; and the Indian votaress all but an immortal. Therefore, as we watch Titania and her loved friend laughing at the 'traders on the flood', imitating their 'voyage' on the waters of life, we see fairyland laughing at storm-tossed mortality. We must not forget the universal suggestion with which voyages are impregnated in Shakespeare. This is, indeed, an exquisite prologue to the middle action, where Puck befools poor mortals: [quotes III ii 114–5]. Titania's merchandise speech beautifully reflects this essential spirit, as a prologue to our middle scenes.

For humanity here indeed suffers some cruelly comic distresses. In the first scene we find tragic tempests: [quotes I i 128–31]. In this play passionate love gives vent to 'showers of oaths' [I i 245], and Bottom by the power of his acting will 'move storms' [I ii 23–4]; while in the midnight wood the troubles of Hermia and Helena are increased. These scenes are dark; dark with distress of lovers, dark with the shadowed and gnomish fearsomeness that reigns through a woodland night. Lysander and Hermia have lost their way in the forest [II ii 42]; Hermia is 'faint' with wandering [II ii 41]. Helena follows Demetrius, imploring pity, receiving curses from the love-tormented and distracted youth. She is 'out of breath' with her fond chase [II ii 94]. Then she finds Lysander, sleeping: [quotes II ii 106–8]. 'Dead', 'blood'; this play is full of fears, and such satanic suggestions are frequent. . . . The play continually suggests a nightmare terror. It is dark and fearsome. The nights here are 'grim-look'd' [V i 167]. And yet this atmosphere of gloom and dread is the playground for the purest comedy. Romance and fun interthread our tragedies here. So, too, a pale light falls from moon and star into the darkened glades, carving the trees into deeper darkness, black voiceless giants; yet silvering the mossy slopes; lighting the grass with misty sparkles of flame; setting green fire to the glimmering eyes of prowling beasts; dissolving Oberon and Puck invisible in their magic beams. . . .

This play has many tempest-beasts: beasts fearsome, ravenous, and grim. So Demetrius threatens to run from Helena and leave her 'to the mercy of wild beasts' [II i 228]; but she answers that his scorn shows him to have a heart more cruel than the wildest, thus contrasting love with fierce beasts. It is significant, too, that to Oberon the leviathan comes as a natural image: [quotes II i 174]. The bear, the most usual tempest-beast, is frequent. Helena cries:

> No, no, I am as ugly as a bear,
> For beasts that meet me run away for fear.   [II ii 100–1].

She is a 'monster' [II ii 103]. The bear is found in other passages where there are significant groups suggesting fearsome animal-life. Oberon wishes that Titania may love a 'monster' [III ii 377]:

> The next thing then she waking looks upon
> Be it on lion, bear or wolf, or bull,
> On meddling monkey or on busy ape,
> She shall pursue it with the soul of love.   [II i 179–82]

The second line clearly contains the usual tempest-beasts; as for the third, we may remember the part played by apes in *Othello* and *Timon*. Oberon varies his animals a little when he speaks the actual charm: [quotes II ii 36–9]. The ounce and pard are new, but clearly in the usual tradition; the cat recalls the 'wild-cat' to which Katharina, the Shrew, is compared; the boar and bear are old friends – or enemies. The bear especially hardly ever fails to put in an appearance on these occasions. Such are the nightmare beasts Oberon's tempestuous jealousy would introduce to a Fairy Queen's love. And all these suggestions build an atmosphere of fearsomeness in our play. . . .

Oberon charms Titania to 'wake when some vile thing is near': he expects a tempest-beast, but instead she wakes to love Bottom, ass-headed. Throughout we must see an exquisite contrast between these two, Bottom and Titania. The one is 'the shallowest thick-skin of that barren sort' [III ii 13]; the other, all queenly, feminine, and fairy grace. . . . It is a symbolic union: symbolic of the whole play where opposites are so exquisitely blended in unity.

This is a union of the material and the spiritual; or the bestial and the birdlike. Birds in Shakespeare suggest spiritual essences: both through their ethereality and their song-music. They are thus to be contrasted with rough beasts. And the bird-beast opposition is vivid here: [quotes II i 232–3]. Bottom's heavy wit or blundering ignorance gives us other examples. [Quotes I ii 77–8 and III i 27–30]. The humour in these clearly depends on the bird-beast contrast. Rough beasts are ever to be contrasted with ladies. Now much of our paradoxical comedy turns on the bird-beast opposition, if we remember always to regard Bottom himself as a beast. We often hear of his voice. 'He is a very paramour for a sweet voice' [IV ii 11–12]. He will 'sing' the tale of his dream before the Duke [IV i 214]. He clearly prides himself on his voice. And when he finds himself deserted by his companions he passes off an embarrassing situation by singing, and all about birds too: [quotes III i 116–7]. So he sings two stanzas of the 'ousel cock', 'the throstle with his note so true', the 'wren', the 'finch', 'sparrow' and 'lark', and the 'plain-song cuckoo'. They are all song birds. And this music enraptures Titania: [quotes III i 130–1]. Ass-headed Bottom, song-birds, and Titania: the union of these is profoundly comic, depending for our full understanding on full awareness of the bird-beast opposition. For Titania, also, must clearly be directly associated with birds and contrasted with evil beasts. Consider the lovely song invoking 'Philomel' to sing 'with melody' in the 'sweet lullaby' of the Fairy Queen [II ii 9–30]. 'Snakes', 'hedgehogs', the 'newt', and 'blindworm', 'spiders', 'beetles', the 'worm' and 'snail' – these are to be charmed away: they are evil, reptilian, of *Macbeth* suggestion. . . . Instead, the nightingale's music. And all this is a contrast between the gross and ethereal; which contrast is exquisitely imagined in the love of Titania for Bottom: [quotes III i 148–52] . . .

[Discusses 'the sparkling jewel-imagery applied to grass and flowers . . . the dawn-poetry, the waking back to human life', and references to music, quoting IV i 105–26.] The music thought here is most interesting, especially in its blending of diversity – which gives tempests – with unity, which is music. We have a 'musical confusion', 'so musical a discord', and 'such sweet thunder': clearly this is another variation being played on our tempest-music opposition, and one which reflects the final impression of the whole of Shakespeare's work: tempests dissolved in a sublime unity of music. Observe here, too, how our most eminent tempest-beast, the bear, is aptly attacked by these more musical beasts of Theseus. The 'bells' are also important, since 'jangling' is a recurrent word for human discords – thus Hamlet's madness is as 'sweet bells jangled'. Also we may observe, what is characteristic of Shakespeare always, that though this speech is universally and typically Shakespearian, it is yet woven in a fabric peculiar to its own play. Notice the forester, groves, fountains, morning-dew – all, especially if we remember the varied nature-images of Titania's tempest speech, are particular to this vision. Finally, note especially how these lovely speeches of discords resolved in music are blended with dawn, 'the vaward of the day', and exquisitely prelude the awakening of the lovers whose long night of jangling [III ii 353] is to be now harmonised in the music of love. . . .

Three persons here have especial autonomy, existing, as it were, in their own right: Theseus, Oberon and Bottom. Each is sovereign in his sphere, king over his companions, and demands our respect. Nor can we, who watch, say with confidence that one is more real than the others. And the remarks I am to make on Theseus and the fairies must not be taken to mean that those fairies are purely unreal. Rash fancies may be dangerous, inexpedient to man: it does not follow that they are untrue. Now at the start we have a discord, among men and fairies, and in each world the discord may be said to derive from the other. The Athenian lovers and Egeus find their imaginations and desires conflicting with actualities; that is, their fairy dreams of happiness will not materialise. And in the wood Oberon and Titania quarrel, and their dissension is due wholly to their contact with humanity – rivalry for the Indian boy, jealousy respectively of Theseus and Hippolyta. Oberon accuses Titania of leading Theseus 'through the glimmering night' and making him break faith with Perigenia, Aegle, Ariadne, and Antiopa – is she then a personification, from a mortal's view, of the unrestful fancy and love-longing which torments mankind? And Titania also accuses Oberon of disguising himself as Corin and piping love to 'amorous Phillida' [II i 61–80]. Oberon cures Titania of her violent love for the boy by making her love the ass-headed Bottom: after that, she suffers a revulsion from excessive mortal desire. Dissension thus enters fairyland through the fairies' love of mortals; there is dissension at Athens through the mortals aspiring to the fairyland of their love. The lovers then violently pursue their love into the magic wood, and find themselves in confusion. Thus the action shows us first the clash, then the reharmonising of fairyland and human life. So the original tempest gives place finally to music, revelry, and feast.

But of all our persons Theseus is the calmest and wisest. Whatever old unrest he has endured is now over; and he will not believe in the lovers' story. Why? He shows an exquisite and wide love and deep human knowledge; witness his remarks to Hippolyta before the play. But he groups the lunatic, the frenzied lover, and the poet together as untrustworthy and fantastic story-tellers. He is greater than they. For such deal in pure fancies: whereas Theseus himself blends all such imaginations with life. Poetry is to him thus purely fanciful: [quotes V i 208–9]. Set midway between the two kings Bottom and Oberon, himself a mightier king than they, he is master of all that is best in either.[1] Living, then, the life of inward music, Theseus himself makes no division between fairyland and actuality: therefore fairyland is, to him, non-existent, and he can smile at the extravagances of undisciplined fancy. And yet it is Theseus who gently introduces the fairies at the end: [quotes V i 354]. And it is right that the words should be his.

For, on the bridal night if never else, the lovers all enjoy this harmony natural to Theseus, this peace, this blending of spirit-dreams with their own lives; and this it is that is symbolised by the fairies' final entry, song and dance, to honour, without wrangling, their loved ones on earth. These wayward spirits and mankind here blend in one harmony, and the two words, fact and fairyland, which have been divided in tempest, now embrace to music.

SOURCE: extracts from *The Shakespearian Tempest* (1932), pp. 142–6, 151–2, 154–6, 164, 166–8.

NOTE

1. The Bottom-Oberon contrast repeats that of Falstaff and the fairies in *The Merry Wives of Windsor*. Theseus holds the balance exact of earthliness and spirituality, Caliban and Ariel.

Ernest Schanzer   The Moon and the Fairies
(1955)

. . . In this play we are given three wholly distinct kinds of fairies, provided we can speak of Puck as a fairy at all. He was not considered so in popular superstition, but was thought of as a spirit of another sort, whose merry pranks made him the most popular of all the sprites that haunted the English countryside . . . he considers himself to be a fairy, as his 'And we fairies, that do run By the triple Hecate's team' [v i 373–4] shows. (Cf. also III ii 110). He is the complete opposite of the tiny fairies with whom Shakespeare fills Oberon's and Titania's train, being gross and earthy, boisterous, rough and boyish, where the tiny fairies are aerial, timid, and courteous. Nothing could be more misleading than to speak of them as irresponsible children, as so many critics do. . . .

[The attendant fairies] are conscientious and very much overworked servants of the queen, with little time for idle gossiping. [Quotes II i 14–7]. The time employed on these errands is very carefully apportioned by their exacting mistress: [quotes II ii 1–8].

Life among the fairies smacks more of Aldershot than of Cockaigne. In their encounters with Bottom, the tiny fairies, so far from being like children, show themselves accomplished and ceremonious courtiers. To see them otherwise robs the scene of much of its humour. For Bottom, with his customary adaptability to any part he is called upon to play, at once fits himself to his new role of Prince Consort, and proceeds to hold a levée. As we would expect, he plays the part to perfection. He is courteous without condescension, well informed about each fairy's family, genuinely interested in their affairs. . . .

Oberon and Titania, though very different in kind from their attendant fairies, are no more childlike or irresponsible than they. When commentators speak of 'little Titania', or when Professor Charlton, lamenting the undomesticated life led by Oberon and Titania, tells us that 'acorn-cups impose no fellowship',[1] it is evident that these critics take the King and Queen of fairyland to be of the same miniature brand as their attendant spirits. That Shakespeare did not think of them in that way is plain enough. The Titania who winds Bottom in her arms is clearly a full-grown woman. Not only would it be unactable to have a tiny Titania make love to Bottom, but it would also be unthinkable. For the humour of their love-scenes depends on our realisation that it is a supremely beautiful woman who is enamoured of this weaver turned ass. (Had Shakespeare thought of the fairy queen as diminutive in size, 'Titania' would have been a most unhappy choice of name for her.) Shakespeare clearly thinks of Titania and Oberon as of the same stature as the traditional English fairies, who were considered to be of normal height or slightly below it. Nor are they depicted as ethereal, mere gossamer and moonlight. Not only Titania's 'Sleep thou, and I will wind thee in my arms', but also Oberon's

> Come my queen, take hands with me
> And rock the ground whereon these sleepers be
>
> [IV i 84–5]

make against this impression. But more harmful than the notion of Oberon's and Titania's diminutive size is the notion of their childlikeness and irresponsibility. Of this I can find no trace in the play. They are the counterpart in the spirit-world of Theseus and

Hippolyta, like them full of stateliness and dignity, though more ceremonious and distant. Their quarrel is not a children's squabble, no sooner engaged in than forgotten, . . . but a quarrel which, if we are to credit Titania, has been in progress for many months, disrupting the whole body politic of fairyland. Only thus can we understand Titania's speech about the chaos in nature, which has arisen out of their quarrel: [quotes II i 115–7]. This is more than a merely poetic allusion to a year of unusually bad weather. It is rather the disorder in the macrocosm which, in so many of Shakespeare's plays, accompanies disorder in the body politic, here the state of fairydom. Of irresponsibility I can find no more sign in Oberon and Titania than of childlikeness. Neither Titania's rearing of the little changeling boy for the sake of his mother, and her refusal to buy domestic peace at the price of parting with him, nor Oberon's treatment of the Athenian lovers suggests irresponsibility.

Shakespeare has been sometimes reproached with having gelded the English fairy, having robbed it of its fearfulness and hence its reality, and turned it into a trifle light as air, the mere plaything of the imagination. We can see why he should have done so for the purposes of this play. He probably felt that the traditional English fairy was too uncanny and fearful a creature to be accommodated in this scene of tragical mirth. And so, in creating the attendant fairies in this play, Shakespeare drew on a *jeu d'esprit*, written probably a few months earlier, Mercutio's Queen Mab speech. But the miniature and flower-like fairies had been created for a special purpose in a particular play, and in no way ousted the traditional English fairy from the poet's imagination. Not until *The Tempest* does he return to the 'Shakespearean' fairy; all the references in the intervening plays are to the conventional fairies of English folklore . . . [quotes *Antony and Cleopatra* IV viii 12; *Hamlet* I i 166; *Cymbeline* III vi 42; *Pericles* V i 155, and *Cymbeline* II ii 9–11]. In all these instances Shakespeare has the traditional English fairy in mind to whose demise in the popular imagination he so largely contributed. . . .

While the theme of love-madness weaves together various apparently unrelated portions of *A Midsummer Night's Dream*, Shakespeare creates unity of atmosphere chiefly by flooding the play with moonlight. There is only one daylight scene in the entire play, part of the first scene of Act IV, where we watch the coming of dawn and with it the arrival of Theseus' hunting party. And here the coming of daylight and the sounding of the hunting-horns announce the return of sanity, the dispersal of magic and illusion, the end of the dream. Theseus and Hippolyta are both daylight characters. Neither of them is unimaginative, and Theseus, at least, is depicted as an ardent lover. But he has wooed Hippolyta with his sword, in a fashion very different from Lysander's wooing of Hermia:

> Thou hast by moonlight at her window sung,
> With feigning voice, verses of feigning love.
>
> [I i 30–1]

And the Duke's cool reason and good sense throw into relief the lovers' absurdities. They have their natural existence by moonlight, which propagates phantoms and illusions, the world of dreams.

With Shakespeare, and, it would seem, with the Elizabethans generally, the Moon is never the great aphrodisiac that she became in later literature. She could not become so as long as poets continued to think of her as the Goddess Diana, the virgin huntress and jealous guardian of chastity. Only through the Endymion myth was the moon connected with love for the Elizabethans, but this story alone could not overcome the predominant association of the 'cold, wat'ry moon' with chastity. Shakespeare only once refers to the Endymion story, in Portia's 'Peace ho! the moon sleeps with Endymion And would not be awaked' [*Merchant* V i 109–110], while there are many references to the moon's association with chastity [quotes I i 73–4; II i 161–2; III i 193–5].

Nor could the predominant association of the moon with chastity be overcome by another conception of Diana not unfamiliar to the Elizabethans. Like Artemis, Diana was originally worshipped as a fertility goddess, the special protectress of women, particularly in procreation and childbirth. Only under Greek influence, as a result of her identification with Artemis, did she later become a moon-goddess, the virgin huntress, and the jealous guardian of virginity. Lucina, who, as a goddess presiding over childbirth, had been frequently identified with Diana (as well as with Juno), and aided by her name, became also a moon-goddess, so that Dunbar, for instance, can write of 'Lucina schynning in silence of the nicht' [*Poems* XXXV, 1]. The association of the moon with procreation and childbirth and all that pertains to growth finds its most famous expression in Elizabethan poetry in Spenser's address to the moon in his *Epithalamion* [372 ff.]:

> And sith of wemens labours thou hast charge,
> And generation goodly dost enlarge,
> Encline thy will t'effect our wishful vow,
> And the chast wombe informe with timely seed,
> That may our comfort breed:
> Till which we cease our hopefull hap to sing,
> Ne let the woods us answere, nor our Eccho ring.

And the same attribution is found in George Wither's *Epithalamion* [199 ff.]:

> But thou, Luna, that dost lightly
> Haunt our downs and forests nightly,
> Thou that favour'st generation
> And art help to procreation
> See their issue thou so cherish,
> I may live to see it flourish.

But this association of the moon with procreation and childbirth was not sufficiently widespread in literature to overcome the dominant image of the cold, fruitless moon, the stern guardian of virginity.

Where the moon, for Shakespeare, is associated with love, it seems to be rather with fickle, inconstant love, because of the moon's changes. Thus in that great antiphonal love-chant between Jessica and Lorenzo the two scenes suggested by the moonlight to Lorenzo deal both with deserted and wronged lovers, Troilus and Dido. To Jessica the moonlight calls up the fateful meeting of Pyramus and Thisbe at 'Ninny's tomb', but the second of her scenes no longer deals with lovers at all, but with Medea gathering enchanted herbs by moonlight. Here the suggestion comes from the association of the moon with magic and witchcraft, because of her identification with Hecate. There is another association with the moon, that of madness, which makes the moon's omnipresence in *A Midsummer Night's Dream* add meaning to its main theme. Inconstancy, magic, madness, all could be suggested to Shakespeare's audience by the many moon-references in the play. But it seems unlikely that the poet relied much on these associations. Though inconstancy, madness, and magic, all play a dominant part in the drama, Shakespeare makes no allusions to them in his moon-references. . . .

On the whole, it seems that Shakespeare's moon-references are designed to create atmosphere rather than to underline a theme. As far as they suggest a theme at all it is . . . that of chastity at war with love, the chaste beams of the watery moon quenching young Cupid's fiery shaft, Diana's bud undoing the work of Cupid's flower. It is surprising that neo-Hegelian Shakespeare critics, who like to discover a play's inner meaning in the tension developed between two abstractions at war with each other, have so far overlooked *A Midsummer Night's Dream*. But in fact the choice of the two ways of life never becomes a real issue. As far as there is a choice presented in the play it is between two kinds of love, the love of seething brains of the young Athenians, and the more balanced and rational love of Theseus and Hippolyta. . . .

SOURCE: extracts from 'The Moon and the Fairies in *A Midsummer Night's Dream*', *University of Toronto Quarterly*, XXIV (1955), 234, 235, 235–7, 238, 238–40, 240–1.

NOTE

1. H. B. Charlton, *Shakespearean Comedy* (London, 1938), p. 117.

Paul A. Olson   The Meaning of Court Marriage (1957)

. . . Commensurate with its origins in a court marriage, this drama speaks throughout for a sophisticated Renaissance philosophy of the nature of love in both its rational and irrational forms. Even Bottom the fool observes that 'reason and loue keepe little company together, now a daies' [III i 147–8].* His sententious surmise – and it has been taken as the drama's theme – is best understood in terms of sixteenth-century marriage doctrines. . . .

The guests at the wedding may have been reminded of the intellectual function of the new playwright's poetry – if they needed such reminding – through the definitions of Duke Theseus's speech: [quotes V i 12–7]. Theseus's lines have been interpreted in their context as a jocular degradation of the poet to the level of lover and madman. Poets do not often sell their craft so short, and Shakespeare is not, I think, doing so here. First of all, one must note that Theseus makes some implicit distinctions between the poet and his mad colleagues. It is only lovers and madmen who are said to exhibit fantasies which descend beyond the comprehension of reason [V i 4–6]. Implicitly, poets, however much they are possessed by a *furor poesis*, may deal in imaginings apprehensible in more rational terms. The speech quoted above perhaps makes clear how this happens. Its syntax suggests that what the poet sees, in glancing to heaven, is the 'ayery nothing' or 'forme' which his imagination is then empowered to body forth.[1]

In looking back to earth, he bequeathes to this Form a 'locall habitation and a name'. In a similar vein, Neoplatonic criticism in the time spoke of the artist's duty to incarnate the universal (or 'form') in the concrete visual emblem. Professor E. H. Gombrich recently used much the same language as Duke Theseus to summarise the rationale of such Renaissance visual symbols:

They are the forms which the invisible entities can assume to make themselves understood to the limited human mind. In other words, the idea of Justice – be it conceived as a member of the celestial hierarchy or as an abstract entity – is inaccessible to the senses. At best we can hope to grasp it in a moment of ecstasy and intellectual intuition. But God has decreed in His mercy that these invisible and abstract entities whose divine radiance no human eye could support may accommodate themselves to our understanding and assume visible shape.[2]

Professor Gombrich treats of the figure of justice; the theory could as

* Olson's quotations from Shakespeare are taken from the First Quartos of *A Midsummer Night's Dream* and *Two Noble Kinsmen*, and from the First Folio for the other plays. [Ed.] The form 'Hippolita' is here retained.

well be used to explain the '*Cupid* painted blinde' [I i 235] placed in *A Midsummer Night's Dream* to embody earthly as opposed to heavenly love. In fact the entire play may be seen as a skilfully composed fabric of iconological referents giving local habitation to the 'invisible and abstract entities' which would be likely to claim the attention of a marriage audience. Thus, while the aesthetic of the work implies a surrender to modes of looking at the world which do not derive their sustenance from phenomenal fact, it also demands a return to this kind of fact for their expression. . . .

The Elizabethan poet who wished to bring before an aristocratic group the 'formes of things Vnknowne' in describing the function of marriage, could refer to an old and dignified philosophy of its purposes. This thought had come down to him from the middle ages, but he could have found it in sixteenth-century sermons, scriptural commentaries, marriage manuals, or encyclopedias of general knowledge. According to its doctrines, the love found in well-ordered marriage was regarded – in the words of Chaucer's Theseus – as part of the 'fair cheyne of love' which 'bond/The fyr, the eyr, the water, and the lond/ In certeyn boundes' [*KT* 2988–92].[3] This divine love, this 'perfect harmonie, like as in musicke . . .'[4] also maintained the patterned hierarchy of society and kept the stars in their paths. Wedlock fulfilled its part in the concord of things when the male ruled his mate in the same way that reason was ordained to control both will and passions. It was argued that, before the Fall, men propagated their kind according to the promptings of charity. But with the first temptation, Eve's sensuality overcame Adam, and Adam's reason.[5] The fall transformed all divine, rational love in man into unreasonable and selfish lust. In Bottom's words, 'Reason and Love keep little company together'. Afterward, man's desire sought more to please itself than to follow God's plan for the world in general, especially for the procreation of the race. Since a link in the 'faire cheyne' had been broken, the marriage of the first garden was kept as an institution, a fragment shored against the complete ruin of rationality in man.[6] It could in a poetic sense allow Adam's intellect again to rule Eve's willfullness. *The Comedy of Errors* makes Luciana speak no more than the commonplace wisdom of the sixteenth century when she advises Adriana concerning woman's liberty:

> Why, headstrong liberty is lasht with woe:
> There's nothing situate vnder heauens eye,
> But hath his bound in earth, in sea, in skie.
> The beasts, the fishes, and the winged fowles
> Are their males subiects, and at their controules:
> Man more diuine, the Master of all these,
> Lord of the wide world, and wilde watry seas,
> Indued with intellectuall sence and soules,
> Of more preheminence then fish and fowles,
> Are masters to their females, and their Lords:
> Then let your will attend on their accords.   [C of E II i 15-25]

Marriage was assigned not only a positive social value, but various spiritual symbolisms were found in it. The meeting of God and the soul, the relationship of Christ and the Church, these also involved bonds of loue which were described in marital terms.[7] The view of wedlock outlined here was expressed in Chaucer by the Knight and the Parson [KT 2986-3108; PT. 260-70, 321-48, 836-957], repeated in La Primaudaye's The French Academie, dramatised in Ben Jonson's Hymenaei. It was in part further popularised by the manuals which followed Bullinger's The Christen State of Matrimony. The popular manuals added some practical strictures conducive to order which are relevant to A Midsummer Night's Dream. Parents were advised not to force unpleasant matches upon their offspring, but to 'haue respect to gods ordinance, & to the right ordinate consent of the parties. . .'[8]. Children on the other hand were counselled that marriage must be undertaken only with the permission of their parents.[9] The modern interpreter needs to be aware of these ideals throughout the play, for they, I think, control the pattern of its action and modify the meanings of individual words and images.

In terms of such concepts, A Midsummer Night's Dream discloses a three movement pattern similar in outline to that which Nevill Coghill finds implicit in the mediaeval foundations of Shakespearean comedy.[10] The work begins with order [Act I], then passes through the cycle of a Fall which brings the domination of unbridled passion [Acts II-III]. Finally, it returns to a realisation of the charity and cohesive community morality in which it began [Acts IV-V]. . . .

The first movement, the movement toward an orderly subordination of the female and her passions to the more reasonable male, is epitomised at the beginning of the first scene with the announcement of the prospective marriage of Theseus and Hippolita. Long before Shakespeare wrote, Theseus had come to embody the reasonable man and the ideal ruler of both his lower nature and his subjects. Chaucer's Theseus, to whom the ruler of *A Midsummer Night's Dream* is indebted had conquered 'all the regne of Femenye' with his wisdom [*KT* 865–6]. Shakespeare and Fletcher, in forming *The Two Noble Kinsmen* out of *The Knight's Tale*, pointed up the same conception; there the women of Thebes name the duke as one whose 'first thought is more,/Then others laboured meditance', whose 'premeditating/More then their actions' [*TNK* I i 135–7]. He gives substance to their observations with his own remarks that the conquest of the lower affections is a man-like task: 'Being sensually subdude/We loose our humane tytle' [*TNK* I i 232–3]. . . .

Hippolita was not so fortunate. She was remembered as an Amazon, the ruler of a nation who overturned the fixed hierarchy of wedlock. Celeste Turner Wright, in her exhaustive study, shows that the female warriors had the same reputation in the Renaissance as in the Middle Ages for holding up 'a dangerous example of unwomanly conduct, a violation of that traditional order under which "Women are born to thraldom and penance/And to been under mannes governance" '.[11] Specifically, they had come to signify a false usurpation of the duties of the male reason by the lower, female passions. The Pyrocles of Sidney's *Arcadia*, who is costumed as an Amazon, offends Musidorus mainly because he sees in him the overthrow of 'the reasonable parte of our soule' by 'sensuall weakness'.[12] Spenser pictures a similar inversion of the faculties in his Amazonian Radigund [*FQ* V v 25].[13] And John Knox explains the woman: flesh; man: spirit analogy while at the same time attacking the Amazon ruler as transforming men to Circe's brutes, to the 'follishe fondnes ãd cowardise of women'.[14] That Shakespeare and Fletcher had learned to work these correlations we know from the manner in which Hippolita and her marriage to Theseus are described in *The Two Noble Kinsmen*:

> Most dreaded *Amazonian*, that ha'st slaine
> The Sith-Tuskd-Bore; that with thy Arme as strong
> As it is white, wast neere to make the male
> To thy Sex captive; but that this thy Lord
> Borne to uphold Creation, in that honour

> First nature stilde it in, shrunke thee into
> The bownd thou wast ore-flowing; at once subduing
> Thy force, and thy affection . . .   [*TNK* I i 78–85]

The meaning of the rulers' marriage is here explicit; it is even directly related to the prelapsarian relationship in which man and woman, or the analogous inner faculties, were rightly oriented [*TNK* I i 83].

It is, I think, with some such associations in mind that the more literate members of the initial audience of *A Midsummer Night's Dream* would have viewed its opening action. Theseus, King of Order, has come to rule an all-too-passionate queen. The duke appears to announce the date of the coming marriage; presumably his undisciplined desires will end when the new moon, Chaste Cynthia, replaces the old stepdame whom Renaissance classicists would have recognised as distraught Hecate. There is to be a season of ceremony and pageantry, a pageantry announced by the formal movement of the verse [quotes I i 16–9].

Such stable conditions could not long remain. If they did, there would be no play. But the set presentation of Hippolita and Theseus and their marriage plan states the ethic which is to govern the rest of the work. The action then begins to tumble toward the chaos of the second movement. Egeus interrupts to announce that Lysander has won the young Hermia against his wishes. Egeus's problem is essentially one for the marriage manuals, a question of the 'right ordinate consent of the parties. . .'. Theseus is quick to affirm the principle of order; the child must obey the father or 'liue a barraine sister . . ./Chaunting faint hymnes, to the colde fruitlesse Moone' [I i 72–3]. Athenian law [I i 119] is possibly here the law of hierarchy which Plutarch's Theseus introduced.[15] However, Shakespeare's ruler forgets that divine order is maintained by Divine Love and not by law in any mechanical sense. And so there is a failure on both sides, a failure of charity in Theseus, a lack of reason in the lovers. This in turn prepares the way for the break to the woods and the heightening of the drama's psychological tensions.

The duke's exit leaves Lysander and Hermia without an effective guide, and for a time the positive values of the play must necessarily be stated primarily through the imagery. Immediately, the development of disorder shows in images of tempests and of fading roses, and this is intensified by a series of inverted religious allusions which follow. The irony of Lysander's lines, 'The course of true love

neuer did runne smoothe' [I i 134] lies, of course, in the recognition
that if one takes charity and its functions for true love, the reverse is
obviously true.[16] The comparison of class difference, as the hindrance
of lovers, to a cross turns upside down the conception of the first cross
where One above class was 'inthrald to loue' [I i 136]. Later, the
cross as an emblem for patience in suffering becomes a customary
thing 'As dewe to loue, as thoughts, and dreames, and sighes . . .'
[I i 154]. That the Christian cross has some association with heavenly
love is evident, as is also the paradox of its connection with Hermia's
amorous resignation. Essentially, the argument of the *tête-à-tête*
between Hermia and Lysander proceeds along fatalistic lines; the
love of which they speak, being temporal and unreasonable, is
correctly described as bound for confusion [I i 141–9] But the
references to the crucifixion undercut the argument and appeal to the
audience's awareness that there is another kind of love which may
move through higher faculties and is not so bound or so temporal.

Lysander, to escape from Athenian restraint, suggests that Hermia
go with him to the woods outside the city and attempt a clandestine
marriage. Generally such unions were described as illicit in the
sixteenth century, and they would hardly be looked on with any favor
by parents at an aristocratic wedding. Hermia is not abashed,
however. She accedes to the proposition with a fine series of oaths
culled carefully from the classics [I i 169–78]. First, she calls on
Cupid, a symbol for the power which preserves form in the universe.
But this same Cupid . . . becomes a furor and insanity when
transferred to the human mind.[17] Then she swears by the simplicity of
Venus's doves, another emblem for unrestrained desire.[18] Finally her
oath includes the fire which burned Dido in her final act of self-
assertion and self-destruction, a fire which did not, in any known
account, either knit souls or prosper loves.

After Helena's entrance, the metaphor returns to a religious area
of reference, now overtly used for ironic purposes; Hermia makes use
of the concept of grace to explain the process by which her Athenian
Paradise was transformed to a more unhappy place as she learned to
worship Lysander [quotes I i 206–7]. . . . Finally, Helena ties
together the whole tenor of the early action with her long closing
speech dissecting the effects of Cupid and Cupid's love; this, of
course, also directs our attention back to the world of the classics. An
early part of her description of the boy's power foreshadows Titania's

relation to Bottom: 'Things base and vile . . ./Loue can transpose to forme and dignitie' [I i 232–3]. At one level, these lines express the will of such infatuates as the queen of fairy to delude themselves. At another, they represent a perversion by Helena of the belief that Love moves always to impress its form upon the base material of Chaos. The central antithesis between love and reason is first stated explicitly and with a touch of comic incongruity in the same speech: 'Loue lookes not with the eyes, but with the minde' [I i 234]. However, the girl makes clear two lines later that love's mind is a little eccentric as minds go, for, she observes, it is altogether lacking in rational judgment. Moreover, Helena bothers to point out that the Cupid who figures the emotions which have been evident on the stage is painted blind [I i 235]. Now in the Renaissance there had come to be two Cupids.[19] One was pictured without the bandage over his eyes and waited upon *Venus Coelestis*, the mother of supernal love. The other was a blind boy associated with *Venus Vulgaris* who shot the hot darts of irrational, earthly desire. By having Helena here speak of the blind member of the pair, Shakespeare explicitly adopts an icon from a sister art to clarify the significance of the lover's emotions and unify the scene. . . .

The shift at the beginning of the second section [Acts II–III] leads from Athens to the woods, from light to darkness. The Athens which Theseus ruled dedicated itself to Minerva, the goddess of wisdom. It became a city of philosophers.[20] In this play, its antithesis is represented by the near-by woods. They belong in a tradition with Dante's 'selva oscura', Spenser's Wood of Error, or the forested, craggy place which Ariosto created for the necromancer, Atlanta. Harington explains Ariosto's allegory as follows: Atlanta is 'that fond fancie we call loue', and this kind of folly is like the 'darkesome wood' in which Dante found himself or the 'wandring wood of which the dolefull *Petrarke* complaines so often in those his sweet mourning sonets, in which he seemes to haue comprehended all the passions that all men of that humour haue felt'.[21] . . . Shakespeare plays upon this convention in one of Demetrius's speeches – 'And here am I, and wodde, within this wood . . .' [II i 192] – through a pun which establishes the association between the woods and unreason. In a more generalised sense, the dark wood could signify the confusions which beset the earthly life.[22] Thus, the contrast between the play's two settings is a stage projection of the thematic center of the entire work, the contrast between reasonable and unreasonable love. To move from the city to the forest is to choose madness. Shakespeare reinforces the symbolic implications of the wood by having the scenes which take place in them occur at night. Hence, he can draw on the traditional associations between darkness, evil and disorder [III ii 378–87]. . . .

Consistent with its dissimilar setting, act two begins by reversing the situation which opened act one. There Theseus had mastered Hippolita; here Oberon, king of fairies, has lost his sovereignty over Titania, and things are topsy-turvy. The fairyland which Shakespeare presents is no more like the Celtic underworld than that in the *Faerie Queene*. Like Spenser, Shakespeare uses the shadow country to represent the 'Other-world of allegory – that is, of Platonic Ideas, which constitute a higher reality of which earthly things are only imperfect copies'.[23] Consequently, the dramatist is able to work the fairy rulers for fairly complex artistic purposes. First of all, they are cosmic or mythological projections of the same qualities which Theseus and Hippolita embody in the world of the state. At the same time, the action of their plot forms a commentary upon the foibles of the lovers. They are the higher reality and the lovers their imperfect copies. This technique Shakespeare may have learned from Chaucer's use of Pluto and Proserpina as analogues to January and May in the *Merchant's Tale*. To understand the significance of the device, however, we must identify the literary traditions [behind] the King and Queen of this otherworld.

In Berners' *Huon of Burdeux*, Oberon is a kind of grace figure who protects Huon, when he is sinless or penitent, on his way to the conquest of Babylon. This Oberon was born some forty years before Christ's nativity and is never to age; his place has been appointed for him in Paradise when he leaves the mortal world.[24] To Huon he gives the cup from which only the guiltless can drink,[25] a vessel which is almost certainly a Eucharistic symbol. Again, the Oberon of Greene's *The Scottish History of James the Fourth*, proclaims himself ruler 'Of quiet, pleasure, profit, and content,/ Of wealth, of honor and of all the world'.[26] His function is to state the play's Boethian moral: content is virtue and the love of worldly things vanity. In the first scene he raises Bohan back to life and gently informs him, 'I visit thee for loue', though the angry Scot objects that true love long since took flight to go to heaven.[27] Ben Jonson's masque of *Oberon* shows the same fairy as king in a celestial palace of those knights who have been 'Quick'ned by a second birth' [line 147].

In this tradition, Shakespeare's king of Shadows is also a delicate figure for grace. He is the play's Prospero. Like Theseus, he may have wandered in the mazes of love and war, but, again like Theseus, he has overcome these. When properly sovereign, Oberon furthers the celestial love which preserves chaste marriages and keeps the cosmos in order. His relation to the higher love is clarified in a late scene. There Puck points to the damned spirits who deliberately exiled themselves 'from light,/And must for aye consort with black browed night' [III ii 386–7]. Oberon immediately objects that he is not the same sort of spirit. By reminding Puck that he has often sported with the morning's love, he introduces an image which has behind it an accumulated tradition of reference to the sun of God's charity.

Since Oberon's mate symbolises the opposite, earthly love, she is of quite a different mold. Her name comes from Ovid, who used Titania most conspicuously as an epithet for Diana [*Met.* III 173]. Donald Miller has observed that Shakespeare's fairy queen does not seem to be the chaste goddess of the hunt, however. 'Oberon is nearer the truth when he calls her "a wanton".'[28] The paradox of a licentious goddess of chastity may be solved if we look at the Diana in Shakespeare's main source, *The Knight's Tale*. There Emelye's prayer addresses her as goddess of heaven and earth, and 'Queene of the regne of Pluto derk and lowe' [*KT* 2299]. In the Renaissance as in the fourteenth century, Diana presented three aspects: '. . . *in heauen she is called* Luna, *in the woods* Diana, *under the earth* Hecate, *or* Proserpina.'[29] Emelye's prayer emphasizes the Proserpina aspects of the goddess, and in Shakespeare's time Thynne described her sacrifice as addressed to Diana Hecate.[30] It is my thesis that Shakespeare, using his Chaucerian sources freely, developed his woodland goddess from such a figure. Like Proserpina in the *Merchant's Tale*, Titania is the 'queene of Fayerye' [*MT* 2316], and like her earlier counterpart she knows something of the ways of lechery. The moon appears in its last phase through most of the play, and so it is appropriate that Diana Hecate should rule. Considering the definition quoted above, she should not be a woodland goddess, yet this mythology could be manipulated in several ways. Lyly creates a Luna in *The Woman in the Moone* who is both queen of the woods and wife of Pluto [V i 281–4]. Some corroborative evidence indicates that writers in the period so regarded Shakespeare's ruler of summer [III i 146]. . . .

Since Prosperina had power over the coming and going of the seasons, she was allegorised from ancient times as a naturalistic representation of the potency of seeds, as a kind of fertility goddess. This traditional interpretation could in turn be easily extended to make her stand for the forces of the lower passions in man. An Ovidian moralisation once attributed to Thomas of Wales emphasises that aspect of the goddess. . . . Similarly, Titania is queen of summer and a goddess of the earth. Its products, Peaseblossom, Mustardseed, and Cobweb, wait upon her court. Following the fashion set by Lyly's Tellus, she is laden with flowers; like Proserpine and Tellus, she becomes in this play a symbol for the earth and its earthly love. . . .

All the objects which surround Oberon's queen befit her station. Her bower is a sensual paradise.[31] Near it, Philomel, the bird of lascivious loves, sings its melody while the wise owl hoots at the 'quaint' spirits which appear [II ii 1–30].[32] Her erotic games with Bottom and the changeling fit the symbolic frame which Shakespeare has placed about her, since she is princess of sensual passion. In the total conceptual scheme of the play, the king and queen of the woods dramatise the two poles of the scales of values which gave meaning to marriage. They are types of the forces of Reason and Passion which in a more complex and human manner move through Theseus and Hippolita respectively.

As we observed earlier, the world of the woods, unlike Athens, is upside down. Oberon, prince of grace, is no longer sovereign over the fertile earth and its characteristic lusts. It is one of the clichés of the Elizabethan period that macrocosm and microcosm mirror one another. Since the rulers of fairyland are Platonic archetypes, their struggle has fairly broad effects. It reflects itself in the chaos of nature, the reversal of the seasons, and so forth [II i 81–117]. A parallel to this appears in Jonson's *Masque of Queenes*. There the witches attempt to raise a spell which will 'strike the World, and *Nature* dead' [line 314] and restore shrunk-up Chaos to his ancient dominions. During their rites of disorder, the hags describe the earth as it appears when triformed Hecate is powerful. As in Shakespeare, the seasons alter, floods come, the corn is removed, the storms trouble the land [lines

221–42]. Jonson specifically attributes this collapse of the natural order to Hecate, and we err if we fail to see the parallel passage in Shakespeare as something similar, as more than a mere versified account of the inclement weather of 1595. The disorders described in both passages are caused by the same figure, and both likewise fit into the conscious intellectual purpose of the larger works in which they are placed.

The battle which makes all the trouble concerns a very elusive changeling boy who was carried into the otherworld by the fairies. In like manner, Ganymede was taken by Jove, and Ganymede's tale was commonly thought to be a parable of the capture of man's rational soul by the love of God.[33] Again, Spenser's Red Cross Knight, who is obviously at one level a symbol for the soul, was as a child a changeling kidnapped into the world of Platonic ideas [*FQ* I x 65–6].

Now to regain this changeling and recover control over Titania, Oberon sends for the obscure flower, love-in-idleness. He informs Puck that it has power to make the fairy queen dote on any creature, 'Be it on Lyon, Beare, or Wolfe, or Bull . . .' [II i 180]. The herb has been suspected by modern critics of containing some superstitious magical potion, perhaps some aphrodisiac. However, the association of love and idleness goes back as far as Ovid's *Remedia Amoris*: 'Otia si tollas, periere Cupidinis arcus . . .' [lines 139; cf. 135–50]. Idleness is porter of the Narcissian garden of self-love in *Le Roman de la Rose*; Spenser calls the same personification the 'nourse of sin' and makes him lead the parade of the seven deadly vices [*FQ* I iv 18–20]. Euphues observes that 'idleness is the onely nourse and nourisher of sensual appetite, the sole maintenance of youthfull affection, the first shaft that *Cupide* shooteth into the hot liuer of a heedlesse louer'.[34] Shakespeare's love-in-idleness takes its color from the same Cupid [II i 165–8], the Cupid whom Helena and Hermia found so attractive. The herb is rather obviously a source of 'sensual appetite', and no one should be surprised when it makes Titania dote on the first beast she sees, Bottom in the role of an ass.

There is an allegory in this doting. As Arthur Golding observes, only those who live under reason's law are to be accounted truly human; those who succumb to their bestial nature must be considered no more than beasts.[35] Bottom's ass head may be the development of several traditions, but a fairly accessible interpretation sees it as the symbol for stupidity and sensuality, for the carnal man as opposed to the spiritual. Bottom, of course, does not stand for such qualities throughout the play, but the Bottom who appears in the dream, the ass who is the object of Titania's seduction is probably such a symbol. He is – in Titania's phrase –as wise as he is beautiful [III i 140]. Rather striking support for this is to be found in St Paul [I Corinthians 2: 7–14]. Bottom says that it is 'past the wit of man, to say; what dreame it was. Man is but an Asse, if hee goes about [to] expound this dreame . . . it shall be call'd *Bottoms Dreame*; because it hath no bottome' [IV i 204–13]. St Paul puts it a little differently (in Tyndale's translation): 'For the sprete searcheth all thinges, ye the bottome of Goddes secretes. For what man knoweth the thinges of a man: save the sprete of a man which is with in him?. . . . For the naturall man perceaveth not the thinges of the sprete of God. For they are but folysshnes vnto him.'[36] It is the bestial or natural man who is unable to see to the bottom of things; he is the fool or ass who cannot expound the dream. This does not mean that Shakespeare denies to the more perceptive spirit of his audience the privilege of perceiving 'these invisible and abstract entities which no human eye could support'.

What then are the invisible and abstract entities which may be seen in the comic fairy plot? Paraphrase is always bad for a stage piece; it tends to impoverish and rationalise the richness of a dramatic symbol. Yet, if one were to apply this malpractice to the Oberon-Titania-Bottom triangle, one might say that celestial love in the form of Oberon attempts to capture the young man (the 'sprete' or the changeling) into his train and bring earthly love under his control in order that the rational and animal in man may form a proper marriage. To accomplish this, Divine Love, 'providentially works through imperfect human love',[37] as in the *Knight's Tale*. That is, Oberon uses love-in-idleness to force Titania to release her hold upon the changeling and to seek only the carnal or physical man, Bottom. Bottom recognises the earthly character of Titania's love when he speaks of her having little reason for loving him, and then tosses off the jest which sets the theme of the play [III i 135–8]. The service which Titania's coterie, especially Peaseblossom, Mustardseed, and Cobweb, pay to Bottom is obviously a miniature picture of the satisfaction which the products of the earth can give to the grosser senses. There is a plot analogous to this one in Lyly's *Endimion*; there Cynthia, the higher love, forces Tellus or earthly pasion to release her hold upon Endimion (the rational soul) but allows her to retain her love for Corsites (the body). Shakespeare was possibly as aware as Lyly that the body quite naturally will have its sexual appetites. He may also have recognised, as more recent dramatists sometimes do not, that these appetites need not undermine man's reason, his social responsibility, or his spiritual seeking.

Thus, having reduced physical love to her proper sphere, Oberon can use '*Dians* budde' to release her from the unchaste power of '*Cupids* flower'. At that point the third movement of the play begins in the fairy plot. Oberon regains his sovereignty over the fairy queen; the two loves are matched as they should be in any true marriage. The pair beats the ground in a circular dance, and Oberon calls for music which strikes 'more dead/Then common sleepe of all these, fi[v]e the sense' [IV i 80–1]. This harmony may be the *mundana musica* which preserves chaste loves and keeps the stars from wrong. The dance was given the same universal significance as a symbol for the concord of divine love in Sir John Davies's *Orchestra* (1595). Finally, all this is knit together when the fairies hear the song of the lark, a bird which sings at heaven's gate and which well into the seventeenth century was a symbol for the ascent of the reasonable soul toward God. Thus the king and queen of the otherworld arrive at the ordered condition which Theseus and Hippolita had reached at the play's beginning. Such an interpretation of the fairy plot may be incomplete, but it seems to me somewhat more consonant with what we know of the literary use of fairies in the 1590s from the *Faerie Queene* than the view we sometimes get that Shakespeare was here a slightly amateurish Warwickshire folklorist.

To see the mythical plot in this way is to see it as an integral part of the total dramatic meaning of the play. It amounts to a stage projection of the inner condition of the lovers, of the pattern of fall and redemption which they experience. Shakespeare is craftsman enough to establish carefully stage links between the two plots. Thus, when Demetrius and Helena first appear in the woods, Helena comes running after Demetrius [II i 188]; ten lines earlier Oberon has predicted that Titania will pursue the first beast she sees with the soul of love. Later Titania sleeps and receives the juice of love-in-idleness upon her eyelids; then Lysander and Hermia sleep, and Lysander is treated with the same philtre. Under its influence, Lysander worships Helena [II ii 109–50]; the next scene gives us a Titania enamoured of

Bottom's shape. Throughout, Shakespeare uses formal parallelism between the scenes from the two plots to stress their inner relationship and to heighten the humor of both.

Though the flight to the woods is obviously the beginning of the lovers' fall, their subjection is not such a serious one. Shakespeare is not writing a serious play in that sense. Hermia preserves her humane modesty though Helena is less worried about the worth of her virginity. In any case, Oberon again providentially works through imperfect human love, using the philtre to transform the initial foolishness into behavior which is more obviously irrational. The ridicule which is the most potent enemy of the wrong kind of love, is intended to act both upon the lovers and, it is hoped, upon their audience. Puck makes a mistake with Lysander, but this only serves to heighten the comedy. The boy sinks to sleep protesting everlasting love for Hermia; he awakens from the herb eager to run through fire for Helena. He has arrived at that unsound condition where he can adduce scholastic arguments for his sanity, and so give the theme of the play another ironic twist [quotes II ii 121–7]. . . . Incidentally, Reason in *Le Roman de la Rose* does not attempt to marshal the will to the eyes of a beautiful woman, but to a different kind of jewel.

However, the climax of the dramatization of the troubles of irrational love is reached in Act III, scene ii. The exaggerated praise and worship of the mistress common in Ovidian satiric love poetry, the suspicions of friends are all there. Hermia even endeavors to tear out Helena's eyes [III ii 298]. A moralist might say that the concupiscible passions have led on to the irascible. This is also what happens to Palamon and Arcite in the *Knight's Tale*. Yet, the troubles of heroic love do not lead the lovers in Shakespeare's work to the same violent end which Chaucer's Arcite suffers. It is part of Shakespeare's art that while the plight of the lovers seems more and more desperate to them, it appears increasingly comic to their audience, possibly because in this play the benevolent Oberon can send in his Robin to rescue the squabbling pairs and apply the *Remedia Amoris* [quotes III ii 448–63]. . . . Thus Oberon, with his servants, returns the lovers to reason; by allowing them to see for themselves the humor of their situation, he makes it possible for them to extricate themselves permanently from the fond fancy which misdirects the will and leaves one enamoured of an ass.

The lovers are ready for the type of 'bond of love' speech which Theseus gives in the third section of the *Knight's Tale*. Here again Shakespeare chooses the appropriate dramatic symbols. The song of the lark, the music and dance symbolise the 'faire cheyne' in the fairy plot; in the other plot Theseus appears at dawn to remark the same effects [quotes IV i 142–4]. . . . This concord is a reflection of the concord between Oberon and Titania, between their loves. It suggests a return of the world of nature from seasonal disorder to a similar harmony. And the state comes to its own order; Theseus now preserves hierarchy by overruling Egeus. His success results from a more profound understanding of the principle of consent as the basis of marriage than he exhibited in the first scene. Finally, he proposes the ritual which will confirm a union not 'Briefe, as the lightning in the collied night . . .' [I i 145] but rather more lasting [quotes IV i 179–80]. . . .

SOURCE: extracts from '*A Midsummer Night's Dream* and the Meaning of Court Marriage', *ELH*, 24 (1957), pp. 95–6, 97–8, 99–101, 101–2, 102–6, 106–10, 110–1, 111–8.

NOTES

[Reorganised and renumbered from the original – Ed.]

1. Pico similarly regards the imagination as the faculty which embodies celestial realities; its purpose is to move the uninitiated to a contemplation of higher things, and this functions particularly in Scriptural allegory. . . . Pico della Mirandola, *On the Imagination*, ed. Harry Caplan (New Haven, 1930), p. 92; cf. 86–92. La Primaudaye treats the imagination, properly used, as the vehicle through which such heavenly visions as Nebuchadnezzar's are communicated; Peter de la Primaudaye, *The Second Part of the French Academie* (London, 1594), sig. [K6]. These ideas may be a development from Boethius, 'De Consolatione Philosophiae' [*Liber* V, *Prosa* IV], where the imagination is assigned a position between the wit which looks on sensate things and the intelligence which contemplates the simple forms.

2. E. H. Gombrich, '*Icones Symbolicae*: The Visual Image in Neo-Platonic Thought', *Journal of the Warburg and Courtauld Institutes*, XI, (1948), p. 180.

3. *The Poetical Works of Chaucer*, ed. F. N. Robinson (Cambridge, Mass., 1953). All quotations and citations from this edition.

4. Peter de la Primaudaye, *The French Academie* (London, 1618), Sig. Ooo2v.

5. This interpretation of the fall, originating as early as St Augustine, *De Trinitate* [Lib. XII, Cap. 12], was popularised in the 12th and 13th centuries by *Sententiae* of Peter Lombard [Lib. II, Dist. XXIV, Cap. VI ff.]. . . . Arnold Williams in *The Common Expositor* (Chapel Hill, 1948), p. 128, has indicated the persistence of this interpretation as a subsidiary moralisation into the Renaissance. . . .

6. Peter de la Primaudaye, *The French Academie* (Newbery, 1586), sig. [Hh8]ᵛ; John Donne, *Works* (London, 1839), IV, 34.

7. Donne, *Works* [IV 40 ff.]; La Primaudaye (1586 ed.), sig. [Ii6]ᵛ.

8. Heinrich Bullinger, *The Christen State of Matrimony*, trans. Myles Coverdale (n.p. 1546), sig. E3.

9. Bullinger, sig. D4.

10. Nevill Coghill, 'The Basis of Shakespearian Comedy', *Essays and Studies* (London, 1950), pp. 12–3 and *passim*, pp. 1–28.

11. Celeste Turner Wright, 'The Amazons in Elizabethan Literature', *SP*, XXXVII (1940), 456 and *passim*, pp. 433–56.

12. Sir Philip Sidney, *The Countesse of Pembrokes Arcadia*, ed. Albert Feuillerat (Cambridge, 1912), p. 77.

13. *The Works of Edmund Spenser*, ed. Greenlaw, Osgood *et al.*, 9 vols. (Baltimore, 1932–45). All citations from this edition.

14. John Knox, *The First Blast of the Trumpet Against the Monstrvous Regiment of Women* (Geneva, 1558), sig. B3.

15. Plutarch, *Lives of the Noble Grecians and Romans*, trans. Sir Thomas North, 5 vols. (London, 1895), I, pp. 153–4.

16. La Primaudaye, *The Second Part of the French Academie*, sig. [S6]–[S6]ᵛ; cf. sig. T2–T4ᵛ.

17. Natalis Conté, *Mythologiae* (Lyons, 1602), sig. C4ᵛ; cf. *A Midsvnmer Night's Dream*, variorum ed. H. H. Furness (Philadelphia, 1895), pp. 23–4, note.

18. '[Venus'] Doues are wanton . . . being meanes to procure loue and lust.' Abraham Fraunce, *The Third Part of the Countesse of Pembrokes Yuychurch* (London, 1592), sig. M3.

19. Erwin Panofsky, *Studies in Iconology* (New York, 1939), pp. 95–128; one should not ignore the ironies which Shakespeare places in the speech, ironies which link it more closely to the 'old' moralisations than Panofsky admits (cf. Panofsky, pp. 123–4).

20. 'Athenes whilom, whan it was in his floures/Was callid norice of philisophres wise, . . .' [lines 4243–4]. John Lydgate, 'The Story of Theseus', *The Fall of Princes*, ed. Henry Bergen, 4 vols. (London, 1924–27).

21. Ludovico Ariosto, *Orlando Furioso in English Heroical Verse*, trans. Sir John Harington (London, 1591), sig. C4ᵛ.

22. Torquato Tasso, *Godfrey of Bulloigne; The Recovery of Jerusalem*, trans. Edward Fairfax (London, 1600), sig. A3ᵛ; cf. George Sandys, *Ovid's Metamorphosis Englished, Mythologiz'd, and Represented in Figures* (London, 1640), sig. Nn[1]ᵛ; Margaret Galway, 'The Wilton Diptych: A Postscript', *Archaeological Journal*, CVII (1950), p. 9, notes that the 'selva oscura' is frequently a meeting place for earthly and celestial beings in later literature.

23. Josephine Waters Bennett, 'Britain Among the Fortunate Isles', *Studies in Philology*, LIII (1956), p. 136.

24. *The Boke of Duke Huon of Burdeux*, trans. Sir John Bourchier [Lord Berners] (London, 1882–87), pp. 71, 74.

25. *Huon of Burdeux*, pp. 76–7.

26. Robert Greene, *The Scottish Historie of Iames the Fourth* (London, 1593) sig. C4ᵛ.

27. Greene, sig. A3.

28. Donald C. Miller, 'Titania and the Changeling', *ES*, XXII (1940), p. 67.

29. Abraham Fraunce, sig. [L4]ᵛ–M.

30. Francis Thynne, *Animaduersions*, ed. F. J. Furnivall (London, 1876), pp. 48–9.

31. It may be related to the Bower of Bliss; cf. Don Cameron Allen, 'On Spenser's *Muiopotmos*', *SP*, LIII (1956), p. 152, note.

32. 'Quaint' is a bawdy pun which comes down from Middle English; cf. Paull F. Baum, 'Chaucer's Puns', *PMLA*, LXXI (1956), p. 243. For the tradition of the nightingale, see D. W. Robertson, Jr., 'Historical Criticism', *English Institute Essays* (1950), pp. 23–4. According to the anonymous author of *The Raigne of King Edward the First* (London, 1596), sig. C[1], 'The nightingale singes of adulterate wrong . . .'; cf. D. Filippo Picinelli, *Mondo Simbolico* (Venice, 1678), sig. 01. The nightingale generally sings, in Shakespeare, in scenes in which desire is getting somewhat out of control [*TGV* V iv; *R&J* III v].

33. Andrea Alciati, *Omnia Emblemata* (Antwerp, 1581), sig. C3ᵛ. Cf. Conté, sig. Rrlᵛ; and Sandys, sig. [Dd4]–[Dd4]ᵛ.

34. Lyly, *Works*, [I, 250].

35. Golding, p. 17; cf. Robert Burton, *The Anatomy of Melancholy*, ed. A. R. Shilleto, 3 vols (London, 1893), III, p. 177.

36. *The New Testament*, trans. William Tyndale (Cambridge, 1938), p. 349.

37. H. S. Wilson, '*The Knight's Tale* and the *Teseida* Again', *U. of Toronto Quarterly*, XVIII (1949), p. 145.

William Rossky 'Renaissance Attitudes to the
Imagination' (1958)

Shakespeare couples lunatic, lover, and poet as 'of imagination all
compact' [*Dream* V i 7–8]; Spenser finds that Phantastes's chamber is
filled with 'leasings, tales and lies' [*FQ* II ix 51 9] and that his eyes
seem 'mad or foolish' [*FQ* II ix 52 7]; Drayton speaks of the 'doting
trumperie' of imagination;[1] when men's minds become 'inflamed',
says Bacon, 'it is all done by stimulating the imagination till it
becomes ungovernable, and not only sets reason at nought, but offers
violence to it'.[2] These views of imagination and its activity, echoed in
other important literature of the age of Elizabeth, hardly suggest a
favorable view of the faculty assigned to the poet. The explanation of
such derogatory views lies in the popular psychology of the
period. . . .

Always the imagination or fantasy[3] is seen as a power operating in
a framework of other faculties and functions. In a definite
hierarchical order of communication, knowledge travels from the so-
called 'outer' senses (the five primary senses), to the 'inner'
(Common Sense, Imagination and/or Fantasy, Sensible Reason, and
Memory, which occupy cells in the brain), and thus to the highest
rational, incorporeal powers (the Intellect or Wit or Understanding,
and the Will). More specifically, the general course of
communication runs from the perception of the outward senses to
common sense, or directly to imagination, which unites the various
reports of the senses into impressions that are in turn submitted to the
examination of a rational power and then passed to memory which
retains the impressions and reflects them back to the Imagination and
Sensible Reason, should they turn to it to recall past incidents.
Beyond these faculties and functions lies the overseeing and judging
power of the highest understanding, which in turn informs the Will.

Ultimately, then, all knowledge, thought, and action depend upon
the transmission of data through a hierarchy of powers. And in this
'instrumental'[4] system, imagination is a key faculty; for, as Thomas
Wright puts it, 'whatsoever we vnderstand, passeth by the gates of
our imagination'.[5] Moreover, by imagination, 'wee apprehend

likenesse and shapes of things of perticulers receyued',[6] the 'formes of things',[7] and a sound, healthy imagination is one which reflects to higher powers only accurate images of reality, else, in the instrumental scheme, sound knowledge, proper thought and action become impossible. Therefore, imagination in its healthy reproductive capacity ought – like a mirror – to reflect accurate sensible impressions of the external world, and upon the need for such accuracy in the images of imagination the greatest stress is placed.

> Knowledges next organ is *Imagination*;
> A glasse, wherein the obiect of our Sense
> Ought to reflect true height, or declination,
> For vnderstandings cleare intelligence,

says Sir Fulke Greville.[8] An 'obiect' must be 'made no greater nor lesse then it is in deed', observes Timothy Bright.[9] The concern of the Elizabethan is that the imagination deliver accurate images. When it faces toward reason, Bacon expects imagination to have 'the print of Truth' [*Works* III, 382].

If the report of the senses is accurately delivered, man's reactions are healthy and proportional; but if false reports are rendered, matters are 'otherwise taken then the object requireth' (Timothy Bright, p. 86), man's reasoning is good 'so farre as the naturall principles lead, or outward obiectes be sincerely taken, & truely reported to the minds consideration' (Bright, p. 73). But when fantasy reports 'mishapen obiects' the mind is off balance and reason is 'troden vnder foote'.[10] If fantasy is 'marred', says Sir John Davies, wit perceives everything falsely.[11] Indeed, as a consequence of the theory that it was the inaccurate report of imagination which misled reason, it was common opinion that injured minds – for example, those of idiots or madmen – could reason as well as those of ordinary men, but were misled by the faulty reporting of faulty imagination. Reason would be only as accurate as the images presented to it. As an instrument for correct reason, then, imagination should present accurate, mirror-like images.

Furthermore, since reason is conventionally described as the power which distinguishes good from evil, the ultimate result of inaccurate images of reality is immorality. Since the higher soul is itself incorruptible, the odium falls on the false images of fantasy. . . .

The widespread disrepute of imagination as a falsifying and misguiding faculty rested, even in its passive functions, upon many elements. A rather obvious one was its close tie to and dependence upon the senses, which had been condemned from classical through medieval times to the Renaissance, their disrepute dramatised in accounts of the conflict of the spirit with the animal flesh or philosophised in Platonic descriptions of the secondary and inadequate reality of sensory objects . . . the fallibility of the senses, since they supply the images of imagination, affects the reliability and hence the reputation of imagination. Moreover, about the senses hangs the suggestion of immorality, in which fantasy, their neighbor, shares: imagination, like the senses, is attracted by things of the body. . . .

. . . as might be expected from Shakespeare's reference to lunatics, perhaps as frequent a disreputable relationship as any is that to madness; 'for', as Batman has it, 'by madnesse that is called *Mania*, principally ye imagination is hurt' [Bk. VII, chap. 6], while Du Laurens refers to the 'foolish and vaine imaginations' of 'franticke' men (p. 79). Indeed, so closely tied to imagination is the frenzy of madness that the prescription for madness is confinement of the patient to a room where there are no pictures to stimulate the imagination [Batman, Bk. VII, chap. 5; Boorde, *Dyetary*, p. 298], and hence, often, to a wholly dark room. It is this conventional association of idiocy and madness with fantasy that Spenser recognises when he tells us that Phantastes 'mad or foolish seemd' [*FQ* II ix 52 7]. As a result of madness, of course, the images of imagination are distorted and the instrumental process is disturbed; for 'frenzy' mangles 'the forms of things', so that fantasy makes a false report to the understanding (Sir John Davies, p. 193). . . .

Hitherto we have considered imagination as acting rather passively so that its disrepute seems to stem chiefly from its very openness to influences which in turn make its testimony unreliable. . . . But imagination is not merely passive. . . . Imagination receives and conveys images, but, as Huarte has it, it also devises 'some others of his own framing' (p. 79). The imagination 'taketh what pleaseth it, and addeth thereunto or diminisheth', says the translator of La Primaudaye (p. 155); and he speaks of the 'newe and monstrous things it forgeth and coyneth' (p. 156): the verbs as well as the adjectives are significant . . . imagination, left to its own devices, may make what it will, creating in almost absolute disregard of the images furnished by the senses and hence fashioning often the fondest impossibilities. . . .

The power of fantasy actively to create monstrously distorted visions, lies about external reality, is, then, a cardinal tenet of Elizabethan psychology. These creations are called 'tales', 'fables', 'fictions', 'lyes', 'leasings'.[12] And although imagination feigns not only the grotesque or the monstrous but also the beautiful, not only 'flying asses' and chimeras but also 'golden hils' and 'castles in the air', all are incredible and therefore disreputable. The bias of the material in the psychological writings stands very heavily against this active function of the faculty. . . .

Conventionally it is imagination, and specifically its images, which stimulate emotion; and the very nature of the emotion, in the theory, depends upon the nature of the images. Even in his definition of passions, Thomas Wright, principal writer on the emotions, reveals how inextricably emotion and imagination are related; for a passion is 'a sensual motion of our appetitive facultie, through imagination of some good or ill thing' (p. 8). Indeed we 'cannot love, hate, feare, hope, &c, but that by imagination' (*ibid.*, p. 31). As he tells us in his chapter 'The manner how Passions are mooved', the objects of imagination are communicated to the heart – generally accepted as seat of the emotions[13] – which is thus aroused to irascible (avoiding) or concupiscible (desiring) reactions with, of course, subsequent appropriate action (Wright, p. 45). . . .[14]

The emotions are not in themselves, then, evil, but the distorted pictures of imagination which are presented to the heart make them so: the distorted images create distorted, excessive emotions. Discussing such perturbations, Burton declares 'that the first step and fountain of all our grievances in this kind is a distorted imagination, which, misinforming the heart, causeth all these distemperatures, alteration and confusion, of spirits and humours'. . . .

Such disrepute, then, creates a formidable problem for the adherents of poetry to which in the Renaissance the faculty imagination is assigned; and, in his *Apologie for Poesie*, it is clearly to the disrepute of imagination that Sidney responds when he declares that poetic imagination 'is not wholie imaginatiue, as we are wont to say by them that build Castles in the ayre' (p. 157), and it is surely the psychological descriptions of imagination which leads Puttenham similarly to distinguish between the good phantasy of the poet and the bad phantasy of others and to defend 'despised' poets and poetry on the grounds that 'the phantasticall part of man (if it be not disordered) [is] a representer of the best, most comely and bewtifull images or appearances of thinges to the soule and according to their very truth. If otherwise, then doth it breede *Chimeres* & monsters in mans imaginations, & not onely in his imaginations, but also in all his ordinarie actions and life which ensues' (pp. 18–9). . . .

Indeed the poetical view insists repeatedly that feigning is the very criterion of what is poetry. He who does not feign is a mere versifier or a historian and no poet; feigning is the poet's function and fiction his product: as Jonson says, 'hee is call'd a *Poet*, not hee which writeth in measure only; but that fayneth and formeth a fable.'[15] With Touchstone's punning verdict that 'the truest poetry is the most feigning' [*AYLI* III iii 19–20], almost every poet and critic of the period would agree. . . .

Poetic imagination is a good imagination. Poetic feigning is feigning with a difference. And the good imagination, which is the poetic, is good and reputable principally because it is controlled. . . . The distortion of the poet's feigning is not haphazard, but deliberate and purposeful, moral and rational; his creations are, indeed, 'true' rather than false. His imaginative creation and its emotional effect are guided by the conscious purpose, ordering, reason and morality of the writer to secure, in turn, directly or indirectly, rational and moral effects. . . . A far cry from the uncontrolled feigning of lunatic and melancholic that leads to the stirring of evil perturbations, the feigned image of poetry is the precisely controlled means of effective persuasion to good: it is the best example; it is the most effective mover. . . .

SOURCE: extracts from 'Imagination in the English Renaissance: Psychology and Poetic', *Studies in the Renaissance*, V (1958), pp. 49, 50–2, 53–4, 54–5, 57, 57–8, 60, 62, 63, 64, 65, 65–6, 73.

NOTES

[Reorganised and renumbered from the original – Ed.]

1. Michael Drayton, *The Tragicall Legend of Robert, Duke of Normandy* (*The Works of Michael Drayton*, ed. J. William Hebel, Oxford, 1931–1941, I, p. 262).

2. Francis Bacon, *Of the Dignity and Advancement of Learning* (*The Works of Francis Bacon*, ed. James Spedding *et al.*, London, 1889–92, IV, p. 406).

3. Although in classical times the functions of imagination and fantasy were carefully distinguished on the bases of passive or active function, by Elizabethan times the distinctions had, for the most part, been lost and terms like 'phantasy', 'fantsie', even 'fancy' are used interchangeably with 'imagination'. Thus in his translation of Grataroli, Fulwood lists as the first faculty of the brain 'Fantasie (or immagination[)]' (sig. Bᵛ). On a single page of *Mirum in Modum* John Davies of Hereford used 'Imagination' and 'Fantasie' interchangeably (*The Complete Works of John Davies of Hereford*, ed. Rev. A. B. Grosart, Edinburgh, 1878, I, p. 6) – this despite his declaration that, unlike others, he will make 'distinction' (I, p. 7). Even though he lists them as separate faculties, Pierre de La Primaudaye concludes that he will 'vse these two names *Fantasie* and *Imagination* indifferently', since so many regard them as 'the same facultie and vertue of the soule', and still later uses the term 'fancie' as a synonym (*The Second Part of the French Academie*, trans. T. B., London, 1594, pp. 155, 157). See also Robert Burton, who discusses the '*Phantasy*, or imagination' (*The Anatomy of Melancholy*, ed. Floyd Dell and Paul Jordan-Smith, New York, 1938, p. 139) and uses 'fancy' as synonym (pp. 222, 223).

4. See, for example, La Primaudaye, p. 149; Timothy Bright, *A Treatise of Melancholie*, printed by Thomas Vautrollier (London, 1586), pp. 77, 104: Levinus Lemnius, *The Touchstone of Complexions*, tr. Thomas Newton (London, 1581), fol. 14ʳ; Juan Huarte Navarro, *Examen de Ingenios*, trans. R.C., Esquire (London, 1594), p. 75.

5. Thomas Wright, *The Passions of the Minde in Generall* (London, 1604), p. 51.

6. Stephen Batman, *Batman vppon Bartholomewe* (London, 1582), Bk. III, chap. 1.

7. André Du Laurens, *A Discourse of the Preservation of the Sight: of Melancholike diseases . . . of Old Age*, trans. Richard Surphlet (London, 1599), p. 8.

8. Sir Fulke Greville, *A Treatie of Humane Learning* (*Poems and Dramas of Fulke Greville*, ed. Geoffrey Bullough, New York, 1945, I, p. 156).

9. Timothy Bright, *Treatise* . . . (op. cit. note 4), p. 86; see also pp. 78–9.

10. Thomas Nashe, *Terrors of the Night* (*The Complete Works*, ed. Rev. A. B. Grosart, London and Aylesbury, 1883–5, III, p. 233).

11. Sir John Davies, *Nosce Teipsum*, in *An English Garner*, ed. Edward Arber (Birmingham, 1877–96), V, p. 193.

12. Bright, pp. 102, 104; Nashe, *Terrors* [Works III, p. 233]; Spenser, *FQ* [II ix 51 9]; Huarte, p. 118.

13. See Ruth L. Anderson, *Elizabethan Psychology and Shakespeare's Plays* (Iowa City, 1927: University of Iowa Humanistic Studies, vol. III, no. 4), p. 73.

14. For parallel accounts, see also Sir John Davies, p. 177; Bright, p. 81; Burton, p. 224; and Huarte, p. 31.

15. Ben Jonson, *Discoveries 1641; Conversations . . . 1619*, ed. G. B. Harrison (London, 1923), p. 89.

Cesar L. Barber   'May Games and Metamorphoses on a Midsummer Night' (1959)

If Shakespeare had called *A Midsummer Night's Dream* by a title that referred to pageantry and May games, the aspects of it with which I shall be chiefly concerned would be more often discussed. To honor a noble wedding, Shakespeare gathered up in a play the sort of pageantry which was usually presented piece-meal at aristocratic entertainments, in park and court as well as in hall. And the May game, everybody's pastime, gave the pattern for his whole action, which moves 'from the town to the grove' and back again, bringing in summer to the bridal. These things were familiar and did not need to be stressed by a title.

Shakespeare's young men and maids, like those Stubbes described in May games, 'run gadding over night into the woods, . . . where they spend the whole night in pleasant pastimes' – and in the fierce vexation which often goes with the pleasures of falling in and out of love and threatening to fight about it. 'And no marvel', Stubbes exclaimed about such headlong business, 'for there is a great Lord present among them, as superintendant and Lord over their pastimes and sports, namely, Satan, prince of hell.'[1] In making Oberon, prince of fairies, into the May king, Shakespeare urbanely plays with the notion of a supernatural power at work in holiday: he presents the common May game presided over by an aristocratic garden god. Titania is a Summer Lady who 'waxeth wounder proud':

> I am a spirit of no common rate,
> The summer still doth tend upon my state . . .   [III i 145–6]

And Puck, as jester, promotes the 'night-role' version of misrule over which Oberon is superintendent and lord in the 'haunted grove'. . . . Next morning, when Theseus and Hippolyta find the lovers sleeping . . . Theseus jumps to the conclusion that

> No doubt they rose up early to observe
> The rite of May; and, hearing our intent,
> Came here in grace of our solemnity.   [IV i 131–3]

These lines need not mean that the play's action happens on May Day. Shakespeare does not make himself accountable for exact chronological inferences; the moon that will be new according to Hippolyta will shine according to Bottom's almanac. And in any case, people went Maying at various times, 'Aginst May, Whitsunday, and other time' is the way Stubbes puts it. This Maying can be thought of as happening on a midsummer night, even on Midsummer Eve itself, so that its accidents are complicated by the delusions of a magic time. (May Week at Cambridge University still comes in June.) The point of the allusions is not the date, but the *kind* of holiday occasion.[2] The Maying is completed when Oberon and Titania with their trains come into the great chamber to bring the blessings of fertility. They are at once common and special, a May king and queen making their good luck visit to the manor house, and a pair of country gods, half-English and half-Ovid, come to bring their powers in tribute to great lords and ladies.

The play's relationship to pageantry is most prominent in the scene where the fairies are introduced by our seeing their quarrel. This encounter is the sort of thing that Elizabeth and the wedding party might have happened on while walking about in the park during the long summer dusk. The fairy couple accuse each other of the usual weakness of pageant personages – a compelling love for royal personages [quotes II i 68–73]. . . . Oberon describes an earlier entertainment, very likely one in which the family of the real-life bride or groom had been concerned [quotes II i 148–50, 156–64]. . . . At the entertainment at Elvetham in 1591, Elizabeth was throned by the west side of a garden lake to listen to music from the water; the fairy queen came with a round of dancers and spoke of herself as wife to Auberon. These and other similarities make it quite possible, but not necessary, that Shakespeare was referring to the Elvetham occasion.[3] There has been speculation, from Warburton on down, aimed at identifying the mermaid and discovering in Cupid's fiery shaft a particular bid for Elizabeth's affections; Leicester's Kenilworth entertainment in 1575 was usually taken as the occasion alluded to, despite the twenty years that had gone by when Shakespeare wrote.[4] No one, however, has cogently demonstrated any reference to court intrigue – which is to be expected in view of the fact that the play, after its original performance, was on the public stage. The same need for discretion probably accounts for the lack of internal evidence as to the particular marriage the comedy originally celebrated.[5]

But what is not in doubt, and what matters for our purpose here, is the *kind* of occasion Oberon's speech refers to, the kind of occasion Shakespeare's scene is shaped by. The speech describes, in retrospect, just such a joyous overflow of pleasure into music and make-believe as is happening in Shakespeare's own play. The fact that what Shakespeare handled with supreme skill was just what was most commonplace no doubt contributes to our inability to connect what he produced with particular historical circumstances.

. . . it was commonplace to imitate Ovid. Ovidian fancies pervade *A Midsummer Night's Dream*, and especially the scene of the fairy quarrel: the description of the way Cupid 'loos'd his love shaft' at Elizabeth parallels the *Metamorphoses*' account of the god's shooting 'his best arrow, with the golden head' at Apollo; Helena, later in the scene, exclaims that 'The story shall be chang'd:/Apollo flies, and Daphne holds the chase' – and proceeds to invert animal images from Ovid.[6] The game was not so much to lift things gracefully from Ovid as it was to make up fresh things in Ovid's manner, as Shakespeare here, by playful mythopoesis, explains the bad weather by his fairies' quarrel and makes up a metamorphosis of the little Western flower to motivate the play's follies and place Elizabeth superbly above them. The pervasive Ovidian influence accounts for Theseus' putting fables and fairies in the same breath when he says, punning on ancient and antic,

> I never may believe
> These antique fables nor these fairy toys.   [v i 2–3]

The humor of the play relates superstition, magic and passionate delusion as 'fancy's images'. The actual title emphasizes a sceptical attitude by calling the comedy a 'dream'. It seems unlikely that the title's characterization of the dream, 'a midsummer night's dream', implies association with the specific customs of Midsummer Eve, except as 'midsummer night' would carry suggestions of a magic time. The observance of Midsummer Eve in England centered on building bonfires or 'bonefires', of which there is nothing in Shakespeare's moonlight play. It was a time when maids might find out who their true love would be by dreams or divinations. There were customs of decking houses with greenery and hanging lights, which just possibly might connect with the fairies' torches at the comedy's end. And when people gathered fern seed at midnight, sometimes they spoke of spirits whizzing invisibly past. . . . one can assume that Shakespeare's imagination found its way to similarities with folk cult, starting from the custom of Maying and the general feeling that spirits may be abroad in the long dusks and short nights of midsummer. Olivia in *Twelfth Night* speaks of 'midsummer madness' [III iv 61]. In the absence of evidence, there is no way to settle just how much comes from tradition. But what is clear is that Shakespeare was not *simply* writing out folklore which he heard in his youth, as Romantic critics liked to assume. On the contrary, his fairies are produced by a complex fusion of pageantry and popular game, as well as popular fancy. Moreover, . . . they are not serious in the menacing way in which the people's fairies were serious. Instead they are serious in a very different way, as embodiments of the May-game experience of eros in men and women and trees and flowers, while any superstitious tendency to believe in their literal reality is mocked. The whole night's action is presented as a release of shaping fantasy which brings clarification about the tricks of strong imagination. We watch a dream; but we are awake, thanks to pervasive humour about the tendency to take fantasy literally, whether in love, in superstition, or in Bottom's mechanical dramatics. . . .

Theseus and Hippolyta have a quite special sort of role: they are principals without being protagonists; the play happens for them rather than to them. This relation goes with their being stand-ins for the noble couple whose marriage the play originally honoured. In expressing the prospect of Theseus's marriage, Shakespeare can fix in ideal form, so that it can be felt later at performance in the theater, the mood that would obtain in a palace as the 'nuptial hour/Draws on apace'. Theseus looks towards the hour with masculine impatience, Hippolyta with a woman's happy willingness to dream away the time. Theseus gives directions for the 'four happy days' to his 'usual manager of mirth', his Master of the Revels, Philostrate [quotes I i 11–15]. . . . The whole community is to observe a decorum of the passions, with Philostrate as choreographer of a pageant where Melancholy's float will not appear. After the war in which he won Hippolyta, the Duke announces that he is going to wed her

> in another key,
> With pomp, with triumph, and with revelling   [I i 18–19]

But his large, poised line is interrupted by Egeus, panting out vexation. After the initial invocation of nuptial festivity, we are confronted by the sort of tension from which merriment is a release. Here is Age, standing in the way of Athenian youth; here are the locked conflicts of everyday. By the dwelling here on 'the sharp Athenian law', on the fate of nuns 'in shady cloister mew'd', we are led to feel the outgoing to the woods as an escape from the inhibitions imposed by parents and the organized community. And this sense of release is also prepared by looking for just a moment at the tragic potentialities of passion. Lysander and Hermia, left alone in their predicament, speak a plaintive, symmetrical duet on the theme, learned 'from tale or history', that 'The course of true love never did run smooth' [quotes I i 135–8]. . . . Suddenly the tone changes, as Lysander describes in little the sort of tragedy presented in *Romeo and Juliet*, where Juliet exclaimed that their love was 'Too like the lightning, which doth cease to be /Ere one can say "It lightens" ' [II ii 119–20; and quotes I i 141–9]. . . . But Hermia shakes herself free of the tragic vision, and they turn to thoughts of stealing forth tomorrow night to meet in the Maying wood and go on to the dowager aunt, where 'the sharp Athenian law/Cannot pursue us'.

If they had reached the wealthy aunt, the play would be a romance. But it is a change of heart, not a change of fortune, which lets love have its way. The merriments Philostrate was to have directed happen inadvertently, the lovers walking into them blind, so to speak. This is characteristic of the way game is transformed into drama in this play, by contrast with the disabling of the fictions in *Love's Labour's Lost*. Here the roles which the young people might play in a wooing game, they carry out in earnest. And nobody is shown setting about to play the parts of Oberon or Titania. Instead the pageant fictions are presented as 'actually' happening – at least so it seems at first glance. . . .

The lovers . . . are unreservedly *in* the passionate protestations which they rhyme at each other as they change partners [quotes II ii 108–9]. . . . The result of this lack of consciousness is that they are often rather dull and undignified, since however energetically they elaborate conceits, there is usually no qualifying irony, nothing withheld. And only accidental differences can be exhibited, Helena tall, Hermia short. Although the men think that 'reason says' now Hermia, now Helena, is 'the worthier maid', personalities have nothing to do with the case: it is the flowers that bloom in the spring. The life in the lovers' parts is not to be caught in individual speeches, but by regarding the whole movement of the farce, which swings and spins each in turn through a common pattern, an evolution that seems to have an impersonal power of its own. . . .

In *Love's Labour's Lost* it was one of the lovers, Berowne, who was aware, in the midst of the folly's game, that it was folly and a game; such consciousness, in *A Midsummer Night's Dream*, is lodged outside the lovers, in Puck. It is he who knows 'which way goes the game', as poor Hermia only thought she did. As a jester, and as Robin Goodfellow, games and practical jokes are his great delight: his lines express for the audience the mastery that comes from seeing folly as a pattern.

> Then will two at once woo one.
> That must needs be sport alone.   [III ii 118–9]

Like Berowne, he counts up the sacks as they come to Cupid's mill:

> Yet but three? Come one more.
> Two of both kinds makes up four.

> Here she comes, curst and sad.
> Cupid is a knavish lad
> Thus to make poor females mad.   [III ii 437–41]

Females, ordinarily a graceless word, works nicely here because it includes *every* girl. The same effect is got by using the names Jack and Jill, *any* boy and *any* girl [quotes III ii 458–63]. . . . The trailing off into rollicking doggerel is exactly right to convey country-proverb confidence in common humanity and in what humanity have in common. The proverb is on the lovers' side, as it was not for Berowne, who had ruefully to accept an ending in which 'Jack hath not Jill'. A festive confidence that things will ultimately go right supports the perfect gayety and detachment with which Puck relishes the preposterous course they take:

> Shall we their fond pageant see?
> Lord, what fools these mortals be!   [III ii 114–5]

The pageant is 'fond' because the mortals do not realise they are in it, nor that it is sure to come out right, since nature will have its way. . . .

The woods are a region of passionate excitement where, as Berowne said, love 'adds a precious seeing to the eye'. This precious seeing was talked about but never realised in *Love's Labour's Lost*; instead we got wit. But now it is realised; we get poetry. Poetry conveys the experience of amorous tendency diffused in nature; and poetry, dance, gesture, dramatic fiction, combine to create, in the fairies, creatures who embody the passionate mind's elated sense of its own omnipotence. The woods are established as a region of metamorphosis, where in liquid moonlight or glimmering starlight, things can change, merge and melt into each other. Metamorphosis expresses both what love sees and what it seeks to do.

The opening scene, like an overture, announces this theme of dissolving, in unobstrusive but persuasive imagery. Hipployta says that the four days until the wedding will 'quickly *steep* themselves in night' and the nights 'quickly *dream* away the time' [I i 7–8] – night will dissolve day in dream. Then an imagery of wax develops as Egeus complains that Lysander has bewitched his daughter Hermia, 'stol'n the *impression* of her fantasy' [I i 32]. Theseus backs up Egeus [quotes I i 47–51]. . . .

The supposedly moral threat is incongruously communicated in lines that relish the joy of composing beauties and suggests a godlike, almost inhuman freedom to do as one pleases in such creation. The metaphor of sealing as procreation is picked up again when Theseus requires Hermia to decide 'by the next new moon,/The sealing day betwixt my love and me' [I i 83–4]. The consummation in prospect with marriage is envisaged as a melting into a new form and a new meaning. Helena says to Hermia that she would give the world 'to be to you translated' [I i 191], and in another image describes meanings that melt from love's transforming power [quotes I i 242–5]. . . . The most general statement, and one that perfectly fits what we are to see in the wood when Titania meets Bottom, is

> Things base and vile, holding no quantity,
> Love can transpose to form and dignity.   [I i 232–3]

'The glimmering night' promotes transpositions by an effect not simply of light, but also of a half-liquid medium in or through which things are seen:

> Tomorrow night, when Phoebe doth behold
> Her silver visage in the wat'ry glass,
> Decking with liquid pearl the bladed grass,
> (A time that lovers' flights doth still conceal) . . .   [I i 209–13]

Miss Caroline Spurgeon pointed to the moonlight in this play as one of the earliest sustained effects of 'iterative imagery'.[7] To realise how the effect is achieved, we have to recognise that the imagery is not used simply to paint an external scene but to convey human attitudes. We do not get simply 'the glimmering night', but

> Didst thou not lead him through the glimmering night
> From Perigouna, whom he ravished?   [II i 77–8]

The liquid imagery conveys an experience of the skin, as well as the eye's confusion by refraction. The moon 'looks with a wat'ry eye' [III i 193] and 'washes all the air' [II i 104]; its sheen, becoming liquid pearl as it mingles with dew, seems to get onto the eyeballs of the lovers, altering them to reshape what they see, like the juice of the flower with which they are 'streaked' by Oberon and Puck. The climax of unreason comes when Puck overcasts the night to make it 'black as Acheron' [III ii 357]; the lovers now experience only sound and touch, running blind over uneven ground, through bog and brake, 'bedabbled with the dew and torn with briers' [III ii 443]. There is nothing more they can do until the return of light permits a return of control: light is anticipated as 'comforts from the East' [III ii 432], 'the Morning's love' [III ii 389]. The sun announces its coming in a triumph of red and gold over salt green, an entire change of key from the moon's 'silver visage in her wat'ry glass':

> the eastern gate, all fiery red,
> Opening on Neptune, with fair blessed beams
> Turns unto yellow gold his salt green streams.   [III ii 391–3]

Finally Theseus comes with his hounds and his horns in the morning, and the lovers are startled awake. They find as they come to themselves that

> These things seem small and undistinguishable,
> Like far-off mountains turned into clouds.   [IV i 186–7]

The teeming metamorphoses which we encounter are placed, in this way, in a medium and in a moment where the perceived structure of the outer world breaks down, where the body and its environment interpenetrate in unaccustomed ways, so that the seeming separateness and stability of identity is lost.

The action of metaphor is itself a process of transposing. There is less direct description of external nature *in* the play than one would suppose: much of the effect of being in nature comes from imagery which endows it with anthropomorphic love, hanging a wanton pearl in every cowslip's ear. Titania laments that

> the green corn
> Hath rotted ere his youth attain'd a beard;

while

> Hoary-headed frosts
> Fall in the fresh lap of the crimson rose . . .   [II 94–5, 107–8]

By a complementary movement of imagination, human love is treated in terms of growing things. Theseus warns Hermia against becoming a nun, because

> earthlier happy is the rose distill'd
> Than that which, withering on the virgin thorn
> Grows, lives and dies in single blessedness.   [I i 76–8]

Titania, embracing Bottom, describes herself in terms that fit her surroundings and uses the association of ivy with women of the songs traditional at Christmas[8] [quotes IV i 41–3]. . . .

One could go on and on in instancing metamorphic metaphors. But one of the most beautiful bravura speeches can serve as an epitome of the metamorphic action in the play, Titania's astonishing answer when Oberon asks for the changeling boy [quotes II i 121–37]. . . .

The memory of a moment seemingly so remote expresses with plastic felicity the present moment when Titania speaks and we watch. It suits Titania's immediate mood, for it is a glimpse of women who gossip alone, apart from men and feeling now no need of them, rejoicing in their own special part of life's power. At such moments, the child, not the lover, is their object – as this young squire is still the object for Titania, who 'crowns him with flowers, and makes him all her joy'. The passage conveys a wanton joy in achieved sexuality, in fertility; and a gay acceptance of the waxing of the body (like joy in the varying moon). At leisure in the spiced night air, when the proximate senses of touch and smell are most alive, this joy finds sport in projecting images of love and growth where they are not. The mother, having laughed to see the ship a woman with child, imitates it so as to go the other way about and herself become a ship. She fetches trifles, but she is also actually 'rich with merchandise', for her womb is 'rich with my young squire'. The secure quality of the play's pleasure is conveyed by having the ships out on the flood while she sails, safely, upon the *land*, with a pretty and swimming gait that is an overflowing of the security of make-believe. The next line brings a poignant glance out beyond this gamesome world: 'But she, being mortal, of that boy did die.'

It is when the flower magic leads Titania to find a new object that she gives up the child (who goes now from her bower to the man's world of Oberon). So here is another sort of change of heart that contributes to the expression of what is consummated in marriage, this one a part of the rhythm of adult life, as opposed to the change in the young lovers that goes with growing up. Once Titania has made this transition, their ritual marriage is renewed [quotes IV i 86–9]. . . .

The final dancing blessing of the fairies, 'Through the house give glimmering light' [V i 381], after the lovers are abed, has been given meaning by the symbolic action we have been describing: the fairies have been made into tutelary spirits of fertility, so that they can promise that

> the blots of Nature's hand
> Shall not in their issue stand.   [V i 399–400]

When merely read, the text of this episode seems somewhat bare, but its clipped quality differentiates the fairy speakers from the mortals, and anyway richer language would be in the way. Shakespeare has changed from a fully dramatic medium to conclude, in a manner appropriate to festival, with dance and song. It seems likely that, as Dr Johnson argued, there were two songs which have been lost, one led by Oberon and the other by Titania.[9]

There were probably two dance evolutions also, the first a processional dance led by the king and the second a round led by the queen: Oberon's lines direct the fairies to dance and sing 'through the house', 'by the fire', 'after me'; Titania seems to start a circling dance with 'First rehearse your song by rote'; by contrast with Oberon's 'after me', she calls for 'hand in hand'. This combination of processional and round dances is the obvious one for the occasion: to get the fairies in and give them something to do. But these two forms of dance are associated in origin with just the sort of festival use of them which Shakespeare is making. 'The customs of the village festival', Chambers writes, 'gave rise by natural development to two types of dance. One was the processional dance of a band of worshippers in progress round their boundaries and from field to field, house to house. . . . The other type of folk dance, the *ronde* or "round", is derived from the comparatively stationary dance of the group of worshippers around the more especially sacred objects of the festival, such as the tree or fire. The custom of dancing round the Maypole has been more or less preserved wherever the Maypole is known. But "Thread the Needle" (a type of surviving processional dance) itself often winds up with a circular dance or *ronde* . . .'[10] One can make too much of such analogies. But they do illustrate the rich traditional meanings available in the materials Shakespeare was handling.

Puck's broom is another case in point: it is his property as a housemaid's sprite, 'to sweep the dust behind the door' [V i 380]; also it permits him to make 'room', in the manner of the presenter of a holiday mummers' group. And with the dust, out go evil spirits. Puck refers to 'evil sprites' let forth by graves, developing a momentary sense of midnight terrors, of spirits that walk by night; then he promises that no mouse shall disturb 'this hallowed house'. The exorcism of evil powers complements the invocation of good. With their 'field dew consecrate', the fairies enact a lustration. Fertilising and beneficent virtues are in festival custom persistently attributed to dew gathered on May mornings.[11] Shakespeare's handling of nature has infused dew in this play with the vital spirit of moist and verdant woods. The dew is 'consecrate' in this sense. But the religious associations inevitably attaching to the word suggest also the sanctification of love by marriage. It was customary for the clergy, at least in important marriages, to bless the bed and bridal couple with holy water. The benediction included exorcism, in the Manual for the use of Salisbury a prayer to protect them from what Spenser called 'evill sprights' and 'things that be not' (*ab omnibus fantasmaticis demonum illusionibus*).[12] This custom may itself be an ecclesiastical adaptation of a more primitive bridal lustration, a water charm of which dew-gathering on May Day is one variant. Such a play as *A Midsummer Night's Dream* is possible because the May and Summer Spirit, despite its pagan affinities, is not conceived as necessarily in opposition to the wholeness of traditional Christian life. . . .

The meeting in the woods of Bottom and Titania is the climax of the polyphonic interplay; it comes in the middle of the dream, when the humor has the most work to do. Bottom in the ass's head provides a literal metamorphosis, and in the process brings in the element of grotesque fantasy which the Savage Man or Woodwose furnished at Kenilworth, a comic version of an animal-headed dancer or the sort of figure Shakespeare used in Herne the Hunter, 'with great ragged horns', at the oak in *The Merry Wives of Windsor*. At the same time he is the theatrical company's clown 'thrust in by head and shoulder to play a part in majestical matters' and remaining uproariously literal and antipoetic as he does so. Titania and he are fancy against fact, not beauty and the beast. She makes all the advances while he remains very respectful, desiring nothing bestial but 'a peck of provender'. Clownish oblivion to languishing beauty is sure-fire comedy on any vaudeville stage. Here it is elaborated in such a way that when Titania is frustrated, so is the transforming power of poetry [quotes III i 130–41]. . . . From a vantage below romance, the clown makes the same point as sceptical Theseus, that reason and love do not go together. Titania tells him that she

> . . . will purge thy mortal grossness so
> That thou shalt like an airy spirit go.   [III i 151–2]

But even her magic cannot 'transpose' Bottom.

The 'low' or 'realistic' effect which he produces when juxtaposed with her is much less a matter of accurate imitation of common life than one assumes at first glance. Of course the homely touches are telling – forms of address like 'Methinks, mistress' or words like *gleek* suggest a social world remote from the elegant queen's. But the realistic effect does not depend on Bottom's being like real weavers, but on the *détente* of imaginative tension, on a downward movement which counters imaginative life. This antipoetic action involves, like the poetic, a high degree of abstraction from real life, including the control of rhythm which can establish a blank verse movement in as little as a single line, 'Thou art as wise as thou art beautiful', and so be able to break the ardent progression of the queen's speech with 'Not so, neither'. When Bottom encounters the fairy attendants, he reduces the fiction of their existence to fact [quotes III i 174–9]. . . . Cobwebs served the Elizabethans for adhesive plaster, so that when

Bottom proposes to 'make bold with' Cobweb, he treats him as a *thing*, undoing the personification on which the little fellow's life depends. To take hold of Cobweb in this way is of course a witty thing to do, when one thinks about it. But since the wit is in the service of a literal tendency, we can take it as the expression of a 'hempen homespun'. There is usually a similar incongruity between the 'stupidity' of a clown and the imagination and wit required to express such stupidity. Bottom's charming combination of ignorant exuberance and oblivious imaginativeness makes him the most humanly credible and appealing personality Shakespeare had yet created from the incongruous qualities required for the clown's role. The only trouble with the part, in practice, is that performers become so preoccupied with bringing out the weaver's vanity as an actor that they lose track of what the role is expressing as part of the larger imaginative design.

For there is an impersonal, imaginative interaction between the clowning and the rest of the play which makes the clowns mean more than they themselves know and more than they are as personalities. Bottom serves to represent, in so aware a play, the limits of awareness, limits as limitations – and also, at moments, limits as form and so strength. [Quotes IV ii 23–32]. . . . It is ludicrous for Bottom to be so utterly unable to cope with the 'wonders', especially where he is shown boggling in astonishment as he wordlessly remembers them: 'I have had a most rare vision. I have had a dream past the wit of man to say what dream it was' [IV i 203–4]. But there is something splendid, too, in the way he exuberantly rejoins 'these lads' and takes up his particular, positive life as a 'true Athenian'. Metamorphosis cannot faze him for long. His imperviousness, indeed, is what is most delightful about him with Titania: he remains so completely himself, even in her arms, and despite the outward change of his head and ears; his confident, self-satisfied tone is a triumph of consistency, persistence, existence. . . .

SOURCE: extracts from *Shakespeare's Festive Comedy: A Study of Dramatic Form and its Relation to Social Custom* (New York, 1959; reprinted 1963), pp. 119–23, 123–4, 125–7, 128, 130–1, 132–9, 154–7.

NOTES

[Reorganised and renumbered from the original – Ed.]

1. *The Anatomie of Abuses . . . in Ailgna* (1583), ed. F. J. Furnival (London, 1877–82), p. 149.
2. A great deal of misunderstanding has come from the assumption of commentators that a Maying must necessarily come on May Day, May 1. The confusion that results is apparent throughout Furness's discussion of the title and date in his preface to the *Variorum* edition. . . .
3. See E. K. Chambers, *Shakespearean Gleanings* (Oxford, 1944), pp. 63–4; and Alice S. Venezky, *Pageantry on the Shakespearean Stage* (New York, 1951), pp. 140 ff.
4. The conjectures are summarised in *Variorum*, pp. 75–91.
5. Chambers, *Gleanings*, pp. 61–7.
6. Ovid, *Metamorphoses*, with an English translation by Frank Justus Miller (New York, 1916), pp. 34 and 36–7, Bk. I, lines 465–74 and 505–6.
7. Caroline Spurgeon, *Shakespeare's Imagery and What It Tells Us* (Cambridge, 1935), pp. 259–63.
8. . . . A recurrent feature of the type of pastoral which begins with something like 'As I walked forth one morn in May' is a bank of flowers 'for love to lie and play on'. . . . This motif appears in the 'bank where the wild thyme blows' where Titania sleeps 'lull'd in these flowers by dances and delight'. In such references there is a magical suggestion that love is infused with nature's vitality by contact.
9. See *Variorum*, p. 239, for Johnson's cogent note. Richmond Noble, in *Shakespeare's Use of Song* (Oxford, 1923), pp. 55–7, argues that the text as we have it *is* the text of the song, without, I think, meeting the arguments of Johnson and subsequent editors.
10. *The Medieval Stage* (Oxford, 1903), I, p. 165–6.
11. *Ibid.*, I, p. 122.
12. *Variorum*, p. 240.

Frank Kermode   'Shakespeare's Best Comedy'
(1961)

. . . one could legitimately say that the best of the 'mature' comedies are technically superior to all that came later; I should myself be prepared to maintain that *A Midsummer Night's Dream* is Shakespeare's best comedy.

With this play, and with *Twelfth Night*, criticism – inhibited from the start by an historical failure to take the comedies seriously – has been curiously slow to take the hint of the titles. From the normal licence of St John's Eve to the behaviour of Shakespeare's young lovers in the dark wood is a short step; Hardy must have been aware of it when he wrote the twentieth chapter of *The Woodlanders*, but only recently have critics taken their cue from Frazer and seen something of the full import. What one needs to add to this naïve theme is the recognition of an intense sophistication. It is still probably too much to expect many people to believe that the theme of *A Midsummer Night's Dream* can be explained by references to Apuleius, to Macrobius and Bruno and so forth, and this is not the place to defend such modes of explanation, though they need defending as much as any others, including the view that the play means nothing much at all. Let us, for sake of argument, assume that it is a play of marked intellectual content; that the variety of the plot is a reflection of an elaborate and ingenious thematic development; and that simple and pedestrian explanations of such developments have some value.

☆

A Midsummer Night's Dream opens with a masterly scene which, as usual in the earlier Shakespeare, establishes and develops a central thematic interest. The accusation against Lysander is that he has corrupted the fantasy of Hermia [I i 32], and the disorders of fantasy (imagination) are the main topic of the play. Hermia complains that her father cannot see Lysander with her eyes; Theseus in reply requires her to subordinate her eyes to her father's judgment [I i 56–7] or pay the penalty. She is required to 'fit her fancies to her father's will'. All withdraw save Lysander and Hermia, who utter a small litany of complaint against the misfortunes of love: 'So quick bright things come to confusion.' This recalls not only *Romeo and Juliet* but also *Venus and Adonis* (the passage from line 720 to line 756 is related to *Midsummer Night's Dream*). This lament of 'poor Fancy's followers' gives way easily to their plot of elopement. Helena enters, in her turn complaining of ill-fortune; for Demetrius prefers

Hermia's eyes to hers. Hermia leaves: 'we must starve our sight/From lover's food till morrow deep midnight.' Lysander, remembering that Helena 'dotes/Devoutly dotes, dotes in idolatry' [I i 108–9] on Demetrius, departs, expressing a wish that Demetrius will come to 'dote' on Helena as she on him [I i 225]. The repetition of the word 'dote', the insistence that the disordered condition of the imagination which is called 'love' originates in eyes uncontrolled by judgment; these are hammered home in the first scene, and the characteristic lamentations about the brevity and mortality of love are introduced like a 'second subject' in a sonata. Finally Helena moralises emblematically [quotes I i 230–8]. . . . In love the eye induces 'doting', not a rational, patient pleasure like that of Theseus and Hippolyta. Helena is making a traditional complaint against the blind Cupid[1]; love has nothing to do with value, is a betrayal of the quality of the high sense of sight, and is therefore depicted blind, irresponsible, without judgment. Later we shall see the base and vile so transformed; love considered as a disease of the eye will be enacted in the plot. But so will the contrary interpretation of 'blind Love'; that it is a higher power than sight; indeed, above intellect. *Amor . . . sine oculis dicitur, quia est supra intellectum.*[2]

The themes of the play are thus set forth in the opening scene. Love-fancy as bred in the eye is called a kind of doting; this is held to end in disasters of the kind that overtook Adonis, Romeo, Pyramus; and the scene ends with an ambiguous emblem of blind love. The next scene introduces the play of the mechanicals, which, in a recognizable Shakespearian manner, gives farcical treatment to an important thematic element; for Bottom and his friends will perform a play to illustrate the disastrous end of doting, of love brought to confusion. Miss Mahood has spoken of Shakespeare's ensuring that in *Romeo and Juliet* 'our final emotion is neither the satisfaction we should feel in the lovers' death if the play were a simple expression of the *Liebestod* theme, nor the dismay of seeing two lives thwarted and destroyed by vicious fates, but a tragic equilibrium which includes and transcends both these feelings';[3] and in *Midsummer Night's Dream* we are given a comic equilibrium of a similar kind. The 'moral' of the play is not to be as simple as, say, that of Bacon's essay 'Of Love': there it is said to be unreasonable that a man, 'made for the contemplation of heaven and all noble objects, should do nothing but kneel before a little idol, and make himself subject, though not of the mouth (as beasts are) yet of the eye, which was given them for higher purposes'. Shakespeare's conclusion has not the simplicity of this: 'Nuptial love maketh mankind; friendly love perfecteth it; but wanton love corrupteth and embaseth it.' Yet, for the moment, the theme is blind love; and the beginning of the second act takes us into the dark woods. If we are willing to listen to such critics as C. L Barber,[4] we shall take a hint from the title of the play and attend to the festival licence of young lovers in midsummer woods. Also we shall remember how far the woods are identified with nature, as against the civility of the city; and then we shall have some understanding of the movement of the plot. Puck is certainly a 'natural' force; a power that takes no account of civility or rational choice. He is, indeed, a blinding Cupid; and the passage in which he is, as it were, cupidinised is so famous for other reasons that its central significance is overlooked [quotes II i 155–72]. . . .

The juice used by Puck to bring confusion to the darkling lovers is possessed of all the force of Cupid's arrow, and is applied with equal randomness. The eye so touched will dote; in it will be engendered a fancy 'for the next live thing it sees'. Puck takes over the role of blind Cupid. The love he causes is a madness; the flower from which he gets his juice is called '*Love-in-idleness*', and that word has the force of wanton behaviour amounting almost to madness. The whole object is to punish Titania 'and make her full of hateful fantasies' [II i 258], and to end the naturally intolerable situation of a man's not wanting a girl who wants him [II i 260–1]. Puck attacks his task without moral considerations; Hermia and Lysander are lying apart from each other 'in human modesty' [II ii 63] but Puck has no knowledge of this and assumes that Hermia must have been churlishly rejected:

> Pretty soul! She durst not lie
> Near this lack-love, this kill-courtesy.   [II ii 82–3]

Lysander awakes; his anointed eyes dote at once on the newly arrived Helena. He ingeniously attributes this sudden change to a sudden maturity:

> The will of man is by this reason sway'd;
> And reason says you are the worthier maid.
> . . .

> Reason becomes the marshal to my will
> And leads me to your eyes, . . .   [II ii 121–2, 126–7]

But in the next scene Bottom knows better: 'Reason and love keep little company together nowadays.'

It is scarcely conceivable, though the point is disputed, that the love-affair between Titania and Bottom is not an allusion to *The Golden Ass*. In the first place, the plot of Oberon is like that of the Cupid and Psyche episode, for Venus then employs Cupid to avenge her by making Psyche (to whom she has lost some followers) fall in love with some base thing. Cupid, at first a naughty and indecent boy, himself becomes Psyche's lover. On this story were founded many rich allegories; out of the wanton plot came truth in unexpected guise. And in the second place, Apuleius, relieved by the hand of Isis from his ass's shape, has a vision of the goddess, and proceeds to initiation in her mysteries. On this narrative of Apuleius, for the Renaissance half-hidden in the enveloping commentary of Beroaldus, great superstructures of platonic and Christian allegory had been raised; and there is every reason to suppose that these mysteries are part of the flesh and bone of *A Midsummer Night's Dream*.

The antidote by which the lovers are all restored 'to wonted sight' is 'virtuous' [III ii 367], being expressed from 'Dian's bud', [IV i 72] which, by keeping men chaste keeps them sane. So far the moral seems to be simple enough; the lovers have been subject to irrational forces; in the dark they have chopped and changed like the 'little dogs' of Dylan Thomas's story, though without injury to virtue. But they will awake, and 'all this derision/Shall seem a dream and fruitless vision' [III ii 370–1]. Oberon pities the 'dotage' of Titania, and will 'undo/This hatefull imperfection of her eyes' [IV i 61–2]; she will awake and think all this 'the fierce vexation of a dream' [IV i 68] and Puck undoes the confusions of the young lovers. In the daylight they see well, and Demetrius even abjures the dotage which enslaved him to Hermia; his love for Helena returns as 'natural taste' returns to a man cured of a sickness [IV i 173]. They return to the city and civility. All are agreed that their dreams are fantasies; that they have returned to health. But the final awakening of this superbly arranged climax (as so often in the mature Shakespearian comedy it occurs at the end of the fourth act) is Bottom's. And here the 'moral' defies comfortable analysis; we suddenly leave behind the neat love-is-a-kind-of-madness pattern and discover that there is more to ideas-in-poetry than ideas and verse.

I have had a most rare vision, I have had a dream, past the wit of man to say what dream it was: man is but an ass if he go about to expound this dream. . . . The eye of man hath not heard, the ear of man hath not seen, man's hand is not able to taste, his tongue to conceive, nor his heart to report, what my dream was. . . .   [IV i 203-5, 208-11]

It must be accepted that this is a parody of I Corinthians ii 9 ff.:

Eye hath not seen, nor ear heard, neither have entered into the heart of man the things which God hath prepared for them that love him. . . . Which things also we speak, not in the words which man's wisdom teacheth, but which the Holy Ghost teacheth. . . .

Apuleius, after his transformation, might not speak of the initiation he underwent; but he was vouchsafed a vision of the goddess Isis. St Paul was initiated into the religion he had persecuted by Ananias in Damascus. What they have in common is transformation, and an experience of divine love. Bottom has known the love of the triple goddess in a vision. His dream is of a different quality from the others'; they have undergone what in the Macrobian division (*Comm. in Somn. Scip.* I 3) is called *phantasma*; Brutus glosses this as 'a hideous dream' [*J. Caesar* II i 65]. But Bottom's dream is *oneiros* or *somnium*; ambiguous, enigmatic, of high import. And this is the contrary interpretation of blind love; the love of God or Isis, a love beyond the power of the eyes. To Pico, to Cornelius Agrippa, to Bruno, who distinguished nine kinds of fruitful love-blindness, this exaltation of the blindness of love was both Christian and Orphic; Orpheus said that love was eyeless; St Paul and David that God dwelt in darkness and beyond knowledge.[5] Bottom is there to tell us that the blindness of love, the dominance of the mind over the eye, can be interpreted as a means to grace as well as to irrational animalism; that the two aspects are, perhaps, inseparable.

The last Act opens with the set piece of Theseus on the lunatic, the lover, and the poet. St Paul speaks of the 'hidden wisdom' 'which none of the princes of this world know', which must be spoken of 'in a mystery'; and which may come out of the learned ignorance of 'base things of the world, . . . which . . . God hath chosen' [I Cor. ii]. Theseus cannot understand these matters. In lunatics, lovers and poets, the imagination is out of control; it is the power that makes 'things unknown', as, so this orthodox psychologist implies, these are the disordered creations of the faculty when reason, whether because of love or lunacy or the poetic *furor,* is not in charge of it. The doubts of Hippolyta [V i 23 ff.] encourage us to believe that this 'prince of the world' may be wrong. The love of Bottom's vision complements the rational love of Theseus; Bottom's play, farcical as it is, speaks of the disasters that do not cease to happen but only become for a moment farcically irrelevant, on a marriage day. 'Tragical mirth . . . hot ice and wondrous strange snow' are terms not without their relevance; and the woods have their wisdom as well as the city.

Thus, without affectation, one may suggest the *skopos* of *A Midsummer Night's Dream* – the thematic preoccupation, the characteristic bursting through into action of what seems a verbal trick only (the talk of eyes). Unless we see that these mature comedies are thematically serious we shall never get them right. And it might even be added that *A Midsummer Night's Dream* is more serious in this way than *Cymbeline,* because the patterns of sight and blindness, wood and city, phantasma and vision, grow into a large and complex statement, or an emblematic presentation not to be resolved into its component parts, of love, vulgar and celestial.

SOURCE: extract from 'The Mature Comedies', an essay in *Early Shakespeare*, ed. John Russell Brown and Bernard Harris: Stratford-upon-Avon Studies 3 (London, 1961), pp. 214-20.

NOTES

[Renumbered from the original – Ed.]

1. See E. Panofsky, *Studies in Iconology* (1939), pp. 122–3 and p. 122, n. 74.
2. Pico della Mirandola, quoted in Wind, *Pagan Mysteries of the Renaissance* (1958), p.56.

3. *Shakespeare's Wordplay* (1957), p.72.

4. *Shakespeare's Festive Comedy* (Princeton, 1959). [See extracts from Barber's study above in this selection – Ed.]

5. E. Wind, *op. cit.*, pp. 57ff.

G. K. Hunter   'Contrast Rather than Interaction'   (1962)

. . . *A Midsummer Night's Dream* is best seen, in fact, as a lyric divertissement, or a suite of dances – gay, sober, stately, absurd. Shakespeare has lavished his art on the separate excellencies of the different parts, but has not sought to show them growing out of one another in a process analogous to that of symphonic 'development'. The play is centred on Love, but it moves by exposing the varieties of love, rather than by working them against one another in a process of argument. This is probably another way of saying that the play contains no personalities, no figures like Beatrice, Rosalind or Olivia, who, being self-aware, are also self-correcting; on the whole, the characters remain fixed in their attitudes; those who change, like Demetrius, Lysander and Titania, are lifted bodily, without conflict of characters, and without volition, from one attitude to another. In the case of Titania, the induced passion for Bottom imprisons her but does not infringe her dignity; she can change back without loss of face; in the case of the lovers, the change must be preserved, to complete the pattern, and is accepted in those terms; it is this pattern and the individuals who compose it that is the play's concern . . . the lovers are like dancers who change partners in the middle of a figure; the point at which the partners are exchanged is determined by the dance, and not by the psychological state of the dancers. . . .

The dance is a dance of emotions, but the emotions are not subjected to anything like a psychological analysis; Shakespeare limits our response by showing us the lovers as the mere puppets of the fairies. They act on their emotions, but what is action to them is only 'an act' to those who (invisible themselves) watch, manipulate and comment [quotes III ii 113–4]. . . .

The verse itself helps to 'distance' the scenes of the lovers' cross-purposes. . . . It reduces the passions to a comic level where we do not feel called upon to share them; but it remains poetic and charming. . . .

Seen against the fairies, the lovers are absurd; set against the rational love of Theseus and Hippolyta, the mature and royal lovers who frame and explain the occasion of the play, it is the irrationality of their emotion which is emphasised. This receives its magisterial definition in Theseus's famous speech about 'The lunatic, the lover and the poet'. But even if Theseus had not spoken, or even if we were disposed not to allow the objectivity of what he says, there is plenty of evidence from the lovers' own lips to convict their love of irrationality [quotes I i 232–41]. . . .

This description of love, which Helena puts forward to justify her betrayal of friendship and abandonment of reason, is picked up in the next act in a more obviously fallacious form [quotes II ii 121–8]. . . . Helena remarks on the capacity of love to work without knowing the evidence of the senses (the eyes); in Lysander's case *reason* is only a means of returning to the *eyes* of his mistress, and reading irrational love stories. But the clearest comment on this infatuation comes not in the adventures of the lovers at all, but in the parallel situation of Titania and Bottom. Titania awakes and finds herself in love with Bottom, ass's head and all. Like the other lovers, her first care is to justify the *wisdom* of her choice [quotes III i 132–8]. . . . Just as Bottom is the only mortal to see the fairies, so here he is the only one in the moonlit wood to see the daylight truth about love. But in both cases the knowledge is useless to him, since he supposes that 'man is but an ass, if he go about to expound this'. The advantage he has over the lovers is illusory, for he cannot make use of it.

Seen against the fairies or the royal pair, the lovers – who cannot fight back against either of these – cut rather poor figures. But the play does not leave them in this posture; there is a fourth term which helps to restore their dignity. The play of Pyramus and Thisbe . . . shows a similar situation to that of Hermia and Lysander: lovers obstructed by parental opposition agree to run away from home and meet unobserved, at night. But the mechanicals' monumental unawareness of what is happening in their scene of 'very tragical mirth' makes the Athenian lovers seem, by contrast, to be in control of their destinies. The innocence of the lovers reduces them in a comparison with the mature gravity of Theseus or with the omniscience of Oberon, but innocence is a virtue still, and an effective one when set against the *ignorance* of the mechanicals. Indeed there is one moment in the play where the innocence of the lovers is celebrated on its own account; it is, significantly enough, the moment at which the moonlight world of their illusions is passing into the daylight world of their responsibilities [quotes IV i 186–94]. . . . The humility, the sense of wonder, the hushed note of gratitude here are not available to anyone else in the play.

The contrast between the lovers and the mechanicals is not one which works exclusively by compensating the former at the expense of the latter. In the final scene the lovers make great fun of the ineptitudes in the play being performed: I think we are intended to see the irony of this. Those who were the unwitting performers in a love-play stage-managed and witnessed by the fairies are now, very self-consciously, the superior spectators of another play. We can laugh with them at the mechanicals, but we also laugh at them. Similarly, the aplomb with which Bottom accepts the advances of the fairy queen contrasts in a double-edged way with the frenetic activity of the lovers; immovable ignorance is set against the levity which reacts to every puff of wind, in a fashion which does not redound to the credit of either.

The play is thus a pattern of attitudes, none of which is central and all of which cast light on the others. Shakespeare has obviously laboured (and not in vain) to create complementary visions, and has sought to make each a complete world in itself. . . .

Shakespeare's fairies are not only different in size from those who were part of folk-lore; their rulers are concerned not with mischief, as traditionally, but with *order* in a quasi-human fashion. . . . The quarrel of Oberon and Titania has caused natural havoc, which may serve throughout the play as an image of discord in matrimony, and therefore as a warning to all the intending couples [quotes II i 107–16]. . . .

. . . Another world of the play which Shakespeare has been at some pains to define effectively is the antique heroic world of Theseus and Hippolyta. It is obviously in an effort to create an image of antique chivalry that he gives them their resonant hunting speeches in Act IV [quotes IV i 111–8, 122–5]. . . .

Shakespeare is obviously concerned to fix this image of harmonious control over brute impulse, for his idea of achieved self-possession which Theseus, I take it, represents, cannot be projected through external action, and the psychological dimension of inner debate is not one that this play employs. All Shakespeare can do is to show Theseus and Hippolyta, set in graceful posture of power at rest, like antique statuary, larger than life size. Larger than any other characters, they foreknow the nature of the play between the opening speech and their marriage – the focal point towards which all the action of the play tends [quotes I i 7–19]. . . . The combination of romance and merriment here nicely catches the prevailing tone of the play, and suggests a settled and rational state of loving that has lived through the violent half-knowledge of passion. . . .

Theseus is no Rosalind: he does not control what happens in the wood – that is Oberon's province; and he does not have to deal with the assaults and temptations of other kinds of love – no-one in the play is involved in that kind of interaction. The play is constructed by contrast rather than interaction. . . . The relationship between Rosalind's love and Touchstone's is one which helps to define Rosalind's own nature, for she has to absorb Touchstone's parody (of Orlando's poems, for example) before she can declare her own position. The relationship between Theseus and Bottom is, formally, of a similar kind: the poise and self-confidence of one, in the courtly world of Athens, is met by an equal poise, among 'Hard-handed men that work in Athens here.' Self-knowledge and self-ignorance face one another across the play; but they do not interact; neither learns from the other. The meanings that each establishes only meet in the total meaningful pattern of the play.

SOURCE: extracts from *William Shakespeare: The Late Comedies* (London, 1962), pp. 8–19.

R. W. Dent   Imagination in *A Midsummer Night's Dream* (1964)

For many years editors and critics have customarily praised *A Midsummer Night's Dream* for its artistic fusion of seemingly disparate elements. Sometimes the praise involves little, really, beyond admiring the skill with which Shakespeare interwove the actions of the four lovers, the fairies, and the mechanicals in the first four acts of the play.[1] Usually, quite properly, it moves somewhat beyond this, relating this interwoven action to the thematic treatment of love in the play. But such praise has rarely concerned itself with the play's fifth act; it has tended to treat *A Midsummer Night's Dream* as essentially complete in four acts, but with a fifth act somehow vaguely appropriate in mood and content to serve as a conclusion. 'Pyramus and Thisbe', that rude offering of the mechanicals, has been briefly commended as loosely paralleling in action and theme the problems of the four lovers, and as delightful enough in itself to need no other artistic justification. Despite the consistency with which *A Midsummer Night's Dream* has been admired for its unity, in short, few critics have had much to say about the whole of the play.

The present essay seeks to reexamine the degree and kind of unity achieved by *A Midsummer Night's Dream*. Without pretending to be strikingly original, it approaches the play from a somewhat different angle, suggesting that the heart of the comedy, its most pervasive unifying element, is the partially contrasting role of imagination in love and in art. I do not mean to suggest for a moment that Shakespeare composed this play, or any play, as the result of a single governing conception to which every detail can be effectively related. But I do mean to suggest that *A Midsummer Night's Dream* has a dominant and premeditated conception. Thus, if my argument below appears guilty of the 'intentional fallacy', it is so intentionally. Shakespeare's eye, in creating *A Midsummer Night's Dream*, did not 'roll' in a 'fine frenzy', and my point on imagination's role in the play demands my emphasis.

A prefatory word is necessary. Oversimply, to the Elizabethan the imagination ideally functioned as an essential servant to the understanding, whether as a reporter (the most emphasised function, that of transmitting accurate images of sense data, present or absent) or as a creator or inventor. When, as too frequently happened, it became dominated by passions in conflict with reason, it became a false reporter and/or inventor. In the case of passionate love, for example, one could not say that the imagination actually caused love, but rather that love so influenced the imagination as to have it misreport what it saw, thereby heightening the passion, thereby heightening the imagination, thereby . . . an endless chain reaction to man's ever-increasing peril. In watching the lovers of *A Midsummer Night's Dream*, we tend to be aware of the imagination's activity only when it is thus failing in its proper function. At such times we can scarcely attribute the folly to love or imagination alone, obviously; it derives from their interaction.

Nothing is more common than the observation that *A Midsummer Night's Dream* is a play 'about love', about lovers' lunacy, where 'reason and love keep little company together nowadays', where the follies of imagination-dominated Demetrius and Lysander are reduced to their essential absurdity by the passion of Titania for an ass. It is for the sake of this theme, surely, that Demetrius and Lysander are given so little distinctive characterisation; they cannot contrast like a Claudio and a Benedick, so that a particular pairing of lovers is demanded by the characters of those involved. For the same reason, paradoxically, Hermia and Helena are differentiated, to heighten the puzzle of love's choices (as well as to increase the potentialities for comedy in the play's middle). By all conventional Elizabethan standards, tall fair gentle Helena should be the one pursued, and when Lysander eventually boasts his use of reason in preferring a dove to a raven his argument, by those standards, is indeed rational. Our laughter stems from recognising that it is so only accidentally, as rationalisation.

According to a good many critics, Shakespeare contrasts from the start the irrationality of the lovers with what these critics regard as the admirable rationality of Theseus-Hippolyta. The latter become a kind of ideal which the lovers approach by the end of the play. If so, the role of imagination in love is simple and obvious; it is a disrupting irrational influence which must eventually be purged, and will prove in simple and total contrast to the disciplined use of imagination essential to Shakespeare's art. But I cannot see that any contrast so mechanical as this is intended.

When, thanks to Dian's bud, Lysander returns to Hermia, his 'true love', the return marks a release from dotage but no return to reason as such, any more than does Demetrius's return to Helena by the pansy-juice. Love's choices remain inexplicable, and the eventual pairings are determined only by the constancy of Helena and Hermia in their initial inexplicable choices. As so frequently in Shakespearian comedy, the men fluctuate before finally settling down to a constant attachment such as the heroines exhibit from the start. Men's 'fancies are more giddy and unfirm,/More longing, wavering, sooner lost and won,/Than women's are'.[2] In the case of true love, once stabilised – even as in the case of mere dotage – imagination cannot 'form a shape,/Besides yourself to like of';[3] it 'carries no favour in't' but that of the beloved.[4] Unlike dotage, however, it is in no obvious conflict with reason, either in its object or its vehemence. By the end of the fourth act we are assured that Demetrius and Lysander have come to stability of this kind. But the terminus, I repeat, is not a rationally determined one. Like Theseus at the play's beginning, at the play's ending Demetrius and Lysander are settled. Jill has Jack, nought shall go back, and the prospect of happy marriage is before them all.

Thus in *A Midsummer Night's Dream* the origin of love never lies in reason. Love may be consistent with reason – e.g., Lysander is undeniably 'a worthy gentleman' – and a healthy imagination, although influenced by love, will not glaringly rebel against reason. But as Hermia initially indicates, her choice is dictated not by her judgment but by her 'eyes', by the vision of Lysander as her love-dictated imagination reports it. As Helena says at the close of this same introductory scene, love sees with that part of the mind that has no taste for judgment. Essentially this is as true for Hermia as for the others, although her choice conflicts with parental authority rather than with sound evaluation of her beloved's merits. Despite Egeus's initial disapproval, nevertheless, her choice is eventually confirmed. She is not compelled to 'choose love by another's eyes' [I i 140], to see with her father's judgment (as Theseus at first demanded [I i 57]), nor even to convert her love to one directed by her own judgment. Her love at the end is what it was at the beginning, with the obstacles removed.

Not even Egeus accuses her of dotage although he does think her somehow 'witched' in her refusal to accept his choice rather than her own. 'Dotage', in this play, appears essentially reserved for two kinds of amorous excess approaching madness: the monomaniacal pursuit of an unrequited love (thus Helena 'dotes in idolatry', Demetrius 'dotes' on Hermia's eyes, and Lysander dotes for Helena in the night's comedy of errors), or the ridiculous bestowal of affection upon an obviously unworthy object (most grotesquely in Titania's passion for Bottom, but also in the gross excesses of Lysander and Demetrius during their 'dream').[5]

In the middle of the play, then, when dotage grows more rampant, so too does imagination. The frenzied praises and dispraises of Lysander and Demetrius are exceeded only by Titania's infatuation for Bottom, her hearing beauty in his voice, seeing beauty in his ears, and so on. Were follies so excessive in the cases of the mortal lovers, we could never end as we do in marriage and lasting love. Yet by the end of Act IV, with all obstacles to happily paired marriages removed – no thanks to the behavior of the lovers – the lovers can sound, and behave, rationally enough. Their love, however, is in its essence as inexplicable as ever. . . .

To this question *A Midsummer Night's Dream* perhaps suggests no kind of answer beyond the fact that such true loves do exist, are distinct from the fancy-dominated aberrations that mark inconstancy, and when properly terminating in marriage are part of the natural – and, in that sense, rational – order of things. From the start of the play, the mystery of love's choices (including the attendant male inconstancies) is stressed. Egeus, at least metaphorically, thinks Hermia 'witched', and all Elizabethans would be reminded of disputes on whether love could be caused by witchcraft, or by philtres and charms, whether naturally or supernaturally administered.[6] When the fairies first appear (in II i), and before ever they become involved with the lovers, Shakespeare skilfully prepares us for their role. First, the inexplicable fortunes and misfortunes of housewives are attributed to Puck – this may well receive first mention because it is drawn from folklore, is familiar to the audience, and thus allows the easiest transition into what follows. A few lines later, all the recently experienced disorders of the English-Athenian weather are similarly attributed to temporary discord in the fairy macrocosm:

> And this same progeny of evils comes
> From our debate, from our dissension.   [II i 115-6]

For this night on which we can see fairies, we are allowed to understand, playfully, the cause for otherwise unaccountable phenomena. It is in such a context, too, that we hear the play's only reference to Theseus's well known infidelities preceding his 'true love' marriage to Hippolyta; these too are charged to fairy influence (although Titania discounts the charge). In short, aspects of the inexplicable past, familiar to the audience, have been imaginatively explained as fairy-caused.

Within the play, thus far, we have one similarly puzzling phenomenon, Demetrius's desertion of Helena to pursue Hermia, as well as the less specific mystery of love's choices generally. We have by now a hint that such mysteries – at least that of Demetrius's infidelity – may be similarly explained. The play will never say, understandably. Instead it will allow us for one single night to witness, and thereby understand, 'the mystery of things,/As if we were God's spies'.

The magic charm by which love is to be manipulated on this single night is quite naturally a flower potion administered on the eyes.[7] From the play's beginning we are reminded of the commonplace that, although the eyes are integrally involved in the process of inspiring and transmitting love, nevertheless 'love sees not with the eyes'; instead, the eyes 'see' what the lover's imagination dictates. In *A Midsummer Night's Dream,* at least, this imagination does not misreport sense data, except in the sense that it selects from those data and confers value accordingly. Hermia is never imagined as tall or blond, Bottom as hairless. Titania was 'enamoured of an ass', and knew it, but her selective imagination found beauty in 'fair large ears', 'sleek smooth head', even in its voice. Love, via imagination, transposes 'to form and dignity' by altering the normal evaluation, either in essence or in degree. At its extreme, it sees beauty where others see 'things base and vile', thus finding 'Helen's beauty in a brow of Egypt'. Conversely, it unwarrantedly makes 'base and vile' whatever object love causes it to reject. That the potion should be applied to the eyes was inevitable.

The choice of flower for the potion was almost equally so. 'Maidens call it love-in-idleness.' Perhaps it is foolish to labor over the implications of a flower which the play avoids calling by its most familiar name. But surely most of the audience would recognise the flower as the pansy, and 'That's for thoughts', as Ophelia says, as well as for relief of heart. Cotgrave may remind us of some of the usual associations:

Pensée: f. A thought, supposall, coniecture surmise, cogitation, imagination; ones heart, mind, inward conceit, opinion, fancie, or judgement; also, the flower Paunsie.

Menues pensées. Paunsies, Harts-ease, loue or liue in idlenesse; also idle, priuate, or prettie thoughts.[8]

However, although as Friar Laurence says,

> O mickle is the powerful grace that lies
> In plants, herbs, stones, and their true qualities,

the true dispenser of grace in *A Midsummer Night's Dream* is Oberon. The flower itself, wrongly applied by Puck, can make a hell of heaven rather than a heaven of hell. Both the mispairings and the eventual proper pairings of love, on this single night, we can witness as produced by fairy influence. Oberon wishes true lovers properly paired, and eventually sees that they are. Puck, while not wilfully mistaking, can delight in the consequences of his error, and we do too – the follies of mispaired doting lovers, their excessive praises and dispraises, their broken friendships, even the threat of bloodshed – potential tragedy were it not for Oberon's protection, of which we are so well aware that we can laugh at the folly they themselves take so seriously. The eventual pairings, then, are determined by Oberon, although always with the recognition that the heroines' choices are in some mysterious way right, that the pairings to be 'true loves', must correspond with their wishes. Oberon provides the remedy for the difficulties introduced at the beginning of the play and complicated by the subsequent action; the flower, like the eyes, is but his means.

The necessity of such 'fairy grace' had been suggested from the start. Helena had asked in vain 'with what art' Hermia won the heart of Demetrius. In love there is no art; imagination follows and encourages the mysterious dictates of the heart. Thus Lysander had appropriately wished Helena 'luck' in gaining Demetrius, for only by such good fortune could she conceivably gain the man who found her every advance offensive (no more offensive, of course, than Lysander would later find Hermia, that dwarf, minimus, Ethiope). Helena had herself repeatedly lamented that her prayers were unanswered, that she somehow lacked the 'grace' to be 'happy', 'fortunate', with 'blessed and attractive eyes'. On the night in the wood at last her prayers are answered. Like the rest of the lovers, including Theseus and Hippolyta, she is blessed, and an object of that 'fairy grace' with which the chaos of the first four acts is ended and with which the play concludes [V i 406].

When initially Hermia defied her father's wishes, she said she knew not 'by what power' she was 'made bold'. In similar terms, Demetrius later acknowledges being cured of his dotage for Hermia and restored to his true love for Helena: 'I wot not by what power/(But by some power it is)'. The power is perhaps that mysterious source by which Hermia swore: 'that which knitteth souls and prospers loves' [I i 172]. 'Fairy grace', certainly, removes the external obstacles to marriage for Hermia and Lysander, while at least assisting in the operation of knitting souls for all four lovers.

Initially, Hermia and Lysander had lamented that the course of true love never did run smooth. In the world of tragedy, whether for Romeo or for Pyramus, it does not. 'A greater power than we can contradict' thwarts the plans of Friar Laurence, just as that same Heaven hath a hand in the tragic fortunes of Richard II. Within the complex world of these tragedies written approximately at the same time as *A Midsummer Night's Dream,* the divine will plays an essential role, as critics have long recognised. Within the comic world of *A Midsummer Night's Dream,* where Shakespeare of course avoids so sober an explanation of 'events', we have 'fairy grace'.

In accordance with Oberon's plan, the four lovers awake harmoniously paired and think their whole experience of the night a dream,[9] although a mystifying one with (as Hippolyta says) 'great constancy'. We know it was no dream, at least not in the sense that they regard it as one; we have witnessed its entirety and have even better reason than Hippolyta to reject Theseus's dismissal of lovers' 'shaping fantasies'. What we have seen indeed 'more witnesseth than fancy's images', partly because we are aware that we have been beholding the images of Shakespeare's 'fancy' rather than that of the lovers. Yet we may well ask just how much it 'witnesseth', and we may look to Bottom for a clue. When he awakes, he too thinks he has had a dream, and, as everyone knows, he soliloquises in terms that echo I *Corinthians* ii 9–10. . . .

It used to be customary to see no significance whatever in this echo. One might merely observe, like Dover Wilson, 'that Bottom was a weaver and therefore possibly of a Puritanical turn of mind', apt to recall Scripture. Enticed by Bottom's suggestive malapropism a few minutes earlier ('I have an exposition of sleep come upon me'), it is tempting to look for more meaningful implications, ones that 'expound' Shakespeare's *Dream* if not Bottom's. The lovers, of course, never saw the fairies; their 'dreams' are only of the 'fierce vexation' caused by Puck's mistake in combination with their own folly. Bottom, in turn, had seen the fairies, had been the unappreciative, unimaginative object of Titania's temporary dotage and of the ministrations of her fairies.[10] Unlike either the lovers or Bottom, however, we have ourselves been admitted to a more complete vision, though we may well be asses if we seek to infer from it more than the suggestion of a mysterious 'grace' that sometimes blesses true love. Unlike the lovers and Bottom, we have been witnessing a play, a creation of Shakespeare's imagination. Only a part of the time have we watched imagination-dominated 'dreams'; all of the time we have watched the product of Shakespeare's own imagination. If our attitude to art is that of Theseus, we may, as the humble epilogue encourages us to do, think we

> . . . have but slumb'red here
> While these visions did appear.
> And this weak and idle theme,
> No more yielding but a dream.

But, being good Elizabethans, we may well remember that not all dreams are the product of disordered, passion-stimulated, never-sleeping imagination. Some dreams are divine revelations of truth, however difficult to expound, and we have already seen plays of Shakespeare where dreams contained at least a prophetic, specific truth, if not a universal one. Some dreams are yielding, and *A*

Midsummer Night's Dream – although a poet's revelation rather than a divinity's – may be one of them.

At the same time, when we eventually hear the epilogue's modest disclaimer, we have seen much more than a treatment of 'fairy grace' blessing true love. The 'visions' we have beheld embrace far more than just the 'visions' experienced by Titania, Bottom and the four lovers. Our visions began with the first line of the play, and a good part of our time has been devoted to watching Bottom and his friends prepare and present a play of their own.

As I remarked at the beginning, few critics have had much to say about the relationship of 'Pyramus and Thisbe' to the play as a whole.[11] Undoubtedly Shakespeare's reasons for including this farce were multiple and complex. For one thing, it is impossible to believe that 'Pyramus and Thisbe' is only accidentally related to *Romeo and Juliet*, although we may never be certain which play preceded and provoked Shakespeare's contrasting treatment in the other.[12] Such considerations, however, are wholly external to our present concern with *A Midsummer Night's Dream* as an individual artistic entity. The play, if it was to be conventional, would of course include low comedy, and Shakespeare's problem was to determine what sort of low comedy would be most fitting. An ass like Bottom would serve to develop the love theme effectively, but such an ass could be easily introduced without his fellows. Why have a play-within-the-play, why give it the Pyramus-Thisbe plot, and why develop it in the particular way Shakespeare employed?

To begin with, within his play for a wedding occasion[13] Shakespeare apparently saw the advantages of introducing an inept production for a parallel occasion, the wedding of Theseus. Like Biron, he recognised ''tis some policy/To have one show worse than' his own offering.[14] Of course he could not decide what sort of plot to choose for this contrasting production without at the same time considering what development he would give it. But for the moment we can consider the two aspects separately. In contrast to his own play, the mechanicals should choose for Theseus a plot thoroughly inappropriate for a wedding: love tragedy. Only their ineptitude, and Shakespeare's skill, should make 'Pyramus and Thisbe' fit pastime for a wedding night, both for the newly-weds within *A Midsummer Night's Dream* and those beholding it. Secondly, the plot should be one inviting comparison with the main plot of Shakespeare's play. The moment we meet the mechanicals in I ii we learn they are preparing a play of Pyramus and Thisbe. Even without the early reminder that Pyramus would kill himself, 'most gallant, for love', the audience would at once recognise in the familiar story parallels, actual and potential, to what had begun in I i. Like Hermia and Lysander, Pyramus and Thisbe would run off to the woods in the night, frantically hoping to escape the obstacles to their true love. Unlike Hermia and Lysander (but at this point of the play the audience cannot know of the fairy grace to come), Pyramus and Thisbe, the audience knows, will find their 'sympathy in choice' brought to such sudden catastrophe as Hermia and Lysander had expressly feared [I i 132 ff.].[15]

Most critics who have related 'Pyramus and Thisbe' to *A Midsummer Night's Dream* as a whole have largely confined themselves, very cryptically, to thematic implications of this partial parallel in the action. For E. K. Chambers, 'Pyramus and Thisbe' is 'but a burlesque presentment of the same theme which has occupied us throughout', that 'lunacy in the brain of youth' which is 'not an integral part of life, but a disturbing element in it'.[16] For Arthur Brown, it is 'an integral part of the main theme of the play, which seems to be concerned with gentle satire of the pangs of romantic love'.[17] More soberly, for Frank Kermode it 'gives farcical treatment to an important thematic element; for Bottom and his friends will perform a play to illustrate the disastrous end of doting'.[18] For Paul Olson, most sober of all, it 'fits into the total pattern' because 'it is the potential tragedy of the lovers in the woods', reminding us of the probable consequences of the 'headie force of frentick love'.[19]

Yet in the actual play as developed by the mechanicals, Shakespeare provides a focus that scarcely emphasizes any such parallel to the lovers. The thwarting parents are cast but never given even a line in rehearsal or production; they are referred to in neither Quince's argument nor in the lovers' speeches. In turn, the decision to run to the woods is presented in a single line, and the barrier wall is focused upon as farcical in itself rather than as a cause for action. Lastly, however ridiculous the love poetry of Pyramus and Thisbe, it scarcely seems focused for comic parallel and contrast to the speeches or actions of Shakespeare's four young lovers (except in one possible way, to be examined below).

For Shakespeare's actual development, few critics have much to say. They recognise such external considerations, all undeniably valid, as a possible light mocking of earlier plays, or the demonstration that a Romeo-Juliet plot could be converted to farce by its treatment, or the demands of the low comedy convention. More internally, they recognise the necessity that 'Pyramus and Thisbe' be treated farcically if it is to harmonise in tone with *A Midsummer Night's Dream* as a whole.

But 'Pyramus and Thisbe' is not merely a play about love with a partial resemblance to the love plot of *A Midsummer Night's Dream*. It is, as Shakespeare's original wedding audience would be inevitably aware, a play for a wedding audience. It provides a foil to the entire play of which it is a part, not merely to the portion involving the lovers. And not only Bottom's play, but his audience as well, invites comparison with Shakespeare's.

It is time to turn to the principal member of Bottom's audience, and to his famous speech beginning Act V. Himself a creation from 'antique fable' unconsciously involved in 'fairy toys', Theseus believes in neither. His speech, without appearing improbable or inconsistent with his character, is obviously one demanded by Shakespeare's thematic development. Just as Theseus has no dramatically probable reason to refer to 'fairy toys', so too he has no reason to digress on poetry while discussing the lunacy of love. But by his speech he can provide for Shakespeare a transition from the earlier emphasis of the play upon love to its final emphasis upon art. He can explicitly link the imagination's role in love with its role in dramatic poetry. For him, with his view that 'the best in this kind are but shadows', pastimes to be tolerantly accepted when offered, the imagination of the poet commands no more respect than that of the lover.

Theseus's speech introduces the words 'image', imagine', 'imagination', and 'imagining' to the play. But of course it does not introduce the concepts involved. As we have already seen, and as Theseus reminds us, much of the play has thus far concerned the role of imagination in love. A subordinate part has similarly drawn attention to its role in drama, a role manifested by the entirety of *A Midsummer Night's Dream*.

The success of any play ideally demands effective use of the imagination by the author, the producers and the audience. Perhaps through modesty, Shakespeare gives us little explicit encouragement to compare his own imaginative creation with that initially provided by Quince. We hear nothing, strictly, of Quince's authorial problems prior to rehearsal. The sources of our laughter spring mainly from mutilation of his text in production, by additions and corruptions, rather than from the text with which the mechanicals began. Yet some measure of comparison of *A Midsummer Night's Dream* with their pre-mutilated text is inescapable. 'Pyramus and Thisbe', with nothing demanded beyond the simple dramatisation of a familiar story, could at least have been given imaginative development in action, characterisation, theme, and language. It has none. The first three are less than minimal, and the language – in its grotesque combination of muddled syntax, padded lines, mind-offending tropes, ear-offending schemes – does violence even to what would otherwise be woefully inadequate. We have:

> Anon comes Pyramus, sweet youth and tall,
>   And finds his trusty Thisby's mantle slain;
> Whereat, with blade, with bloody blameful blade,
>   He bravely broach'd his boiling bloody breast,

or

> O grim-look'd night! O night with hue so black!
>   O night, which ever art when day is not!
> O night, O night! alack, alack, alack,
>   I fear my Thisby's promise is forgot!
> And thou, O wall, O sweet, O lovely wall,
>   That stand'st between her father's ground and mine!
> Thou wall, O wall, O sweet and lovely wall,
>   Show me thy chink, to blink through with mine eyne!

Contrasting in every respect we have *A Midsummer Night's Dream*, perhaps the most obviously 'imaginative' of all Shakespeare's plays before *The Tempest*: we have the poetic fusion of classical and native, remote and familiar, high and low, possible and 'impossible', romance and farce – all controlled by a governing intention and developed in appropriately varied and evocative language. Unlike Bottom, if not unlike the Quince who calls his play a 'Lamentable Comedy', Shakespeare knows what is appropriate for his purpose.

He will have infinite variety, but not merely variety as an end in itself. Bottom wishes to have a ballad written of his dream, and 'to make it the more gracious' he will sing it over the dead body of Thisbe at the tragedy's end. Shakespeare, very literally 'to make it the more gracious', will end his comedy with a song bestowing fairy grace. The contrast needs no labouring.

The contrast in authorial imagination, however, is not the principal cause for turning 'Pyramus and Thisbe' from tragedy to farce. In the first appearance of the mechanicals, the largely expository casting scene, we get a hint of the aspect that receives subsequent emphasis: author-director Quince warns that if the lion roars 'too terribly' it will 'fright the Duchess and the ladies', and Bottom proposes as a solution to 'roar you as gently as any sucking dove' (a remedy almost as sound as the later suggestion to 'leave the killing out'). What the mechanicals fail to understand, obviously, is the audience's awareness that drama is drama, to be viewed imaginatively but not mistaken, in any realistic sense, for reality. The idea that these clowns could conceivably create a terrifying lion is in itself ridiculous, but the basic folly lies in their supposing that their prospective intelligent audience will have the naïveté of Fielding's Partridge. And it is this aspect that receives all the emphasis of the mechanicals' rehearsal scene. Except for a very few lines of actual rehearsal, enough to heighten our expectation of the eventual production as well as to allow Bottom's 'translation' to an ass, the whole rehearsal is concerned with how the mechanicals abuse their own imaginations by a failure to understand those of the audience. On the one hand they fear their audience will imagine what it sees is real, mistaking 'shadows' for reality; on the other, they think the audience unable to imagine what it cannot see. Paradoxically, although they lack the understanding to think in such terms, they think their audience both over- and under-imaginative, and in both respects irrational. For each error Shakespeare provides two examples. More would render the point tedious rather than delightful; fewer might obscure it. Thus, to avoid the threat of over-imagination, they resolve by various ludicrous means to explain that Pyramus is not Pyramus and that the lion is not a lion; then, to counteract the audience's under-imagination, they will create Moonshine and Wall. In a play where Shakespeare's audience has been imagining moonshine since the beginning, Bottom and Quince can conceive only of real moonshine or a character to 'disfigure' it. Of course they choose the latter. So too they can think only of bringing in a real wall, weighing tons, or another disfiguring personification.

Significantly, Shakespeare opens the rehearsal scene as follows:

BOTTOM Are we all met?
QUINCE Pat, pat; and here's a marvail's convenient place for our rehearsal. This green plot shall be our stage, this hawthorn brake our tiring house. . . .

The stage is a stage, not a green plot; the tiring house is a tiring house, not a hawthorn brake. The Lord Chamberlain's Men ask us to imagine a green plot and hawthorn brake, just as they ask us to imagine non-existent fog or, on the other hand, imagine the invisibility of an obviously visible Oberon.[20] The play perpetually makes such demands upon us, and even greater ones. It asks us not only to accept mortal-sized actors as diminutive fairies but even to let them be bi-sized, sleeping in flowers and yet engaging in intimate association with ass-headed Bottom. Most basic of all, it asks us to enter imaginatively into a world dominated by fairies, and to accept them as the ultimate source of disharmony and of harmony, while at the same time not asking us to 'believe' in them at all.

When we next see the mechanicals (except for their brief transitional appearance in IV ii) it will be after Theseus's speech, with its condescending attitude toward poetry, and after the prefatory discussion by the court concerning the 'tedious brief . . . tragical mirth' they wish to enact. The emphases in the actual production – including both the production itself and the asides by the audience – are just what we have been prepared for in the rehearsal: not the follies of love but the follies of abused imagination in the theatre. When, for example, Quince concludes his Argument,

> For all the rest,
> Let Lion, Moonshine, Wall, and lovers twain
> At large discourse while here they do remain,

Theseus cannot yet believe that Quince literally means 'discourse':

THESEUS   I wonder if the lion be to speak.
DEMETRIUS No wonder, my lord. One lion may, when many asses do.

But before ever they hear the talking lion they listen to 'the wittiest partition that ever I hear discourse', that 'courteous wall' which provides the 'chink to blink through', only to receive the curses of the frustrated Pyramus.

THESEUS   The wall, methinks, being sensible, should curse again.
PYRAMUS   No, in truth, sir, he should not. 'Deceiving me' is Thisby's cue. She is to enter now, and I am to spy her through the wall. You shall see it will fall pat as I told you. Yonder she comes.

As Theseus says, a few lines later: 'If we imagine no worse of them than they of themselves, they may pass for excellent men.'

There is no danger of wounding the feelings of a Bottom by letting him overhear an aside. His imagination, devoid of understanding, can as easily create beauty in his own mind as it can create unintended farce on the stage. Titania's folly, if possible, was less than what we are now witnessing.

Wall's eventual exit provides further satiric asides, followed by the primary thematic dialogue of the play:

HIPPOLYTA This is the silliest stuff that ever I heard.
THESEUS   The best in this kind are but shadows, and the worst are no worse, if imagination amend them.
HIPPOLYTA It must be your imagination then, and not theirs.

While a successful production depends on the imaginative co-operation of playwright, producers and audience, Bottom's group has placed the entire burden on the audience. Theseus's group quite naturally makes no effort to 'amend them'. The tragedy is too entertaining as farce, too fitting for their nuptial spirits; and besides, it would take an imagination transcending Shakespeare's own to give 'form and dignity' to this 'Pyramus and Thisbe'.

What follows needs no further elaboration. The lion proves 'a goose for his discretion'; the moon, appearing 'by his small light of discretion' to be 'in the wane', ridiculously exits on command from

Pyramus. And so on, until 'Moonshine and Lion are left to bury the dead'. 'Ay, and Wall too.'

But we may return to Theseus's comment that 'The best in this kind are but shadows'. In a sense he is obviously right, as Shakespeare never ceases to remind us, but his estimation of such 'shadows' is consistently deprecating. A noble governor, quite willing to accept poetry for a wedding-night pastime and to acknowledge it as the well-intended offering of his faithful subjects, he at no time implies any respect for it. Shakespeare's entire play implies a contrary view, despite the humility of its epilogue. . . .

A Midsummer Night's Dream could have been defended as indeed a pleasant pastime, especially appropriate for a wedding occasion but fitting for any moment of merriment. It could be further defended, unmistakably, as a delightful exposition of the follies produced by excessive imagination in love and the pleasures produced by controlled imagination in art. Only the most stubborn precisian could have thought poetry 'the mother of lies' after witnessing Shakespeare's thematic distinction, however ambiguous in its ultimate implications, between the worlds of imagination and of 'reality'. Thus, in offering a defence for its own existence the play simultaneously offers us Shakespeare's closest approximation to a 'Defence of Dramatic Poesy' in general.

In some measure, surely, *A Midsummer Night's Dream* is such a defence, although one that expresses its view by indirection and without the emphasis upon strictly moral edification one commonly finds in more formal defences. . . . Theseus links lunatic, lover, and poet indiscriminately. Shakespeare, by contrasting the role of imagination in love with that in dramatic poetry, discriminates. As the play delightfully demonstrates, and lightly satirises, the imagination in love often operates in defiance of 'discretion', especially in creating beauty observable by no one but the creator. Poetic art, distinct from that of a Quince or Bottom, is in accord with discretion, and its creations are capable of universal appreciation, both as beautiful and as meaningful. In love, the ridiculous results from the dominance of imagination over reason, and the lover is unaware of his being ridiculous. In good art, the ridiculous (if it exists) is the product of imagination's cooperation with reason. . . . Rather than being a foe to good living, poetic imagination can be its comfort and its guide, far 'more yielding' than most dreams.

Whether *A Midsummer Night's Dream* has an unplumbed 'bottom' as well as its inescapable Bottom, I hesitate to say. But it provides us 'a most rare vision', one that offers us a disarmingly unpretentious defence of poetry by the greatest of England's poets.

SOURCE: extracts from 'Imagination in *A Midsummer Night's Dream*', *Shakespeare Quarterly*, XV (1964), pp. 115–29.

NOTES

[Reorganised and renumbered from the original – Ed.]

1. The frequency of such praise provoked R. A. Law's denial that the play had any organic unity whatever: 'The Pre-Conceived Pattern of *A Midsummer Night's Dream*', *Texas Univ. Studies in English* (1943), pp. 5–14.

2. *Twelfth Night*, II iv 34–6.

3. To use Miranda's words, *The Tempest* III i 56–7.

4. *All's Well That Ends Well*, I i 93–4.

5. Helena is never so doting that she cannot recognise her apparent folly. Unlike the other victims of dotage, however, her foolish behavior has its root in a true love, once reciprocated and then unaccountably rejected. Thus only Helena can be cured of dotage by Oberon's curing someone else, rather than herself.

6. See Burton's voluminous annotation for *Anat. Mel.*, III ii V iv, or the treatment in such familiar plays as *Endymion*, *Othello* or *The Duchess of Malfi*. See also, in relation to Raleigh, Bruno and Elizabethan preachers, T. Walter Herbert's 'Dislocation and the Modest Demand in *A Midsummer Night's Dream*', *Renaissance Papers 1961* (Durham, N. C., 1962), p. 36.

7. Not surprisingly, 'eyes' appears more frequently in *A Midsummer Night's Dream* than in any other of Shakespeare's plays (with *Love's Labour's Lost* second, for comparable reasons). Like the equally abundant use of 'moon', this frequency is of course partly determined by the story, but the demands of the story are in turn determined by those of the theme.

8. Necessarily, to remedy Puck's error with Lysander, Oberon must use Dian's bud, just as he does for Titania. But the pansy influence, 'Cupid's power', is clearly implied to have as lasting an effect for Demetrius as 'Dian's bud' for Lysander. Witness III ii 88–91 and V i 414–5, for example. Shakespeare's working out of the love theme is perhaps a bit awkward here, but only if we labor the play mechanically in a fashion contrary to its entire spirit. Yet we should not, I believe, do what several critics have done: treat the two flowers as representing opposed kinds of love, irrational and rational, carnal and chaste, etc. . . .

9. Only Hermia has had an actual dream [II ii 147 ff.], a prophetically accurate one to introduce the chaos into which she initially awakes. The

love-threatening serpent of her dream, symbol of male inconstancy, proves more destructive than the literal 'spotted snakes with double tongue' against which we have just heard the fairies sing. For spotted, double-tongued Demetrius, see I i 110, III ii 70–3.

10. Two recent critics have in their different ways been especially anxious to find meaning in Bottom's echo . . . Paul Olson and Frank Kermode. [See preceding excerpts in this selection – Ed.] While very unlike one another in interpretation, Olson and Kermode agree in seeing the play as essentially serious and essentially about love, true and false, earthly and spiritual. However, Kermode . . . seems far-fetched in comparing Bottom's vision to that of Apuleius. . . . Titania violently rejects her dotage when awakened, and Bottom certainly has not profited from any initiation. . . . If I understand Kermode, he appears to confuse Bottom's vision with that of Shakespeare's audience, and to make that vision a product of the 'blindness of love' rather than the art of the poet.

11. Notable exceptions are Paul N. Siegel, '*A Midsummer Night's Dream* and the Wedding Guests', *SQ*, IV (1953), pp. 139–44, and C. L. Barber, *Shakespeare's Festive Comedy* (Princeton, 1959), pp. 119–62. [See excerpt in this selection – Ed.] I am indebted to both, especially for their assuring me that my approach to the play is not wholly idiosyncratic.

12. Not merely the play by the mechanicals but aspect after aspect of *A Midsummer Night's Dream* invites comparison, and contrast, with *Romeo and Juliet:* e.g., on Cupid's arrow versus Dian's wit, on doting versus loving, on love's 'infection' through the eye, on oaths, inconstant moons and male inconstancy, on 'blind love' best agreeing with night, on dreams and fairies as 'begot of nothing but vain fantasy'. The relationship is too complex and too tangential to pursue here, but it once again suggests the need to treat *Pyramus and Thisbe* as an integral part of *A Midsummer Night's Dream*.

13. Alfred Harbage has recently objected to interpreting Shakespeare on the basis of hypothetical occasions for which there is no external evidence: '*Love's Labour's Lost* and the Early Shakespeare', *PQ*, XLI (1962), pp. 19–20. [Editor's note: reprinted in his *Shakespeare Without Words, and Other Essays* (Cambridge, Mass., 1972), pp. 119–21. See Introduction, above.] Nevertheless, the internal evidence that *A Midsummer Night's Dream* was either written or adapted for a courtly wedding seems to me, as to most, overwhelming.

14. *Love's Labour's Lost,* V ii 513–4.

15. For reasons already indicated, I think Pyramus and Thisbe meant primarily to parallel Lysander and Hermia as examples of frustrated true love rather than as examples of folly. Lysander and Hermia may not behave rationally in their flight from authority, but only when misled by pansy-juice does Lysander approach the frenzied passion which so disturbed Friar Laurence. Even in that play, I believe, Shakespeare distinguishes between Romeo's doting for Rosaline and his true but frustrated love for Juliet.

16. *Shakespeare: A Survey* (New York, 1926), pp. 87, 80.

17. 'The Play within a Play: An Elizabethan Dramatic Device', *Essays and Studies*, XIII (1960), p. 47.

18. Kermode, p. 216. [See excerpt in this selection – Ed.]

19. Olson, p. 118. [See excerpt in this selection –Ed.]

20. Modern productions of *A Midsummer Night's Dream*, admittedly magnificent spectacles, often seem to have more in common with the mechanicals than with Shakespeare. Such productions obscure, if not destroy, thematic implications of the kind discussed here. Readers of the play are sometimes subjected to a similar disservice by editors – e.g., the New Cambridge stage direction opening Act II scene i: 'The palace wood, a league from Athens. A mossy stretch of broken ground, cleared of trees by wood-cutters and surrounded by thickets. Moonlight.'

Jan Kott   'Bless Thee, Bottom! . . . Thou Art Translated'   (1964)

. . . The *Dream* is the most erotic of Shakespeare's plays. In no other tragedy or comedy of his, except *Troilus and Cressida,* is the emotion expressed so brutally. . . . There are two different Hermias and two different Lysanders. The Hermia who sleeps with Lysander, and the Hermia with whom Lysander does not want to sleep. The Lysander who sleeps with Hermia,[1] and the Lysander who is running away from Hermia. . . . .

I imagine Titania's court as consisting of old men and women, toothless and shaking, their mouths wet with saliva, who sniggeringly procure a monster for their mistress . . . in this nightmarish summer night, the ass does not symbolise stupidity. Since antiquity and up to the Renaissance the ass was credited with the strongest sexual potency and among all the quadrupeds is supposed to have the longest and hardest phallus. . . .

The slender, tender and lyrical Titania longs for animal love. Puck and Oberon call the transformed Bottom a monster. The frail and sweet Titania drags the monster to bed, almost by force. This is the lover she wanted and dreamed of; only she never wanted to admit it, even to herself. Sleep frees her from inhibitions. The monstrous ass is being raped by the poetic Titania, while she still keeps on chattering about flowers:

The moon methinks looks with a watery eye;
And when she weeps, weeps every little flower,
Lamenting some enforced chastity.
Tie up my love's tongue, bring him silently.   [III i 193-6][2]

. . . Titania wakes up and sees a boor with an ass's head by her side. She slept with him that night. But now it is daylight. She does not remember ever having desired him. She remembers nothing. She does not want to remember anything. . . .

All are ashamed in the morning. Demetrius and Hermia, Lysander and Helena. [*Sic.*]. Even Bottom. Even he does not want to admit his dream [quotes IV i 105-8]. . . .

SOURCE: extracts from *Shakespeare Our Contemporary,* trans. Boleslaw Taborski (London, 1964) pp. 73, 75, 81, 81, 82, 86, 87. Originally published as *Skize o Szekspirze* (Warsaw, 1964).

NOTES

1. [Editor's note: one might well enquire where in the text Kott finds evidence for these assertions, and how he explains their specific denial at II ii 62-7 and 80-3.]

2. [Editor's note: Kott has clearly not read Quiller-Couch (or M. R. Ridley). See Part One above.]

David P. Young   'Picturisation and Panorama'
(1966)

. . . Other unifying features of *A Midsummer Night's Dream* have not received the kind of critical attention lavished on its imagery. To one of these I would give the label 'picturisation'. Again and again, we are given not merely the glimpse afforded by an image, but a fully drawn picture. Often, these are sketches of human activity. Thus, before the play has gone very far, Egeus has given us a picture of Lysander courting; Theseus has sketched for Hermia the life of a nun; Bottom has demonstrated, since he is not capable of describing, the way a tyrant rants; Puck has shown us a gossip drinking from a bowl and an aunt falling from her stool; and Titania has pictured Oberon, disguised as Corin, piping to 'amorous Phillida'. These pictorial effects slow down the action; but in their evocation of the imagination, their illustrations of its follies, triumphs, and possibilities, they realise the play's basic theme in a new and significant dimension.

The most effective and memorable pictures in the play are not the glimpses of single figures and activities described above. They are the larger representations, full landscapes with a remarkable sense of spaciousness and distance. These we might call 'panoramas'. While we catch initial hints of them in Theseus's picture of his wedding with all Athens reveling and in the poignant conversation between Hermia and Lysander that follows, they do not really begin to dominate the play until the entrance of the fairies in the second act. Then, they appear in profusion. Titania's fairy starts things with an extensive answer to Puck's 'Whither wander you?' He counters by summoning up all the places where Oberon and Titania have quarrelled over the changeling boy. Titania and Oberon take it up, she with a reference to 'the farthest steep of India', he with a glimpse of her leading Theseus 'through the glimmering night/From Perigouna, whom he ravished'. The queen then begins her long and Bruegelesque summary of the trouble they have caused in the natural world [quotes II i 81–100]. . . . She goes on to include the different seasons and describe their confusion. Above it all, of course, 'the moon, the governess of floods,/Pale in her anger, washes all the air'. Then, as if she had not been exhaustive enough in her cross section of geography, weather, and natural life, Titania presents in her next speech a seascape, with herself and her 'votaress' in the foreground and the 'embarked traders on the flood' in the distance.

Oberon is not to be outdone at this activity. After his wife has presented her sweeping panoramas for us and left the stage, he has his turn; he even gives us a vantage point for the next great view [quotes II i 148–53]. . . . 'I remember', answers Puck, and we pause to regain control of our dizzying imaginations. But Oberon will not let us rest. He moves on to a vision of even greater proportions [quotes II i 155–68]. . . . We come finally to rest on something small and familiar, the pansy.

Throughout the night in the woods that follows, confined and hectic as it may be, we get echoes and glimpses of these magnificent views and distances. Oberon's description of the bank where Titania sleeps among the flowers is a smaller panorama, but it has its own sweep and detail. Hermia, as if responding to the fairies' talk of girdling the earth [II i 175] and compassing the globe [IV i 96], imagines the moon creeping through a hole bored in the earth and emerging on the other side to shine on the Antipodes [III ii 52–5]. Puck, searching for distance in his description of the fleeing mechanicals, widens the prospect [quotes III ii 20–4]. . . . Even Demetrius, in a flight of passion, can transport us to the mountains of Asia and 'That pure congealed white, high Taurus snow,/Fann'd with the eastern wind' [III ii 141–2].

As daylight returns to the play, the panoramas regain full splendor. First there is Puck's warning of the approaching dawn, with its clouds, shining sky, churchyards, crossways and floods; then Oberon's answer, a brilliant depiction of sunrise over the sea. Theseus's speech, as he enters the play with full daylight, is in the same vein. He is on his way to arrange a panorama of sight and sound [quotes IV i 104–10]. . . . Hippolyta responds with a spacious description of a similar event when Hercules and Cadmus 'bay'd the bear' in 'a wood of Crete', and 'the groves/The skies, the fountains, every region near/Seem'd all one mutual cry'. We are certainly prepared by all these vistas for Demetrius' wondering comment on the night in the woods [quotes IV i 186–7]. . . . The last full panorama in the play comes at Puck's entrance in the fifth act, a night scene with lion, wolf, snoring ploughman, screech-owl, insomniac, gaping graves, and spirits gliding on the churchway paths, the whole coming to rest at the place of performance, 'this hallowed house' [V i 361–78].

The function of these panoramas is not difficult to discern. They provide . . . a contrast to the confinement of the woods, escorting us in and drawing us out again. They create perspective and distance, both in the geographic and aesthetic senses of those words. Through them, we are made aware of both man's pettiness and his grandeur, simultaneous extremes that are also expressed through the fairies. Only such comprehensive vantage points could give us this sense of surveying all of nature in order to discover man's unique position in it.

In their richness and variety, the panoramas become a kind of metaphor for the play: *A Midsummer Night's Dream* is itself a panorama of smaller scenes and characters, a great landscape with cities, woods, fields, mountains, valleys, rivers, ocean, and a host of figures representative of society and the supernatural. Theseus's 'The best in this kind are but shadows' and Puck's 'No more yielding but a dream' take on a perspective of their own when we can link them to Demetrius's 'These things seem small and indistinguishable,/Like far-off mountains turned into clouds'. . . . Like the patterns of imagery, the panoramas contribute significantly to the play's atmosphere of magic, spaciousness and limitless possibility, all attributes of the power of imagination which it both derives from and celebrates.

SOURCE: extract from *Something of Great Constancy: The Art of A Midsummer Night's Dream*, (New Haven & London, 1966), pp.75-81.

Stephen Fender   'Moral Ambivalence'   (1968)

. . . In *A Midsummer Night's Dream* . . . Shakespeare defines his characters according to what they represent, according to their labels. The lovers are not individuals, they are 'lovers', and the definition of that word will determine their behaviour; Puck's actions too are predicated by the definition of 'Puck'. Nor is the process restricted to characters; even places stand for something, are labels. Athens, established in literary tradition as the legendary seat of reason (in Boccaccio's *Teseida* and 'The Knight's Tale') is here almost a byword for rational order. The wilderness outside Athens is called a 'wood' and not a forest, as is the corresponding locale in *As You Like It*, because it must also be a label for 'mad'; and, in case we miss the point, Demetrius is made to pun on 'wood' (for 'mad' and 'forest') and 'wooed'; 'And here am I, and wood within this wood. . . .' With everything so clearly defined and with the infinite complexities of realistic character and 'real life' settings so clearly exercised, no wonder those who came looking for realism go away convinced that the play is a little too simple.

What they have overlooked is perhaps the most important fact of the play: the ideas and forces which Shakespeare makes his characters (and even locales) represent are in every case morally ambivalent. To put it very simply for the moment, the powers which are personified in the figures of Theseus, Hippolyta, the lovers, the fairies, Athens, the wood, are presented as potentially both 'good' and 'evil'. This is the source of the rather unusual complexity of the play.

We might begin to illustrate this point by [considering] the figure of blind love, Cupid [quotes I i 234–6]. . . . The 'mind' with which love 'looks' is not, of course, the rational faculty; this 'mind' is without balanced judgment, and would correspond more to emotional impulses, or the 'will' in Shakespeare's terminology. But the terms as well as the process of 'blind' love in Shakespeare, need some explanation. What follows is a very simplified version, but it will serve for the immediate purpose. The lover's senses, usually represented by the synecdoche 'eye', are affected by a lady's physical attributes:

> Tell me where is fancy bred,
> Or in the heart or in the head?
> How begot, how nourished?
>   Reply, reply.
> It is engender'd in the eyes, . . .

as the song in *The Merchant of Venice* warns Bassanio while he surveys the caskets. 'Fancy' here is a delusory view of the whole person – traits of character as well as appearance – based on a brief assessment of appearance only. But the delusion is a product of what in mediaeval terminology was known as 'ymagynatyf', the mind's power to 'picture' what was not actually before the eyes, and another meaning for 'fancy', is, of course, imagination. The doting lover reacted so strongly to first impressions of appearance that he could go on to construct a synthetic person in his mind's eye after the real person had left his physical field of vision. Later, when he saw the 'real thing' again, he might not recognise it, so strong was the synthetic version built up in his imagination. This is the fullest sense in which 'fancy' is 'engender'd in the eyes', and it explains the apparent contradiction by which 'blind' love could also be called the 'love of the eye'. We are presented with two kinds of blindness, and they are not synchronous: in the early stage of doting love a lover committed the 'sin of the eye' by giving too much credence to visual stimuli, but this could also be called a kind of moral blindness, since the more important attributes of character were being ignored; in the later stage, the lover was cursed with an almost physical blindness, since his imaginative vision of the person (or his delusion) was so strong that he could no longer credit what he saw before him.

This is exactly what happens to Troilus, for instance. He falls in love with Cressida having seen her only, and not met her. While he waits for their first meeting, he worries that the imaginary picture of her in his mind's eye is already so powerful that the real woman will produce stimuli strong enough to overcome him [quotes *T & C* III ii 17–20]. . . . What actually happens is that the imaginary Cressida remains the only one for Troilus, and the character of the real Cressida goes unnoticed. He does his best to remake her in the image of what lives in his fancy [quotes *T & C* III ii 165–7]. . . . But the audience's awareness of the outcome – reinforced by the tentative syntax which Shakespeare gives Troilus in this speech – undercuts the hope heavily. When Cressida finally betrays Troilus and takes up with the Greek Diomedes, Troilus cannot believe his eyes, even when he sees the two of them together [quotes *T & C* v ii 104–69]. . . .

Shakespeare's treatment of blind love owes a good deal to medieval and renaissance moralisers on the theme of *Cupiditas*. The syntactical and verbal similarity between the following and what both Helena and Cresida say about doting love may indicate how closely Shakespeare was working within a tradition:

Now Love is painted as a boy because the desire for lust is foolish and because the speech of lovers is imperfect like the speech of boys . . . he is winged because nothing is lighter or more changeable than lovers. He carries arrows which themselves too are unsure and swift in flight. . . . He is naked because lust is performed by naked people; or because in that turpitude nothing is secret.[1]

Before long Cupid's blindness became his most important attribute. He is blind, to paraphrase Berchorius's introduction to a commentary on Ovid's *Metamorphoses*, because he does not seem to mind on whom he inflicts himself (since love can visit both poor and rich, ugly and beautiful, devout and lay) and also because men are blinded by him (since nothing is more blind than a man inflamed by love for a person or a thing).[2]

The main point to note here is that this form of love was always a 'bad' one and its blindness a distinctly pejorative attribute, stemming from a tradition of medieval iconography which associated blindness with evil, with spiritual and physical death.[3] A poet who wished to assert the enlightening nature of love had to argue against its blindness, to paint the picture of Cupid without the bandage over his eyes, as it were. There seems to have been no argument about possible 'good' and 'bad' meanings of blindness itself.

But in *A Midsummer Night's Dream* Shakespeare adopts this convention in which blind love is unambiguously 'bad' only to qualify it radically. Helena's moral lesson on Cupid is set in a context that gives it a possible 'good' meaning too; just before her lines on Cupid's attributes, she says:

> Things base and vile, holding no quantity,
> Love can transpose to form and dignity.

The fact that love can change the ugly into the beautiful can be condemned or admired, according to one's point of view. Looked at in one way, it is obviously absurd, and Theseus makes it an occasion for satire at the beginning of Act V: 'The lover, all as frantic,/Sees Helen's beauty in a brow of Egypt.' But from another point of view it can be seen as an act of almost divine creativity, the means by which fallen nature can be redeemed, however incompletely and for however short a time. The lightning flash of love, as Lysander calls it [I i] is only 'momentany' and comes quickly 'to confusion', but while it lasts it illuminates 'both heaven and earth' as though in imitation of divine redemption. The act of transposing the ugliness of the world into the beauty of an imaginative construct is very similar to the art of poetry, as described by numerous contemporary essays defending the writing of fiction. Sidney makes a clear distinction between those whose 'Arte' is confined to the works of nature (like historians, astronomers and natural philosophers) and poets, who create their own nature in their imaginations:

Onely the Poet, disdayning to be tied by any such subjection, lifted up with the vigor of his owne invention, dooth growe in effect another nature, in making things either better then Nature bringeth forth, or, quite a newe, formes such as never were in Nature, as the *Heroes, Demigods, Cyclops, Chimeras, Furies,* and such like.[4]

And the lover's 'fancy', which turns the fallen nature of his loved one into something better, is very like the poet's *furor*, which George Puttenham (and others) likened to the creative force of God Himself:

A poet is as much to say as a maker. And our English name well conformes with the Greeke word . . . Such as (by way of resemblance and reverently) we may say of God; who without any travell to his divine imagination made all the world of nought . . .[5]

So Shakespeare's doting love can be ambivalent: a laughable delusion or an intimation of something truer than the literal world. In *Troilus and Cressida* it is important to the strategy of satire that the pejorative nature of blind love be stressed to the exclusion of its other aspect, but in *A Midsummer Night's Dream*, where the tone is more ambiguous, Shakespeare places the traditional moralisers' attack on Cupid in a context in which it is given double value. This ambivalence is thus imparted to the lovers.

Just as it helps to see the lovers . . . as types and the treatment of romantic love as a variant of a tradition, so it is useful to enquire what – if any – traditional ideas lie behind other characters in the play. The traditional ideas about Theseus, for example, were varied and complex. Medieval commentators saw the classical Theseus as a figure of either the rational or the irrational. As the betrayer of Ariadne and the hasty prosecutor of his son Hippolytus, he was an image of treachery and rashness. As the subduer of revolted nature in the shape of the Minotaur, the Centaurs and the Amazons, and as the ruler of Minerva's city, he embodied reason and temperance.

Medieval commentaries developed the idea of Theseus as man of reason,[6] and the *Moralised Ovid* kept the Ariadne story current. Chaucer drew on these sources, and others, for two quite distinct portraits of Theseus – in 'The Knight's Tale' and in Ariadne's story in *The Legend of Good Women*. Lydgate's *Fall of Princes*, paraphrasing a French prose version of Boccaccio's *De Casibus Virorum Illustrium*, recounts Theseus's battles with the monsters and his trip to the underworld with Perithous to rescue Proserpina. Athens is described as sacred to Minerva 'for ther wisdom and ther sapience' and as the fountain, under Theseus's governance, of 'philosophie' and 'knyhthod'. But fortune turned against Theseus when he believed Phaedra's accusation of Hippolytus and condemned his son to death. This was an error of judgement, a departure from the discretion and prudence necessary in the just prince.

The tradition was so varied that even the same events in Theseus's life could be moralised in opposite ways. After pointing out that Theseus's defeat of the monsters provides 'a fit example of valour and justice for Princes to imitate', Alexander Ross considers his descent to the underworld:

[Theseus] going down to hell to ravish *Proserpina*, where he was bound, and from whence he could not be delivered but by *Hercules*, teaches us that lust and venery have brought many a man to sickness, and deaths door as we say.

And yet by this very act Theseus becomes no less than a type of Christ:

Our blessed Saviour is the true *Theseus*, who was persecuted in his infancie, and in his life-time overcame many monsters, but far more in his death; hee went down to hell, and from thence delivered mankinde. . . .[7]

Shakespeare simplifies the issue by choosing, so to speak, the Theseus of 'The Knight's Tale' and excluding his alter ego in *The Legend of Good Women*. Shakespeare's Theseus is the man of reason and good government – both of self and state. His rash acts, though it is important to the play's strategy that we should be reminded of them, are safely in the past. But just as he makes fancy and doting love ambivalent, so Shakespeare also gives a double meaning to the opposite value, reason, and to Theseus its representative. In Shakespeare's hands the very rationality of Theseus becomes ambivalent. However well it fits him for guiding the affairs of men in the world – of governing a city-state – it restricts his view of romantic love, of poetry, or of anything which is at least partly the product of the imagination. In the terms of the play, the worlds of fancy and reason are opposed; hence the representative of reason misunderstands – or chooses to misunderstand – what he discovers in the course of his hunt in the wood, and he says in Act V that he does not believe the lovers' story.

It may be that Shakespeare took the idea of Theseus's ambivalent rationality from 'The Knight's Tale'. Chaucer seems to want to stress the limits of Theseus's 'reason'. The *sentence* of the famous 'Firste Moevere' speech ('Thanne is it wysdom, as it thynketh me,/To maken vertu of necessitee') is a close translation of Boccaccio's 'E però far della necessitate virtù, quando bisogna, è sapienza . . .' [*Teseida* XII 11]. By 'vertu' Chaucer's Theseus, therefore, probably means fortitude or valour, a stoic value in an argument for stoic patience in the face of adverse fate. This is, however, a negative and rather chilly message, quite distinct from Christian patience, which derives from a transcendent view of God's redeeming providence. One mentions the alternative, Christian response to adversity, because Chaucer – as opposed to Boccaccio – seems to remind the reader of it. The story is being told to an audience of Christian pilgrims (to whose response the reader's attention is directed from time to time), and the Knight draws an explicit comparison between their world and the pagan setting of his story when he describes Arcite's death:

> His spirit chaunged hous and wente ther,
> As I cam nevere, I kan nat tellen wher.
> Therfore I stynte, I nam no divinistre;
> Of soules fynde I nat in this registre . . .   [2809–12]

Chaucer's view of Theseus as the enlightened pagan without grace may have given Shakespeare the clue for an enlightened Theseus without imagination. In any case, the Theseus in *The Two Noble Kinsmen* is a prophet of fortune, not of providence, who closes the door firmly on speculations about things metaphysical:

> O you heavenly Charmers,
> What things you make of us? For what we lacke
> We laugh, for what we have, are sorry still,

> Are children in some kind. Let us be thankefull
> For that which is, and with you leave dispute
> That are above our question.

A similar ambivalence is generated in the way the fairies are
presented, although the process is rather different. Whereas in the
case of 'blind' love Shakespeare took a uniformly pejorative tradition
and made it ambivalent, with the fairies he simply embraced all the
meanings which a tradition held for his contemporary audience. . . .

The problem for the modern critic . . . is not only that people seem
to have attributed to the fairies widely differing moral values, but that
the fairies were not, of course, taken uniformly seriously. We may
assume that the less sophisticated among Shakespeare's audience
retained at least a residual belief in the power of fairies, but what
about the more educated? The *Faerie Queene* is hardly the product of a
man who believed in fairies. . . .

For the ignorant, then, the fairies probably retained some of their
power; for the more sophisticated, they became images for abstract
forces, rather as the pagan gods do in 'The Knight's Tale'.
Shakespeare's fairies elicit the widest possible range of responses from
the audience. . . . He makes them small, as though to suggest a
certain beneficence, but retains much of their potential danger as
well. Oberon and Puck, though capable of restoring order in the
wood, also do their best to disrupt it. When Oberon says to Titania:

> Thou shalt not from this grove
> Till I torment thee for this injury,   [II i 146–7]

and:

> What thou seest when thou dost wake,
> Do it for thy true love take;
> . . .
> Wake when some vile thing is near!   [II ii 33–4, 40]

we do not see him as merely impish or mischievous, but downright
malevolent. . . . Again, although the fairies are small, their power
seems limitless; the argument between Titania and Oberon produces

sympathetic dissension in the cosmos, a most awesome 'progeny of evils' of which they are the 'parents and original' [quotes II i 88–100]. . . . The speech is frightening because it suggests the fairies' wide-ranging influence not only over the elements, but – through control of the elements – over human beings too. The really disturbing thought is not that the fairies can create inclement weather, but that they can literally erase any trace of human order. They are, indeed, supernatural forces quite beyond the control of human beings. They, and not Theseus, finally establish order within the wood, and within the lives of the lovers; they, and not the mortals, close the play. Even at the end when they come to bless the wedding, they remind the audience of their potential malevolence; the blessings they promise are negations of the evils that fairies traditionally brought to weddings [quotes V i 393–404]. . . .

The ambivalence of the fairies can be more sharply illustrated by a slightly closer look at Titania. She is associated with the goddess Diana not only by James VI but by Ovid, who uses 'Titania' as an epithet for Diana in her guise as the sister of the Titan Helios, the sun god [*Metamorphoses* III 173]. Diana represented rather contradictory values: she was the moon goddess, the patroness of virginity and of the hunt but also – possibly through association with Lucina – the goddess of erotic love, of child-birth and of mutability. Shakespeare's 'Diana' embodies both the traditional equivalents: she is the chaste wife of Oberon, but she is also the goddess of child-birth of whose order the Indian woman was a votaress. Shakespeare emphasises her contrary roles by bringing them into conflict in the argument over the Indian boy. The ambivalence of Titania may also explain why the moon, Diana's emblem, stands for chastity when Oberon cancels the love juice – [quotes IV i 72–3] – but stands for mutability and erotic love when Egeus accuses Lysander of having enchanted Hermia [quotes I i 30–2]. . . .

This, then, is what one means by the rather special complexity of 'character' in *A Midsummer Night's Dream*. The people in the play may have been given labels rather than personalities, but their labels are ambivalent in every case. The way in which Shakespeare uses the traditions which he and his audience would share shows this ambivalence to be deliberate: he either widens the implications of an idea, such as that of blind love or Theseus's rationality, or accepts all its ramifications, as with the fairies. The process may differ, but the result is the same. Even Bottom's label, his ass's head, might have meant more than just merriment to the audience; they may well have been reminded of Priapus, by virtue of an old iconographic tradition that linked the emblem of the ass with the erotic god.

This double value of character is crucial to the way we respond to a play in which nothing is quite as simple as it seems at first. Much of the play's ironic pressure consists in the audience's awareness, at any one moment, of a character's contrariety: unless we remember the fairies' potential evil even when they are acting graciously, unless we are aware of the limits of Theseus's reason, unless we remember the potential insights of blind love even when love seems most irrational and dangerous, we miss much of the point of the play.

SOURCE: extract from *Shakespeare: A Midsummer Night's Dream*: Studies in English Literature no. 35 (London, 1968), pp. 20–31.

NOTES

[Reorganised and renumbered from the original – Ed.]

1. 'Mythographus III', II, 18, in G. H. Bode (ed.) *Scriptores rerum Mythicarum latini tres Romae nuper reperti* (Celle, 1834), p. 239 Quoted in Erwin Panofsky, *Studies in Iconology* (New York, 1939), p. 105n. [Editor's note: translated by Stephen Fender.]

2. T. Walleys, *Metamorphosis Ovidina moraliter . . . explanata* (Paris, 1515), Fol. VIII, v. Quoted in Panofsky, p. 106n.

3. Panofsky, p. 110.

4. *An Apology for Poetry* (London, 1595); in G. Gregory Smith (ed.), *Elizabethan Critical Essays* (Oxford, 1904), vol. I, p. 156.

5. *The Arte of English Poesie* (London, 1589), Smith, *op. cit.*, vol. II, p. 3.

6. For a brief account of this tradition in the medieval iconography of Theseus, see D. W. Robertson, Jr., *A Preface to Chaucer* (Princeton, 1962), pp. 260–4.

7. Alexander Ross, *Mystagogus Poeticus or The Muses Interpreter*, (London, 1648), pp. 399–401.

Andrew D. Weiner   Multiformitie Uniforme
(1971)

. . . If, like Bottom's dream, *A Midsummer Night's Dream* has no
bottom, we might well turn for the clue to its inexhaustibility to
Bottom's speech upon awakening from his dream [quotes IV i 203–
11]. . . . The lines of course parody I *Corinthians* ii 9. . . .
Shakespeare, however, was not using this passage merely to give
Bottom an opportunity for parody; rather, he uses the passage – and
the context in which it is found – to point to the theme of the play
[quotes I *Corinthians* ii 7–14, in the 1560 Geneva version]. . . . While
the immediate relevance of much of this passage to the play – such as
the unusually low regard in which reason is held and Duke Theseus's
low opinion of the powers of the imagination to penetrate mysteries –
is clear, the connection between the lovers of the play and the things
'which God hathe prepared for them that loue him' must be
elucidated.

From the play's original occasion, a command performance at
some as yet unidentified (and probably unidentifiable) noble
wedding, the play's action took its shape. Relatively quickly we are
presented with four sets of characters: Theseus and Hippolyta, who
are going to be married; the Athenian lovers, who want to be
married, but, because of Hermia's father and Demetrius's dotage,
cannot be; the rude mechanicals, who are to present a play about two
other lovers who could not be married; and Oberon and Titania, who
are married, but who have broken the bonds of matrimony. Through
these four sets of characters and their interaction, Shakespeare
anatomises various facets of the relationships between men and
women (taking, for a moment, Oberon and Titania as man and
woman) as they progress towards the state of husband and wife or
struggle to remain husband and wife or fail to become husband and
wife.

Shakespeare shows us through Theseus and Hippolyta the union
that there is in marriage by showing us how incomplete the speeches
of either one are without the complement of the other. Through the
young lovers, he shows us how the passionate dotage that seems to be

the usual precursor of love – and as Oberon reminds us, even Theseus had to pass through this stage [II i 77–80] – at the same time that he shows us that it must be transposed into a more constant relationship if it is to endure. In Oberon and Titania we see the disharmony that can grow in marriage if either party fails to fulfill his responsibilities and the harmony that returns when they are reconciled.[1] Finally, in the play that the churls present at the wedding, we see the 'wo and payne' that follows when dotage is allowed to be an end in itself.[2]

Beyond its function as a civilising institution, marriage had still greater significance. As Puttenham tells us, marriage is 'the highest & holiest, of any ceremonie apperteining to man: a match forsooth made for euer and not for a day, a solace provided for youth, a comfort for age, a knot of alliance and amitie indissoluable'.[3] The high repute of marriage, 'the holy bond whereof, the earth hath nothing more beautiful or honest',[4] stems from its origin:

First we haue to consider the beginning and antiquitie of marriage, the place where it was instituted, & who was the author therof, & that in the time of innocency . . . Moreover we must remember, that the heavenly word honored with his presence, & set forth a wedding feast with a miracle, euen the first which he wrought in the world. Can any thing then be found more holy, than that which the holy of holies, the Father & Creator of all things hath established, honored & consecrated with his presence?[5]

It is in this sense that the civil war between Oberon and Titania is the cause of the disorder in nature. Just as Adam and Eve, 'The first original of holy wedlock'[6] brought disorder into nature and caused God to institute the seasons through their sin, which was against the order of marriage as well as the command of God, so too, says Titania,

> this same progeny of evils comes
> From our debate, from our dissension;
> We are their parents and original.   [II i 115–7]

If the created universe is held together by the mutual love of its parts, dissension anywhere along the chain must spread throughout the whole.[7]

The greatest significance of marriage, however, is that it figures forth the love that God has for man. As Henry Smith, perhaps the most popular preacher and author of devotional writings of the Elizabethan period, wrote in *A Preparative to Marriage* (1591): 'We read in Scripture of three marriages of Christ. The first was when Christ and our nature met together. The second is, when Christ and our soul join together. The third is, the union of Christ and his church.'[8] It is in this sense that the noble lovers of the play, by preparing themselves for marriage, are also preparing themselves to receive the things 'which God hathe prepared for them that loue him'. Calvin's commentary on this phrase is instructive:

I had rather to understand symply the graces of God, which are dayly bestowed vppon the faythfull: in these we may always behold the cause: but cannot possibly behold them. The cause is the free goodnesse of God, by which he hath adopted vs into the number of his sonnes. He therefore which will ryghtly consyder of them, shall not consider them as naked: but shall cloth hym with the fatherly loue of God, as with a garment: and shall therefore bee dyrected from temporall giftes to eternall lyfe.[9]

The faithful, of course, are those who have partaken of the second of Christ's marriages. As Smith puts it in a sermon on *Romans* 13, 14 ('Put ye on the Lord Jesus Christ'), which is entitled, 'The Wedding Garment':

This garment Paul hath sent unto you, to go before the king of heaven and earth, a holy garment, a royal garment, an immaculate garment, an everlasting garment; a garment whereof every hem is peace of conscience, every plait is joy in the Holy Ghost, every stitch is the remission of some sin, and saveth him which weareth it. . . . So if we put on Christ, we are clothed with his obedience, whereby our wickedness is covered; we are clothed with his merits, whereby our sins are forgiven; we are clothed with his Spirit, whereby our hearts are mollified, and sanctified and renewed, till we resemble Christ himself.[10]

These are the graces of God which are signified to us through the mystery of marriage.

As a mystery, however, one of 'the deepe things of God', the 'whole doctrine of saluation'[11] cannot be comprehended by the wisdom of man. Bottom's dream is thus 'past the wit of man to say what dream it was', and 'Man is but an ass if he go about to expound this dream'. Calvin says much the same thing in explaining why 'the natural man' cannot understand:

By the natural man, he meaneth not one addicted to gross concupiscences, or to his own sensualitie: but euery man which is endued with the gifts and powers only of nature. The which appeareth by the opposite or contrary: for he compareth the natural man with him which is spirituall. Seeing by this natural man he [*i.e.* the spiritual] is vnderstoode whose mynd is gouerned by the illumination of Gods holy spirite, there is no doubt but that the same [*i.e.* the natural man] signifieth a man left in his natural corruption. For the soule is proper to nature, but the spirit cometh of a supernaturall gifte.[12]

Bottom, the natural man *par excellence* [cf. IV i 1–38], can only marvel in ignorant wonder at what has happened to him, but the audience, swept up by the poet's imagination and responding to the 'most rare vision' which has been implanted in their own, are free to respond in a different manner.

In view of the tradition, current in the Renaissance, that Oberon could stand as 'a delicate figure for grace',[13] it is doubly significant that he untangles the confusion caused by Puck's errors and that he presides over the blessing of the marriage while the house sleeps.[14] Even without this identification, however, the argument holds. Although we may not know (and, according to Calvin, 'cannot possibly behold') the operations of God's grace, we can see its effect in the blessing Oberon bestows at the end of the play.[15]

The leap between occasional play and public theatre play, then, is not a very great one. The noble audience could come away having seen their sovereign complimented, their hosts flattered, and their own worthiness assured. A popular theatre audience could leave the theatre with a strengthened belief in the beneficent powers of poetry (thereby helping them to justify continued attendance at the playhouse) and a new understanding of the significance of marriage. All alike, however, may depart with the hope that, like the 'couples three' of the play,

The blots of Nature's hand
Shall not in their issue stand.

If, as I have suggested, the central thematic interest of *A Midsummer Night's Dream* is the celebration of the mysteries signified by and associated with marriage, there is nonetheless much more going on in the play. The multiplicity of incident, allusion, characterisation, and comment is sufficient to justify any number of essays on the play as Shakespeare's *Defence of Poesie*, or his examination of the power of the imagination, or his condemnation of dotage in love. How, then, does he combine these disparate elements into a unified whole and how are we to perceive the unity in this multiplicity? Puttenham's discussion of the creative process is useful here:

For as the euill and vicious disposition of the braine hinders the sounde iudgement and discourse of man with busie & disordered phantasies, for which cause the Greekes call him *phantasixos* [sc. *phantastikos*;], so is that part being well affected, not onely nothing disorderly or confused with any monstrous imaginations or conceits, but very formall, and in his much multiformitie *vniforme*, that is well proportioned, and so passing cleare, that by it as by a glasse or mirrour, are represented vnto the soule all maner of bewtifull visions, whereby the inuentiue parte of the minde is so much holpen, as without it no man could deuise any new or rare thing.[16]

Just as the poet's imagination, when it is 'well affected', renders the 'bewtifull visions' it sees to the soul and reduces multiformity to unity by enfolding them in form, so the spectator's mind, moved by the visions it in turn sees, proceeds by way of its apprehension of the formal structure of the play to the 'new or rare thing' that the poet had devised. Although each of the elements of the play, taken out of context, may give rise to its own set of visions, those elements are firmly linked together through the structure, which relates our reactions to the parts to our comprehension of the whole.

SOURCE: extracts from ' ''Multiformitie Uniforme'': *A Midsummer Night's Dream*', *ELH*, 38 (1971), pp. 336–49.

NOTES

[Reorganised and renumbered from the original – Ed.]

1. Cf. IV i 80–91; and Sandys, *The Sermons of Edward Sandys*, ed. John Ayre (Cambridge, 1842), p. 329: 'The company and fellowship of marriage

folks, if discretely, lovingly and religiously they perform those needful duties each unto other which God requireth at the hands of both, then no doubt both their estate is blessed of the Lord, and deserveth to be honoured amongst men. But if there want discretion in them, we see what contentions, strifes, and heart-burnings are wont to grow between couples, to the great disquieting of their own minds inwardly, and if things do chance to break out, as such flames commonly do, to the discrediting also of their persons openly in the world.'

2. The story that Bottom and company choose to present at the wedding would be highly inappropriate were it not transformed by their incompetence into a ludicrous farce. The explanation for their choice may lie in the epithets with which Puck delights in describing them: 'a crew of patches, rude mechanicals', 'hempen homespuns'. As Madeleine Doran has shown [in ' "Yet am I inland bred" ', *SQ*, 15 (1964), p. 104], in the 16th century the state that was opposed to the civilised was the rustic, which was defined as 'rude, without courtesy, churlish' – a state in which one would be unlikely to find a knowledge of the qualities necessary in a marriage.

3. Sig. G4^v.

4. Peter de la Primaudaye, *The French Academie*, trans. T. B. (London, 1618), p. 197.

5. La Primaudaye, p. 199.

6. Heinrich Bullinger, *The Christian State of Matrimony*, trans. Myles Coverdale (London, 1575), sig. A7.

7. Cf. Sears Jayne, ed. and trans. 'Ficino's Commentary on Plato's *Symposium*', *University of Missouri Studies*, 19 (1944), pp. 149–52.

8. In *The Works of Henry Smith*, ed. Thomas Smith (Edinburgh, 1866), I, pp. 6–7. On Smith's popularity see Louis B. Wright, *Middle-Class Culture in Elizabethan England* (Ithaca, N.Y., 1958), pp. 284–5.

9. Jean Calvin, *A Commentarie vpon S. Paules Epistles to the Corinthians*, trans. Thomas Timme (London, 1577), sigs. D2–D2^v.

10. *The Works of Henry Smith*, I, pp. 151.

11. Calvin, sig. D3.

12. Calvin, sigs. D4^v–D5.

13. Paul Olson [see excerpt in this selection – Ed.].

14. Those given to allegorising might have wished to see Titania's ultimate reconciliation with Oberon and rejection of Bottom as the soul's movement from the natural to the spiritual.

15. Oberon's blessing parallels that which Spenser begs from the heavens in the penultimate stanza of the *Epithalamion* (1595) . . . [lines 413–23].

16. Sig. D3^v.

Anne Barton   'The Ending'   (1974)

. . . Theseus may speak somewhat slightingly of 'the lunatic, the lover, and the poet', beings 'of imagination all compact' whose fantasies are literally incredible: 'more strange than true' [V i 2 ff.]. The play as a whole takes a far more complicated view of the matter. Theseus himself, for Shakespeare as for Chaucer and Sophocles, is pre-eminently the hero of the daylight world of practicalities, of the active as opposed to the contemplative life. His relationship with Hippolyta in the comedy presents an image of passion steadied by the relative maturity of the people involved. There are ages of love as well as of human life and Theseus and Hippolyta represent summer as opposed to the giddy spring fancies of the couples lost in the wood. Theseus is a wise ruler and a good man, but Shakespeare makes it plain that there are other important areas of human experience with which he is incompetent to deal. When Theseus leads the bridal couples to bed at the end of Act V with the mocking reminder that 'tis almost fairy time' [V i 354] he intends the remark as a last jibe at Hermia and Lysander, Helena and Demetrius: people who, in his estimation, have been led all too easily by darkness and their own fear to suppose a bush a bear [V i 22]. The joke, however, is on Theseus. It is indeed almost fairy time. In fact, Puck, Oberon and Titania have been waiting for this moment in order to take over the palace. For a few nocturnal hours the wood infiltrates the urban world. Even so, years before, a Titania in whom Theseus apparently does not believe led him 'through the glimmering night/From Perigenia, whom he ravished' and made him 'with fair Aegles break his faith,/With Ariadne and Antiopa' [II i 77–80]. The life of the self-appointed critic of imagination and the irrational is permeated by exactly those qualities he is concerned to minimise or reject. Gently, the comedy suggests that while it is certainly possible to mistake a bush for a bear, one may also err as Theseus does by confounding a genuine bear with a bush. The second mistake is, on the whole, more dangerous. . . .

For the theatre audience, granted a perspective wider than the one enjoyed by Theseus and his court, the Pyramus and Thisby story of love thwarted by parents and the enmity of the stars consolidates and in a sense defines the happy ending of *A Midsummer Night's Dream.* It reminds us of the initial dilemma of Hermia and Lysander, and also of how their story might have ended: with blood and deprivation. The heavy rhetoric of the interlude fairly bristles with fate and disaster, introducing into Act V a massing of images of death. The entire action of the play within the play is tragic in intention, although not in execution. Without meaning to do so, Bottom and his associates transform tragedy into farce before our eyes, converting that litany of true love crossed which was rehearsed in the very first scene by Hermia and Lysander to laughter. In doing so, they recapitulate the development of *A Midsummer Night's Dream* as a whole, reenacting its movement from potential calamity to an ending in which quick bright things come not to confusion, as once seemed so inevitable, but to joy. An intelligent director can and should ensure that the on-stage audience demonstrates some awareness of the ground-bass of mortality sounding underneath the hilarity generated by Bottom's performance, that a line like Lysander's 'He is dead, he is nothing' [V i 300-1] is not lost in the merriment. Only the theatre audience however, can capture the full resonance of the Pyramus and Thisby play. . . .

Puck's speech picks up and transforms precisely those ideas of death and destruction distanced through laughter in the Pyramus and Thisby Play [quotes V i 361–72]. . . . All the images here are of sickness, toil, and death. Even the wasted brands, in context suggest the inevitable running down of human life as it approaches the grave.

Once again, Shakespeare has adjusted the balance between art and life, reality and illusion. Puck's hungry lion is something genuinely savage, not at all the 'very gentle beast, and of a good conscience' [V i 223] impersonated by Snug. Even so, his talk of graves and shrouds, drudgery and exhaustion, brings the sense of mortality kept at bay during the Pyramus and Thisby interlude closer, preparing us for the true end of the comedy after so many feints and false conclusions. Puck's speech begins a modulation which will terminate some fifty lines later in direct address to the audience and in a player's request for applause. Actors and spectators alike will be turned out of Athens to face the workaday world. Yet Shakespeare refuses to concede that Theseus was right. In the first place, Puck's account of the terrors of the night is not final. It serves to introduce

Oberon and Titania, the most fantastic characters in the play, and in their hands Puck's night fears turn into benediction and blessing. About the facts of mortality themselves the fairy king and queen can do nothing, even as Titania could do nothing to prevent the death, years before, of the votaress of her order. All they can do is to strengthen the fidelity and trust of the three pairs of lovers, to bless these marriages and to stress the positive side of the night as a time for love and procreation as well as for death and fear. Certainly, the emphasis on the fair, unblemished children to be born is not accidental, something to be explained purely in terms of the possible occasion of the play's first performance. These children summoned up by Oberon extend the comedy into the future, counteracting the artificial finality which always threatens to diminish happy endings. A beginning is made implicit in the final moments of the play, a further and wider circle.

SOURCE: extracts from her Introduction to the play in *The Riverside Shakespeare*, ed. G. Blakemore Evans and others, (Boston, Mass., 1974), pp. 219–20.

Alexander Leggatt   'Organised Disorder'
(1974)

. . . When Titania meets Bottom in the wood near Athens, we see a fairy confronting a mortal, and finding him more wonderful than he finds her. For Titania, Bottom – ass's head and all – is an object of rare grace and beauty; for Bottom, the queen of the fairies is a lady he has just met, who is behaving a bit strangely, but who can be engaged in ordinary, natural conversation [quotes III i 130–40]. . . . Behind the sharply contrasted voices are two utterly different kinds of understanding, and each one comically dislocates the other. Titania's love is addressed to a hearer who uses it simply as the occasion for a bit of cheerful philosophising. And the philosophy, in turn, is wasted on the listener. It is all very well for Bottom to chatter away about reason and love; he has the detachment of the totally immune. But Titania is caught up in the experience of which Bottom is only a detached observer, and, ironically, his cool philosophy only gives her one more reason for adoring him.

But while the essential technique is familiar [from earlier plays], there is a difference in the way it is used. When Speed and Launce commented on the loves of their masters, or when the ladies of France mocked the men who were courting them, we felt that the mockers had (temporarily, at least) a special authority, that they were sharing with the audience a more sophisticated awareness than that of their victims. In the confrontation of different understandings, we felt able to take sides. But in the confrontation of Bottom and Titania, the audience's judgement is delicately suspended between both parties. Each one's assessment of the other is amusingly wrong: Bottom is hardly an object of beauty and grace, nor is plain 'mistress' an adequate form of address for Titania. On reflection, there is something to be said for each of these mistaken views: for all his mortal grossness, Bottom has been touched by magic; and the fairy queen is in the grip of a passion we have already seen affecting mortals, and affecting them in a similar way. Yet this only compounds the joke, for while both have been transformed, shifted from their true natures, both are unaware of being anything but their normal selves. The special, sophisticated awareness of the ladies in *Love's Labour's Lost* made the dislocations of that play critical and satiric. But in *A Midsummer Night's Dream* no character has that kind of awareness: each is locked in his own private understanding, confident, self-enclosed and essentially innocent. The closest analogy, perhaps, is with *The Comedy of Errors*, where one brother thought he was subjected to enchantment, the other appeared to be going mad and only the audience knew the true state of affairs. But there at least the characters knew that something very strange was happening: Bottom and Titania, in a situation more genuinely fantastic than anything in *The Comedy of Errors,* accept it without bewilderment, Titania moving to gratify her love at once, and Bottom accepting his new role with cheerful equanimity. The keynote, again, is innocence.

Bottom and Titania present the play's most striking image, a pairing of disparate beings whose contact only emphasises the difference between them. It looks for a moment as though the barrier between the mortal and immortal worlds has fallen; but on inspection, the barrier proves as secure as ever. Instead of a fusion of worlds we are given a series of neat comic contrasts. And throughout the play, we see four different groups of characters – the lovers, the clowns, the older Athenians and the fairies – each group preoccupied with its own limited problems, and largely unaware of the others. When they make contact, it is usually to emphasise the difference between them. All are to some degree innocent, though . . . the degree of innocence varies. But the play weaves them all together. Each group, so self-absorbed, is seen in a larger context, which provides comic perspective. Each in turn provides a similar context for the others, and if here and there we feel tempted to take sides, we can never do so for very long; for while each group has its own folly, it has its own integrity as well, and its own special, coherent view of life.

We are reminded throughout of the workings of perception, and in particular of the way we depend on perception – special and limited though it may be – for our awareness of the world. When Hermia finds Lysander, who has run away from her, her first words appear to be a digression [quotes III ii 177–82]. . . . The natural question – 'But why unkindly didst thou leave me so?' – is asked only after she has discoursed in general terms on how the senses work. In the clown scenes, there is a recurring joke by which the senses are comically transposed . . .[1] For the most part, however, the general point is absorbed into the particular dramatic situations of the play. The conflict between Hermia and her father, for example, is seen as a difference of perception [quotes I i 56–7]. . . . When Hermia and Egeus look at Lysander, they see two different people, for she sees with the eyes of love, he with the eyes of cantankerous old age, obsessed with its own authority. . . .

The lovers see their experiences in the forest as chaotic; but for the audience the disorder, like the disorder of a Feydeau farce, is neatly organised, giving us pleasure where it gives them pain.[2] When Hermia accuses Demetrius of killing Lysander, the patterned language and the rhymed couplets cool the emotional impact the scene might have had [III ii 43–81]. Over and over, the violence of the ideas is lightened by jingling rhythm and rhyme: 'I'll follow thee, and make a heaven of hell,/To die upon the hand I love so well' [II i 243–4] . . . the manner of the action in itself ensures that the passion is convincing only to the characters. They lash out frantically at each other, but the audience is too far away to share in their feelings. Our detachment is aided by the presence of Puck and Oberon, acting as an on-stage audience and providing a comic perspective. What is serious and painful to the lovers is simply a 'fond pageant' of mortal foolishness to the watchers [III ii 114]. Puck in particular regards the whole affair as a show put on for his amusement (and incidentally if we can remember this in the final scene it adds a level of irony to the lovers' laughter as they watch Pyramus and Thisbe: they too, not so long ago, amused an audience with antics that they thought were serious). The irony is compounded when the lovers indignantly accuse each other of playing games with serious feelings: 'Wink at each other; hold the sweet jest up;/This sport, well carried, shall be chronicled' [III ii 239–40]. Helena's accusation is very close to the truth – except that it should be directed at the audience.

But our feelings are subtly managed here: there are two watchers – Puck, with his delight in chaos, and Oberon, who wishes to bring chaos to an end. We share in both these attitudes. . . .

In his dealings with the lovers in the first scene, Theseus can also be seen as exerting an authority that has no final validity. In preparing to enforce the harsh Athenian law, and urging Hermia to recognise her father's power, he is counselling patience and submission of a kind that he himself finds difficult [quotes I i 3–6]. . . . It seems ironic that as he himself is about to seal an 'everlasting bond of fellowship' [I i 85] he is prepared to allow a loveless match to take place. But to do him credit, he enforces the law with evident reluctance: he tactfully leaves the lovers together, and behind the mask of authority we can detect other feelings. In asking Demetrius and Egeus to go with him, he says 'I have some private schooling for you both' [I i 116], suggesting that he may want to talk them out of the match. And his words to Hippolyta, 'Come, my Hippolyta; what cheer, my love?' [I i 122] suggest a recognition that she too is upset by what is happening. Like the Duke of Ephesus he is trapped by a cruel law 'Which by no means we may extenuate' [I i 120]; and like that other Duke he brushes the law aside with a wave of his hand once the action of the comedy has taken its course: 'Egeus, I will overbear your will' [IV i 178]. It is part of the peculiar logic of comedy that rules which seem rigorously binding in the first act suddenly appear trivial when it is time to end the play. The mere sight of the lovers happily paired has become a force stronger than the law of Athens.

Theseus enforces the law with reluctance; Egeus insists on it with a grim fanaticism that makes him the only unsympathetic figure in the play; and a comparison between the two men helps us to see the value of Theseus's kind of authority. In the scene of the lovers' waking, the rich harmony of Theseus's speech on the hounds establishes an atmosphere in which Egeus's jerky, irritable style is utterly out of place [quotes IV i 153–8]. . . . In the text as normally printed, Egeus does not appear in the last scene; his fussy, sterile concern with his own power is the one kind of mentality the play's final harmony can find no room for. Theseus, on the other hand, is allowed considerable authority in the final scene. For all his limits as a commentator on art and love, he is not to be brushed aside as the representative of a worn-out order. His urbanity, common sense and good temper are necessary ingredients in society, as we see when he attempts to soften the conflict between generations, and when he accepts the lovers' union as a *fait accompli*. Throughout the final scene, Theseus and Hippolyta suggest not only mature love but a general principle of balance: he disbelieves the lovers, but she is more open-minded; conversely, he is the more tolerant with the players. Each corrects the other's excesses, but with tact and affection. They are not the play's final spokesmen, for they have no means of comprehending what goes on in the woods; but their cool wisdom is as necessary to the play's total harmony as the desire of the lovers or the earnest good intentions of the clowns. . . .

Through much of the play the worlds of Theseus and Oberon – rulers, respectively, of the day and the night – are opposing and complementary. While other characters mingle, the two rulers never share the stage. In Theseus's city, order and rationality are temporarily dominant, with suggestions of a period of chaos in the past (and with some laws from the past that still need reforming: Egeus invokes a barbaric 'ancient privilege' [I i 41]). Though the point is not stressed, this is consistent with the familar legends of Theseus. In the fairy kingdom disorder is temporarily dominant: the mutual reproaches of Titania and Oberon suggest that this is hardly a normal state of affairs: 'Why should Titania cross her Oberon?' [II i 119]. But while Shakespeare exploits this kind of contrast all through the play, he can also bring its various worlds together in more intimate and sympathetic contact. In the final scene, with the peace of his own kingdom restored, Oberon uses his blessing to forestall any approaching disorder in the mortal world [quotes

V i 397–400]. . . . The two worlds, though not intermingled, are finally brought to rest side by side.

SOURCE: extracts from *Shakespeare's Comedy of Love* (London, 1974), pp. 89–92, 96–7, 101–3, 105–6.

NOTES

1. This appears to have been a standard comic routine. In *Mucedorus* the clown Mouse declares, 'I can keepe my tongue from picking and stealing, and my handes from lying and slaundring, I warrant you, as wel as euer you had man in all your life' [I iv 128–31] – *The Shakespeare Apocrypha*, ed. C. F. Tucker Brooke (Oxford, 1967). But in *A Midsummer Night's Dream* – as in Costard's 'mistaking words' in *Love's Labour's Lost* [I i 292–4] – the stock device is used to serve the play's special comic vision.

2. There are similar effects in *The Comedy of Errors* and *Love's Labour's Lost*, in which the scenes of most intense confusion – such as Antipholus of Ephesus's vain attempt to break into his own house, and the Russian masque in which the men court the wrong ladies – contain some of the most patterned writing in their respective plays.

Noel Purdon   'The Mythological Psychomachia'
(1974)

. . . Shakespeare appears to have used his Plutarch associatively rather than logically. Lots of the sub-mythology in *A Midsummer Night's Dream* comes directly from the *Life of Theseus*: the nymphs loved by Theseus such as Aegle, Ariadne, Antiope and Perigenia; the battle of the Lapithae; the hunt for the Caledonian boar. But the only gods that appear in this section of Plutarch are Apollo and Venus. There is no Cupid, no Dian, no Moon. The virgin goddess appears instead in the parallel life of Romulus: 'And fearing lest his brother's daughter might have children which one day might thrust him out again, he made her a nun of the goddess Vesta, there to pass her days in virginity, and never to be married.' And the Moon, and the notion of the changing of the moon and the reforming of the almanac, occur four lives later, in the life of the other great Athenian duke, Solon.

Even in Shakespeare's other probable source, Chaucer's *Canterbury Tales*, it is merely stated that Theseus 'weddede the queene Ypolita / With muchel glorie and solempnytee'. The only goddess that appears is the 'goddesse Clemence'. As for the fairies, the King and Queen of Fayerye who quarrel in the garden and comment on the mortals in *The Merchant's Tale*, these are identified by Chaucer with Pluto and Proserpina.

Shakespeare has preferred to change all this, to relate time, space, heroes, fairies, lovers, imagery, all, to the central emblem of the moon. As far as time and space go, it is obvious from the opening that this is a world in which happenings are regulated by the moon. Yet it is completely useless to say 'the world of the play is bathed in a gentle atmosphere of moonlight', as if Shakespeare had nothing better to do with his intellect and his poetry than provide a sort of gigantic whitewash in which to make anything he had to say vague and nursery-like, a gentle heaven for Victorian children.

The calendar speech at the beginning, on the contrary, is an important device for indicating that time in the play is under the control of the moon. Lysander has charmed Hermia by singing at her window at *moonlight*; Theseus and Hippolyta regulate their nuptials by the phases of the moon; Lysander tells Helena that he and Hermia will begin their flight 'when Phoebe doth behold/Her silver visage in the watery glass'. Titania's fairy tells Puck that she travels 'swifter than the moon's sphere'. Quince makes appointments by the moon. Oberon and Titania collide accidentally by moonlight, etc., etc. In its genre and used without pattern, this is merely a *Chronographias*,[1] one of the many rhetorical devices for setting a night-piece.

Yet even in cases like this it gains resonance by the opposition of appropriate images with appropriate intellectual or emotional ideas. Ovid uses the moon-calendar reckoning continually to denote the passage of time in the *Metamorphoses,* particularly in Book VII, where there is a prolonged night-piece involving Medea as a votary of the triple Diana, with a dragon chariot, and the gathering of magical herbs.[2] The opening similarly awaits the coming of the full moon. 'It wanted three nights, that the horns of the moon would be rounded into its full circle, when it would shine, very full, looking down on earth with complete face.'[3]

The world of the play is under the influence of the moon in two other senses. It is the kingdom of *metamorphosis* (the Moon in Lyly's *The Woman in the Moone* boasts 'For know that change is my felicity' [V i 307]), and it is *lunatic*, as Pandora is in the same play when the Moon is in the ascendant. . . . Events that happen in it will be deliberately speeded up like those of farce, and given the structure of unreality, symbolised by Shakespeare in the frame of the dream.

The date of the play, whatever the actual season of the year, is also given a symbolic May-Day setting: a setting in which the homage to a Virgin goddess is ambiguously combined in Elizabethan ritual with the marriage of the May-King and the May-Queen.[4] This sets up in Shakespeare's mind a whole train of images by which love is linked to religion. Lysander calls Hermia 'my surfeit and my *heresy*'; there are several references to the observance of the May morning by lovers; Helena is said to 'dote in *idolatory*' upon Demetrius; the moon will receive *hymns*; the night will be *blest* with carols – climaxing in the *hymenal* delivered by Titania and Oberon.

Most of the fairy scenes operate as a masque, in which the events that actually happen in the rest of the play receive the allegorical and abstract treatment expected from this form. Purcell's librettists later found it easy to remove and assemble them as such.

Shakespeare's handling, though, is especially clever in the way in which it combines action and commentary in an almost imperceptible join, in the riding-over of the fairy plot with the lovers' plot. Because the fairies are delightful, as the sylphs in *The Rape of the Lock* or the Lilliputians in *Gulliver's Travels* are delightful, critics have been led into making a Christmas pantomime of *A Midsummer Night's Dream* as fatal to art as the children's book that has been made of *Gulliver's Travels*. None of Shakespeare's plays has suffered so constantly as this one from the refusal of critics to give it the same kind of attention as a work of art that they would give the others.

As for the spirit mythology, for instance, I would suggest that the fairies are not quite so native, vague and haphazard as is generally supposed.[5] Titania is an avatar of Diana, Puck is linked directly to Cupid, the fairies themselves are devotees of Diana – an idea not found in Shakespeare alone, but part of the general educated Renaissance attitude towards the derivation of native myths from classical ones. Nashe clearly points out the equivalence:

The Robbin-good-fellowes, Elfes, Fairies, Hobgoblins of our latter age, which idolatrous former daies and the fantasticall world of Greece ycleaped *Fawnes, Satyres, Dryades & Hamadryades.*[6]

In this way the Elizabethan spirits are linked with the classical mythology of nymphs, dryads, hamadryads, oreads, naiads and pygmies who come from the Indies. 'Pygmei', the omniscent Batman told his fascinated readers, 'be little men . . . and they dwell in mountaines of *Inde*, and the sea of ocean is nigh to them'.[7] Even the specific association with Diana can be demonstrated to be a Renaissance commonplace. No less a classical scholar and authority on spirits than James I himself writes of 'That fourth kind of spirits quhilk be the gentiles was called Diana and her wandering court, and among us called the Phairie.'[8]

It is this classical tradition that Shakespeare chooses to allude to (after all, he might have as easily called the Queen of Fairy 'Mab' rather than giving her an Ovidian name), and the critic's emphasis might more sensibly be on Shakespeare's theatrical artistry rather than the charms of the Warwickshire woods.

One has only to compare the presence and function of the fairies in this play with their presence in something which does not have a strong pattern of debate or ideas to put across – e.g. Drayton's *Nymphidia* or Greene's *Scottish History of James IV*, where they are an excuse for dances and cuteness – to realise in what way Shakespeare has injected the classical ritual and the moon-emblem with a pattern. And this pattern [is] the psychomachia. . . .

In Shakespeare, this psychomachia is set allusively in *Much Ado About Nothing*, where all the mythology is lightly handled in two delicate echoes in the songs. Benedick's

> The god of love,[9]
> That sits above

is counterparted by Claudio's solemn chant to Diana:

> Pardon, Goddess of the night,
> Those that slew thy virgin knight;
> For the which, with songs of woe,
> Round about her tomb they go.

Midnight, assist our moan,
Help us to sigh and groan,
Heavily, heavily;
Graves, yawn and yield your dead,
Till death be uttered,
Heavily, heavily.

Of course, immediately after this Hero is 'restored'.

The Venus-Diana psychomachia, the ritual battle between lust and chastity that will be resolved in terms of love within marriage, begins already in the imagery of the first scene of *A Midsummer Night's Dream*. In the very first speech, the formal identification of the moon with Diana is prepared for in Hippolyta's use, as a similitude, of one of the goddess's iconological attributes, the silver bow. Even here, however, the moon as chastity is performing a function that is inimical to the full life and expression of the human personality. Theseus and Hippolyta are impatient to consummate their marriage and chafe under the inhibition of the moon [quotes I i 4–6]. . . .

A world in which Diana dominates emotion, and a moon-calendar regulates time, is a world in imbalance, and the establishment of balance is one of the things that the play works towards. Already our expectations that Diana will be overthrown are set up by the frame of Theseus's marriage. He has conquered an Amazon, a virgin warrior queen, always associated by the Elizabethans with militant chastity, and we are now to see her bedded with her full consent. Diana is already losing one votary. But the other possibility, that Diana will triumph, is set savagely before us. If Hermia refuses to obey her father's marriage choice, she will live the stunted and inadequate life of a virgin, a devotee of Diana and the moon. The imagery here creates a pattern of sterility: 'a *barren* sister . . . chanting *faint* hymns to the *cold fruitless* moon'

> Or on Diana's altar to protest
> For aye *austerity* and *single* life.

The condemnation of the way of Diana is unequivocal. Yet the other tradition of the praise of chastity, particularly with a rampant and emblematic virgin on the throne of England, survives. The Pauline doctrine is re-affirmed by Theseus [quotes I i 74–8]. . . .[10]

Shakespeare's point is the ancient one – that enforced chastity is abhorrent to the gods, and he returns to this again and again in the imagery.

Against this dominance of Diana in Athens, only individual lovers can give service to Venus. Hermia swears by the simplicity of Venus's doves. It is marvellous here that Shakespeare's selection of language and attributes gives to Venus all the purity that might have been associated with Diana, and none of the sterility. She places her promise in Cupid's strongest bow, his best arrow, and Dido's funeral pyre.

Yet a dominance of Venereal love is shown to be just as inadequate as the dominance of Diana. Shakespeare expresses this initially in as formal a way as he had previously presented the emblem of the moon for our contemplation, in terms of an iconographical commentary on the figure of Cupid in his attributes of being blind, winged and a boy. In respect of each of these attributes he is shown to be deficient. Once again, Shakespeare has selected attribute and interpretation most carefully to fit his particular need [quotes I i 234–41]. . . . Cupid is painted blind because Love, looking with the mind's eye, lacks judgment, and his wings give him a haste that because of his blindness is liable to be fatal. He is an inconsistent little boy playing at a game, without intelligence or comprehension. It is one of Shakespeare's games with the spectator within this play to invent his own Cupid.

Puck to all intents and purposes *is* Cupid, and plays the role that Cupid would have undertaken in Lyly or one of the court masques. . . . Significantly Shakespeare's is made even more of a blind and haphazard agent than the conventional Cupid, and typically the servant of a master, so that he stands midway between Ariel-Prospero and the Plautine and Lylian master-servant relationship. Shakespeare invites us to speculate on the relationship between his new creation and the older myth on which it is based, as Spenser does in *The Faerie Queene*.

The psychomachia is carried on in a minor key between Puck and the Fairy on their first meeting. Shakespeare deliberately exploits the device of pairs of characters in visual and verbal opposition on the stage, to further the opposition of the themes that are at the centre of his interest. So here Puck fulfils the role of Cupid, and the Fairy that of a Vestal. She serves the Fairy Queen – the associations to an audience that had read Spenser would be unequivocal – and travels swifter than the Moon's sphere. Puck, on the other hand, serves a master, and travels 'swifter than arrow from Tartar's bow'. Yet the world in which the spirits themselves act out the psychomachia that is preoccupying the human characters is clearly, like the city of Athens, under the dominance of Diana. Cupid is at a disadvantage. Time and space (the moon and the woods) are in the hands of Diana, in terms of two of her chief attributes.

This predominance is strengthened by another of Shakespeare's 'Spenserian' creations. We must unequivocally associate Titania with Diana.[11] 'Titania' appears nowhere in English literature before Shakespeare invents her as an avatar of Diana, and the title itself is unquestionable proof that he read Ovid in Latin as well as using Golding's translation, since Golding never uses the name but always a paraphrase such as 'Titan's daughter'. In Ovid it occurs four times, as an epithet of Latona, Pyrrha, Circe and Diana, all of them night-creatures. The most interesting appearance in the *Metamorphoses* is Titania as Diana, and this occurs in Book III in a sequence in which she changes Actaeon into a stag. (One thinks at once of Bottom with the ass's head.) Ovid's verse runs [in Purdon's translation]:

Now while Titania was bathing there in the stream as usual, the grandson of Cadmus, who had for the present abandoned his hunting, wandering with hesitant steps, came to this unknown grove: so were the fates directing him.

[*Ovid. Met.* III 173–6].

She, like the moon, is in ascendance – it is she who controls the Indian boy at the moment, and Oberon who must play beggar; it is she who, like Dian herself, has an 'order' with 'votaresses'; she who reminds Oberon that their neglect of the rituals due to the Moon has resulted in disorder and chaos.

We are at this stage presented with an emblematic catalogue of the Moon as destroyer. The images of sterility already present in Theseus's speeches on Diana are here realised further in images of cold and destruction [quotes II i 103–7]. . . . It is against this pattern of moon-cold-unnatural sterility associated with Diana that Shakespeare now clashes the Cupid pattern in a direct emblem that works in several ways. Since this very complicated icon is a hinge on which both the action and the poetry turn, it may be as well to bring out the magnifying glass in order to look at it.

The elements in the icon[12] are roughly these: in the foreground a promontory with a figure contemplating the sea. In the sea, riding on a dolphin's back, is a mermaid singing, while from the spheres above her, stars are represented as shooting down, attracted by her song. Side by side with this is another icon, which, taken with the other, makes up the pattern and the story. Here a flying Cupid is placed between the moon and the earth, where he has shot an arrow at the heart of a virgin queen. The parabola of the arrow has, however, passed through the sphere of the moon, missed the moon-vestal, and fallen on a flower which it has dyed purple. . . .

If the icon is viewed in terms of the structure we have been examining . . . , it opens up vistas of speculation in terms of the presentation of the Diana-Cupid psychomachia. What in fact both icons represent is the restoration of equilibrium, one through the power of harmony, and one through the counterbalance of strong opposite forces. They form a composite emblem of the sub-pattern of the play. The first icon is one which might have been turned into a *tableau vivant* at any Renaissance pageant. It would be an illustration of the theme 'The Power of Music', and it would operate to suggest the beauty of harmony as a state of being – used as panegyric, it could illustrate the power of a prince, for example, in achieving concord within his realm. . . .

The other icon is much more original – Shakespeare here designs his own *impresa* – and shows an application of this general principle to a specific case. Several elements are set in opposition – earth and moon, hot and cold, fire and water, Cupid and Vestal, Vestal and Flower – and the connecting harmony is achieved by the parabola of the arrow.

Cupid's hot, fiery energy comes into direct conflict with the Moon's cold, watery chastity. Diana protects her vestal Cynthia – and the panegyric reference to Elizabeth seems inescapable. Cupid appears to have been defeated in this first confrontation. The terms of reference of chastity seem to be extremely complimentary [quotes II i 163–4]. . . .

Yet this *is* seen as a unique case – Elizabeth is the only one of her kind, the virgin ʾphoenix, *semper eadem*. Her gentleman poets are prepared in art to celebrate her court as a shrine of vestals, though in fact they tend to speculate rather greasily about her virginity in private, and even to get the vestals pregnant. What is moral for the queen may be dangerous for other men and women.

Diana's apparent victory has been counterbalanced by the creation of a most potent new weapon for the armoury of love, a flower as purple as the ones dyed in Ovid by the amorous blood of Venus and Pyramus; it breeds rampant eroticism, 'love-in-idleness', the kind of blossom that, to the Elizabethans, exploded in Italian courts where youth had nothing to do except play at games of love. If anything, then, this second icon has been the locus of the tipping of the scales in battle. From now on love will rule, yet rashly, energetically, bizarrely.

Now begins a series of comically reversed erotic chases, like the ones in the *Metamorphoses*, deliberately placed on their heads by Shakespeare, and equally deliberately referred to [quotes II i 230–1]. . . . One of the things which Puck, as Cupid armed with juice instead of arrow, must immediately do, is to set the direction of the chase right again [quotes II i 245–6]. . . .

The other pair of lovers reflects the other direction: of movement towards marriage through an observance of the rites of love. This period before their marriage is, however, the most dangerous of all, and they must, like Ferdinand and Miranda, observe a ritual chastity and decorum of behaviour [quotes II ii 62–5]. . . . Their very observance of Diana is the cause of their undoing, since Puck mistakes their discretion for an unnatural lack of affection, and squirts his love-juice around in the best classical tradition of the blind Cupid.

A further monstrosity in the kingdom of love ungoverned by reason and chastity now occurs, as the votaress of Diana, Titania herself, is stricken with lust for what Shakespeare suggests is in fact the same as that part which Alison sticks out of the window to be kissed in the *Miller's Tale*.

Two mythological analogues are combined in this Puck-Bottom-Titania scene:

1. The tale of an over-presumptuous man being given animal attributes; e.g. Actaeon, Midas, etc.

2. The motif of the goddess or queen being punished by being made to fall in love with a mortal or animal; e.g. Venus, Pasiphae, Selene, etc.

Shakespeare's fusion of the two is interestingly paralleled in iconographical experiments of the same kind. Thus we have seventeenth-century chimney pieces showing a reclining Diana embracing a stag, French canvases of Cupid shooting bestial satyrs who remove the clothes of a sleeping Diana, Faenza plates depicting Cupid on a hobby horse firing at a donkey-headed Actaeon, all involving the same sort of play with the basic material of the myth.

In Shakespeare the metamorphosis of the mortal assumes secondary importance to the punishment of the queen. This is Love's terrible humiliation of his rival, and the former devotee of the moon can now quite prettily present that Moon, combined with flower imagery, as an argument *against* chastity:

> The moon, methinks, looks with a watery eye;
> And when she weeps, weeps every little flower,
> Lamenting some enforced chastity.

There is double comedy in this, of course. Whereas it is perfectly true applied to the case of Hermia, it is outrageously ridiculous when applied to Titania's designs on a hairy Bottom.

Unquestionably, erotic love has been allowed too full play. Demetrius compares Hermia to a glimmering Venus, and Oberon, taking the image up, chants [quotes III ii 102–3, 106–7]. . . . Love is running amok, and enjoys the disorder he is causing:

> Cupid is a knavish lad
> Thus to make poor females mad

says Puck, and from his own part exults

> And those things do best please me
> That befall preposterously.

The lovers are in a dark night of ungoverned and misdirected passion – unlike the 'fancy-free' votaress Elizabeth, they are 'fancy-sick'. The spirits that do battle in their souls are, at this stage, of dubious benignity. They are associated with 'night's swift dragons' and they 'run by the triple Hecate's team'. Perhaps they serve a witch goddess. Puck for a moment raises the question of their identification with the 'damned spirits all' that wander the night and flee at dawn [quotes III ii 386–7]. . . . But this is the sort of imagery that the playwright has been reserving for the adherents of the implacably chaste Diana [quotes I i 71, 73]. . . . Oberon makes it instantly clear that these spirits, though they serve a night-goddess, are celebrators of physical love, and of daylight [quotes III ii 388–93]. . . .

This image of Oberon as forester prepares the way for the shift of function that Shakespeare wishes his dominant emblem to have, a shift which he effects simply by selecting the right mythological attributes at the right time. Diana the moon becomes Diana the huntress, who comes with Aurora at dawn to course the glades, bringing light and the music of hounds.

Whereas the other Diana has been of dubious, and often destructive influence, this one is unquestionably a balancer, like the mermaid in the icon. Erotic love can go too far and must be balanced by moderation and chastity. Symbolically, the psychomachia receives the resolution in a final confrontation of the forces of Cupid and the forces of Diana, and Love must yield to a new flower which is characterized by strength and religious sanction [quotes IV i 73–4]. . . . Titania will be saved from a monstrous lust, and Demetrius and Lysander from selecting the wrong mate. Once again, the symbolic restoration of harmony is accompanied by music, which continues into the next scene as 'horns sound within'. Theseus and Hippolyta enter as hunters and as restorers of equilibrium. Their music is an heroic clarion one: 'gallant chiding', 'musical confusion', 'mutual cry', 'sweet thunder'.

Shakespeare is here turning to new account the conventional hunter's entry of the Twelfth Night masque, when the courts round the audience would ring to the baying of eager hounds. With it now he ties up threads of imagery and ideas that have been stretching to this point. In terms of action, it advances the play only slightly, but as an emblematic tableau, it operates as the mermaid did, with splendid poetry and appropriate mythologising. Theseus as hunter Shakespeare knew from Ovid, but he is careful to make Hippolyta as well a huntress of heroic stature, like Atalanta or Diana. This he achieves by associating her poetically with heroes, and by the invention of a mythological scene which she can refer to, as Spenser uses such scenes of reference for his inventions [quotes IV i 111–3]. . . . These royal and heroic hunters operate as marriage-mongers. An observance of Diana is seen to be valuable only as part of the pre-marriage ritual. On seeing the lovers, Theseus observes complacently: 'No doubt, they rose up early to observe / The rite of May.'

Chastity is here, however, celebrated only in its aspect of being a delightful state for two people who are about to mate. The youth and virgins of the city who are mystically celebrating May-Day are indulging in a rite where chastity and fertility are strangely mixed. His next remark is more urbane and to the point:

> Good morrow, friends. Saint Valentine is past;
> Begin these wood-birds but to couple now?

The proper harmony and pairing has been achieved, and Theseus makes it clear that the two pairs of lovers must now be wedded with him in the temple. . . .

It remains now only for the marriages to be celebrated and then solemnised magically with pagan ritual. The fairies return to fulfil the function that Shakespeare has already prepared for them in the earlier part of the play. Both sets of mythological creatures have come from the Indies to be present at the marriage of mortals whom they love. We have already had Oberon presented to us as a pastoral lover piping to a shepherdess, and Titania as a protectress of Theseus in his amorous adventures. But Shakespeare emphasises that even in this role of marriage sanctifiers, the spirits are devotees of Diana [quotes V i 373–6]. . . .

Yet with no incongruity they perform the function that the more conventional masque of Hymen operates for the marriages of *As You Like It*. The adaptation of pagan and mythological ritual to Renaissance marriage is complete.

The house in which the newly-weds have retired to consummate their marriages, a mirror of the house where the play was probably performed first, is 'hallow'd', and the fairies 'bless' the bride-beds. Instead of the holy water of the Christian tradition, there is 'field dew consecrate', and as Diana in another of her curious aspects is the goddess of childbirth[13] (since she assisted her mother Latona in delivery of Apollo), these her votaries enact in mime and dance a ritual to safeguard the fruit of the marriages from deformity [quotes V i 401–4]. . . .

Ben Jonson in the *Hymenaei* uses a similar pattern of mythological marriage ceremonies, but characteristically draws much of his material from contemporary and scholarly works of archaeology. Shakespeare, on the other hand, takes a single mythic tradition, presents it in terms of emblems and tableaux, and uses it as a commentary on the action rather than as a development of the action itself.

It remains to consider the function of the play-within-the-play to all this. What I wish to advance and illustrate is the notion that Shakespeare, both in the events and language of 'Pyramus and Thisbe', is parodying the play that he himself is writing. If we read the play-scene as his comment on his own efforts to provide a marriage-play, it has double point.

The author and producers of this play are as obsessed as he is with moonlight setting. They will rehearse by moonlight, they have set the action of their play by moonlight, they will perform it by moonlight, and they end up by trying to represent Moonlight on the stage, a mistake in taste that Shakespeare is careful to avoid in his own play – Diana and the Moon exist only in terms of the imagery; there is no theophany. Quince, on the other hand, is preoccupied, as Lyly was, with the theatrical problem of bringing 'moonlight into a chamber'. Lyly, in one of his later plays, actually sets up on the stage a kind of giant astrolabe, in which the planets, including most importantly the Moon, move through a cycle of ascendancy and dominate the action on the stage before them. They exist as visible emblems which the spectators have to contemplate, hieratically enthroned in an upper gallery, and loaded with iconographical attributes (which Lyly probably took from Hyginus) to make them readily identfiable.[14] This is what Quince proposes to do – he will have an actor represent an icon [quotes III i 53–5]. . . .

Already Shakespeare indicates that he thinks this is liable to be poor dramatic practice – the notion illustrated will indeed be 'disfigured' rather than 'presented'. The whole statement is a criticism of the theatrical technique of using actors as mythologised icons, a technique [which] Lyly had established in elaborately formal masques, and which Jonson was to continue to the point of apoplexy, as mythological figure after figure trudged in, loaded with such a quantity of symbolic ironmongery that the actors must have found it difficult to move, let alone deliver their lines. Shakespeare himself prefers to use the poetry, not the actor, to represent the icon, and this is another concomitant of his moving away from overt mythological representation to an embodiment of it *within* the form.

Lyly presents on the stage characters who *are* Cynthia and Tellus, who *are* the Moon and the Earth, and who enact their battle for the heart of Endymion. Shakespeare puts the same thing in a miniature icon in Oberon's speech about the promontory. Lyly depicts Cupid and Diana doing direct battle on the stage as personages. Shakespeare expresses the battle in terms of their attributes, such as the bud and the flower, used as images in the poetry.

Shakespeare doubly despises the sort of devices Quince is using, since Quince and his actors don't know how to use them well. . . . One of his favourite ways of scoring off this amateur company of tradesmen is to indicate that they don't know their mythology, and that this is surely fatal in the context of a mythological play. When Phoebus becomes Phibbus, Hercules Ercles, Ninus is a Ninny, Thisbe Thisny, Leander Limander, Hero Helen, Cephalus Shafalus and Procris Procrus, any other attempt at Lylian devices is liable to prove a mess.[15] Shakespeare allows the courtly spectators to mirror his amusement, and they are particularly outspoken on Quince's unfortunate decision to have an icon of Moonshine.

The Moon that plays such an important off-stage role in Shakespeare's own comedy is here made uneasy quivering flesh in the person of a stage-struck tailor. Quince has tried to construct a hieroglyph according to the best Renaissance conventions, but the courtiers are quick to pounce on the result. The actor carries a lantern and a dog, two of the attributes of Diana as moon and huntress, and found as such in Cartari and many other iconographies, but he has forgotten the horns which were the third attribute that would have completed the emblems. This provides an opportunity for Demetrius to deliver himself of one of those jokes on cuckoldry which the Elizabethans seem never to have found tiresome. Theseus then suggests that perhaps he doesn't represent the crescent moon at all, but a full moon, since he is moonfaced and the horns are therefore sunk in the rest of the circle [quotes V i 235–6]. . . .

But both spectators are, of course, also pointing out that the icon itself is ludicrously wrong, and when the actor stammers on to insist that he is the man in the moon, Theseus roars out that he should then be sitting inside the lantern. 'This is the greatest error of all the rest', he observes technically. Pyramus commits a still further lapse of decorum in attributing golden glittering streams to the moon.

Hippolyta now in game treats the Moon stomping round on the stage before them as if it were the same moon of chaste Diana that the lovers had fidgeted under in Act I [quotes V i 244–5]. . . . But with infinite courtesy she then applauds the moon's brilliant acting [quotes V i 259–60] . . . a statement that only increases the comedy and reduces the status of the icon still further. Shakespeare is parodying not only the man-in-the-moon devices that appeared in the Whitehall shows, complete with thorns, or in City triumphs of the sort that Middleton was later to write, but the whole vogue for theatrical hieroglyphs used in a clumsy way. . . .

Shakespeare's point is the shrewd one that it is a dangerous practice for a poet to set in motion as a dramatic being something that has its real substance as poetic metaphor, and he clinches it tellingly, when, in response to Pyramus's death-cry 'Moon, take thy flight', the Moon obediently shambles off the stage, to the complete collapse of the spectators. . . .

Shakespeare uses Quince's play for a manifoldly rich effect. Firstly, it is a statement of what he hopes he has avoided, and he presents it as such for the spectator's contemplation. Secondly, it operates dramatically as a kind of emotional release for the lovers, who having passed through the dream and the ritual, can now sit back and watch squeaking Cleopatras boy their passion, as they are shown what might have happened in their love entanglements if something had gone wrong. Yet the whole suggestion of possible tragedy in love has to be immediately discounted. They fall gratefully on the play and tear it apart until the comedy laughs out of existence any notion that lovers could really die. All the monsters and beasts that Hermia and Helena had feared in the woods finally appear as the Lion and pursue their stage counterpart. But what a Lion! Quince proudly believes that he has created a 'grisly beast' but Theseus immediately recognises that it is a 'very gentle beast, and of a good conscience'. Quince's fear that illusion will be taken as reality[16] is made more ridiculous by the fact that he tries to merge the two. . . . . .

The court prologue to *Sapho and Phao* insists that 'whatsoever we

present . . . our intent was at this time to move inward delight; . . .
we all . . . entreat that Your Highness imagine yourself to be in a
deep dream, that in your rising Your Majesty vouchsafe but to say,
And so you awaked' – a statement which Shakespeare has parodied in
Quince's prologue but used seriously for his own Epilogue . . .

As in Lyly, the mistake that sets the action in motion is not the
Plautine one of identity but of emotional direction, and the device
used to carry the emotion is the psychomachia. But in Shakespeare,
the whole relationship between appearance and reality, reason and
imagination, play and truth is probed much more deeply, particularly
by the introduction of a marriage-play which parodies the main
action.

SOURCE: extracts from *The Words of Mercury: Shakespeare and English
Mythography of the Renaissance,* Institut für Englische Sprache und
Litteratur, Universität Salzburg (Salzburg, 1974), pp. 178–82,
184–7, 187–9, 189–90, 190–1, 199–200, 201, 202, 203

NOTES

[Reorganised and renumbered, from the original – Ed.]

1. Hilariously parodied in Armado's letter in *Love's Labour's Lost* [I i 233–
68]. 'The time when: About the sixth hour; when beasts most graze, birds
best peck, and men sit down to that nourishment which is called supper: so
much for the time when.' Slightly more serious exemplars are provided in
Aphthonius (London, 1575), p.192 v, and Erasmus, *Copia* (London, 1573)
p.126 v.
2. Surely the impetus for many of Shakespeare's ideas for *MND* comes
from this book of his favourite reading, and from the next book, which bears
the association: Theseus, Diana and hunting.
3. Ovid, *Metamorphoses,* Book VII.
4. Doubly appropriate if the play was indeed for Southampton's
mother, whose re-marriage to Sir Thomas Heneage took place on May 2.
The ritualisation of the May holyday extended throughout Elizabethan
social amusements, from plays to folklore. Elizabeth herself as an old woman
rode to the woods on May day and came home with the May boughs, and
the young people of Warwick spent the evening in the woods together rush
gathering.
5. Most criticism of the fairy motif really is a case of Hobgoblin run away
with the garland of Apollo. For a sensible discussion of a subject that
otherwise borders on the tweely silly, see K.M. Briggs, *The Anatomy of Puck*
(London, 1959).

6. T. Nashe, *Terrors of the Night* (1594), ed. R.B. McKerrow (Oxford, 1956), vol. I, p. 347.

7. S. Batman, *Uppon Bartholome* (London, 1582), p. 377.

8. James I, *Daemonologie* (Edinburgh, 1597), p. 73.

9. Note that in figuring Love for the Psychomachia, the Elizabethans, finding something innocent and pleasing in the image of the boy over the carnal image of his mother, usually chose Cupid rather than Venus. . . . .

10. An equivocal compliment. One surmises that Shakespeare was writing for an occasion when Elizabeth would not actually be in the audience.

11. Even Fuseli, illustrating *MND* two centuries later, was careful to give Titania a hat with the crescent moon and stars of Cartari and the myth manuals. Olson [see excerpt in this selection – Ed.] connects Shakespeare's Titania, on Lylian precedents, with the earth and flower goddesses Prosperpina and Tellus. While it is true that Titania's pregnant vestal is indulgently described in a way that has very little to do with Diana's (or Elizabeth's!) treatment of their Callistos, the play hinges on this duality of the two functions of the moon-goddess as restrainer and midwife. . . .

12. I am not simply punning or adopting a recent fashion in speaking of this as an *icon,* incidentally. In terms of Renaissance rhetoric this is exactly what it is, and it functions more as a picture than most other rhetorical devices. See Puttenham, *Eng. Poesie III*, XIX (Arber p. 250); E.K.'s Glosse to February in Spenser's *Shepheardes Calender*; Blount's *Glossographie.*

13. Recorded as such by Sandys, *Metamorphoses* (1632), p.100: '*Iuno* in *Lucian* upbraides *Latona* that her daughter *Diana* . . . being so farre from a Virgin as continually conversant at the labours of women, like a publike midwife.'

14. Shakespeare had already used (and simultaneously mocked) this iconographical and mythographical method of composing scenes and staging.

> All hid, all hid, an old infant play,
> Like a deimi-god here sit I in the sky,

says Biron, in the complicated IV iii of *Lovers Labours Lost.*

15. This seems an obvious glance at Golding's habit of rendering classical proper names by Elizabethan slang diminutives, with often disastrous results for the dignity of the myth. Thisb, Augi, Penthy, Orphey and Morph sound like a fine collection of bussing English yokels.

16. Note: that did occur! In 1594 the Scots King and Queen had to be entertained by a blackamoor instead of a lion, in case they were frightened, and at one of Elizabeth's water pageants involving Arion on a dolphin's back, the actor tore off his mask and said he was really 'honest Henry Golding'.

PART THREE

Twentieth-Century Productions

Robert Speaight   Granville-Barker's Production in 1914   (1973)

Barker's third Shakespearian revival was *A Midsummer Night's Dream*, which opened on 6 February 1914. This would always be remembered for its 'ormolu fairies, looking as if they had been detached from some fantastic, bristling old clock'.[1] Barker admitted that the fairies were the 'producer's test', and that it was partly in the hope of passing that test that he had decided to produce the play at all. They could not sound too beautiful, but 'how should they look? –. They must not be too startling. But one wishes people were not so easily startled. I won't have them dowdy. They mustn't warp your imagination – stepping too boldly between Shakespeare's spirit and yours. It is a difficult problem.' It certainly was, and not even Barker himself was sure that he had solved it. Theseus's palace was . . . in black and silver, its definition contrasting sharply with the diaphanous wood. . . . There was all of Robin Goodfellow in Donald Calthrop's Puck, a creature of medieval folk-lore brewing his mischief from the vantage point of some Gothic cathedral, and none the less closely bound to the earth for his ability to survey it. Mendelssohn was discarded in favour of Cecil Sharp; and the rustics, with Nigel Playfair in command as Bottom, had to rely upon Shakespeare for their laughs. The production aroused furious controversy. To some it was too metallic to the eye and insufficiently melodious to the ear. One or two people suspected that those gilded sprites were the creations of a man who did not believe in fairies. . . .

. . . the productions at the Savoy have become a part of theatrical legend, influencing all who saw them, and many who did not. They were a crucial break-through in the evolution of Shakespeare on the stage. Perhaps, as Bridges-Adams has suggested,[2] the challenge to tradition was too strident. . . .

SOURCE: extracts from *Shakespeare on the Stage: An Illustrated History of Shakespearian Performance* (London, 1973) p. 144.

NOTES

1. Desmond MacCarthy, *Theatre* (London, 1964), p. 53.
2. 'The Lost Leader' from *A Bridges-Adams Letter Book* (London, 1972).

George C. D. Odell   Granville-Barker in America
(1915)

On February 16, 1915, Mr Granville Barker presented at Wallack's Theatre his London production of Shakespeare's play. . . . Let it be said that it represented the last cry in the new stage decoration.

Mr Barker divided his play into three parts; the first dealing with the 'mortals' – Theseus and his court, Quince and the other hardhanded men; the second running together without break the fairy episodes and the affairs of the perplexed lovers, as well as the transformation of Bottom; the third showing all the characters again in the palace of Theseus. The stage was built out far into the auditorium, and the huge apron thus formed was used as a place for posing actors in effective groups; the part behind the proscenium was used for whatever 'decoration' was required. The fairy scene was built up to a round mound in the middle of the stage, and covered with bright green velvet carpet. Just above the mound was suspended a large terra-cotta wreath of flowers that would have been the envy of a German pastry cook, and from it depended a veil of white gauze, lighted within by vari-colored electric bulbs, hanging at irregular lengths. At the back and sides of the stage fluttered curtains of chintz or silk, designed to suggest forest branches. Like forest branches they waved vigorously in the breeze, so that one felt disposed to ask some one to shut the windows of heaven in order that the trees might not blow out so violently into Titania's bower (the gauze canopy aforesaid). The scene of Theseus's palace in the last act, however, was a very solidly-built affair, with steps and many heavy columns of black and silver, and with a door at the back letting in much red light. It was evidently quite Egyptian in its mass and design. The other changes of scene were indicated by curtains that waved, to the loss of all illusion. The first, Theseus's palace, was of white silk, with conventional gold design. The Quince curtains were of salmon pink silk, with steel-blue masses supposed to represent the roofs of the city. There was another curtain of electric blue, heavily spangled with silver stars and moon. This was all supposed to be very much more artistic than the kind of thing Augustin Daly aimed at, and far more suggestive. It was thought to be full of illusion. Of course, it was not. Any one who has imagination can get the poetic illusion by seeing these things acted on a bare stage or on a stage hung with curtains or with just a conventional unchanged setting, such as Mr Ben Greet has used. No human being, however, can be expected to be anything but worried and annoyed by pink silk curtains that are supposed to be the roofs of houses, or green silk curtains that are supposed to be forest trees; especially when they blow and stream out in the gales of the stage. . . .

Perhaps no feature of this 'show' awakened more discussion than Mr Barker's fairies. From head to foot they were differentiated by a coat of bronze paint, that made them look precisely like something you might buy to set up in the corner of the parlor; their dresses exactly corresponded. These fairies clanked as they walked. Viewed just as decoration, without regard to time, place or sense, they were very pretty; groups of them were novel and interesting. Their dancing under and around Titania's gauze bower was really a pleasing sight. By the aid of their bronze you could tell at a glance whether any person in the play was a fairy or a mortal, and as Mr Barker evidently had no faith in Shakespeare or the imagination of the audience, this was an advantage. Let it be admitted, then, that in his way he solved the problem of making the fairies seem different. He also gave the part of Oberon and Puck to men, for which I thank him; I hope the silly custom of the Nineteenth Century, in this regard, has been broken forever.

With the time-saving device of the curtains Mr Barker was able to give the play entire. The verse was delivered at a rapid pace. None of it was spoken well. . . . And when one grew weary of trying to understand what Puck was saying, he could find solace in wondering why the sprite was not gilded like the other fairies but made to look like a toy Loge in the Rheingold, flaring, flaming hair and all. I hope this is not indicative of what will happen when stage setting ceases to be scenery, and becomes only decoration.

SOURCE: extract from Odell's 1915 review, reprinted in his *Shakespeare from Betterton to Irving* (New York, 1920; reprinted 1966), vol. II, pp. 467–8.

Harcourt Williams   Music for the Old Vic Production of 1929–30   (1949)

[At the Old Vic in 1929–30] we made a Jacobean masque of it inspired by Inigo Jones, and Paul Smyth our designer painted a glorious wood with a sky of silver. I threw Mendelssohn overboard, and used the arrangement of English country airs put together by Cecil Sharp for the Granville-Barker production in 1914 at the Savoy. This caused no end of a sensation . . . and letters of protest rained upon me. . . . One letter, I remember, complained that the writer had been used to telling her friends that when she took them to see *A Midsummer Night's Dream*, she took them to an opera as well as a play – on the principle of two treats for the price of one, I suppose! . . .

Let me confess at once that I do not like Mendelssohn's incidental music . . – that is, when it is played as such. I think I may have had too much of it in the Benson company, especially as in those days the 'Spring Song' and 'The Bees' Wedding' were added to the score, not to mention T. S. Cooke's 'Over Hill, Over Dale', sung by the first fairy. Worst of all Oberon's exquisite speech, 'I know a bank where the wild thyme blows', was sung to C. E. Horn's music by two well-developed fairies obviously of the female sex. Oh, those muslin-clad fairies from the bottom of the garden and the suburban dancing school! One has to sacrifice, I am willing to admit, the entrance music of the Clowns with its ass's bray, but the Wedding March is too redolent of confetti and old satin slippers to adorn a sixteeth-century masque.

However, when [Tyrone] Guthrie revived the play in 1937 at Christmas time, with decor by Oliver Messel, and the fairies were straight out of an early Victorian ballet and of the Mendelssohn period, then the music was delightful, as indeed was the whole production. [Robert] Helpmann as Oberon, looking like some strange, sinister stag-beetle, was indeed a spirit of another sort. His speech and his movement, as one would expect, were beautiful. Vivien Leigh as his consort looked like one of those delicious coloured prints of the period.[1]

SOURCE: extracts from *Old Vic Saga* (London, 1949), pp. 84, 157.

EDITOR'S NOTE

1. The photograph of Guthrie's production reproduced by Harcourt Williams shows Demetrius and Lysander, in their quarrel scene, holding their swords in the manner of early Victorian 'Penny Plain – Tuppence Coloured' prints.

Robert Speaight   The Actors' Workshop Production of 1966   (1973)

. . . the Actors' Workshop production of *A Midsummer Night's Dream* in San Francisco [in 1966] was inspired – disastrously – by Jan Kott, for whom that particular dream is an erotic nightmare. The set and costumes were designed by the pop artist, Jim Dine. Music by Mendelssohn and Mahler came from a jukebox; Hippolyta appeared in a cage; a light bulb flashed on and off in Demetrius' codpiece;[1] and Helena was played by a man six feet four inches tall.

SOURCE: extract from *Shakespeare on the Stage, An Illustrated History of Shakespearian Performance* (1973), p. 240.

EDITOR'S NOTE

1. Stephen Fender (see excerpt in Part Two above) comments: 'It might have surprised the fourth forms, but it came closer to the truth of the play than the sort of production which causes words like "delightful" and "enchanting" to spring to the lips of the critics.' (*Op. cit.,* p. 13).

Benedict Nightingale (1970)   Brook's Perverse Dream

Only a humourless man could have staged this. There are also times when one feels that only a cynical one could be in control. . . . Does the verse limp, the acting labour? Very well, put the speaker on a swing or stilts, make him scramble up ladders or wrestle with his betrothed on the ground, let him deliver his lines as if they are a pop-song, or, if they're meant to be sung already, sob them like a raga. All this happens in Brook's perverse dream, and more.

. . . The oddity of it is that Brook's controversial friend and influence, Professor Kott, is never more persuasive than when he condemns the sentimentality with which the *Dream* has been swaddled since Mendelssohn and before: in no other Shakespeare play (he suggests) is 'eroticism expressed so brutally'. The effect of Brook's interpretation is to sentimentalise it once again, and in a new, more insidious way. His manic decoration has deprived it of suffering, fear, horror, and, apart from one moment, when Bottom's phallus is crudely mimed by the fairies, even of lust.

SOURCE: extracts from a review in the *New Statesman* (4 September 1970).

John Russell Brown   'A Machine for Acting In': Peter Brook's Production of 1970   (1974)

Sally Jacob's set for Peter Brook's production . . . (1970) took the [Royal Shakespeare] company style still further [than in previous productions]. Her innovations were to make the acting space smaller, insetting a three-sided white box so that around it and above it there was an area in which music could be played, stage tricks set in motion, and actors be seen to prepare, or to watch and react to their fellows in the play itself. The stage properties and representations of bushes and trees were still less realistic: trapezes, wooden stilts, coiled wires, two plain oblong white doorways of equal size and spacing, black metal ladders down the front at either side of the stage, a black handrail round the top. This was a machine for acting in. A white light remained almost unchanged throughout the play, whether in Athens or wood, by night or day. Actors were again exposed in sharpest outline, and this effect was accentuated by costumes of simple cut, many of them in white and one or two sharp colours. The lack of realistic or atmospheric illusion, together with the obvious inventiveness of the stage-business and the new antics of the performers, were a constant challenge to the audience. Never could they imagine that they had strayed into a slice of life, nor even into an enlarged, simplified and more essential version of aspects of real life. The ingenious, theatrical construction had to be taken – or rejected – as a transformation of life. Not surprisingly Meyerhold was quoted in the printed programme:

There is a fourth *creator* in addition to the author, the director and the actor – namely, the spectator . . . from the friction between the actor's creativity and the spectator's imagination, a clear flame is kindled.

By creating a kind of clean, stark gymnasium or circus for the setting of this production, the director and designer ignored many of the words of the text, especially the ambiguous, gentle and homely words in which the play abounds.

SOURCE: extract from *Free Shakespeare* (London, 1974), pp. 27–8.

Sally Jacobs   Designing Peter Brook's Production of 1970   (1974)

. . . Peter wanted to investigate all the *ideas* of the play, such as the variations on the theme of love, with a group of actors – always inter-relating so that they could play each other's parts – in a very small, very intimate acting area. So the story would remain clear. It wouldn't be blown up into a big production number, with fogs, forests, and Athens, and all of that pretense. We would just keep it very, very simple and make it *a presentation of actors performing a play*. In doing 'The Dream' that way, we could let it be surprising, inconsistent, the source material always being the text rather than a 'scheme'. . . .

The white space gave us a sense of distance, but at the same time it was very intimate. Actors could speak very quietly, if they wanted to. Acoustically, it worked quite well, especially on the large Stratford stage, where voices can get lost. But acoustics was not the major concern. Mainly, it was to create an intimate acting area, which would nevertheless give us a place where the rest of the actors who were not in the scene could surround the action and continue to watch it. So that's how the top gallery came about. You see, the actors are never uninvolved. The tension never lets up. They're *there*. Both on and off-stage – or gallery – areas can be seen. One is aware of the actors' presences whether they are on-stage in a scene or off-stage watching. They can come and go freely. And, when not in a scene, they can interact in the same way the audience does. That creates a further 'surround' for the action.

We were also absolutely certain that to be able to get that beautiful shock of catching your breath, we couldn't produce the magic in the way that it had always been produced. That the familiar would kill the magic. There's no such thing as the Magic Flower. We've already seen it too many times on stage. It's not magic: we know it's only a prop. So what to replace such objects with? To find the right device, to bring back the gasp of joy, of pleasure? It had to be the *right* thing, to delight and still suggest what it was supposed to be. We remembered the spinning plates from the Chinese Circus – the whirling plate on the stick works very well for the Flower. Before you know it, there's that humming sound and the spinning dish. I still get a very nice feeling from that which no prop flower would ever give me.

It's the same with the trees in the forest. I knew that when they went into the forest, the white space would have to be broken *vertically*, both to change the look of the space from the previous scene and to suggest the forest. I found the coiled wires did this for us, without having to bring in trees – which would have been very boring. While you can look through the coiled wires, they still represent obstructions we can all understand.

Somewhat malign in their movement, with the fairies controlling them? Yes, that's right. But once you have a device like that, you can use it various ways to develop the drama. But originally the coils of wire were just to have some place for the characters to *go*. When you're in a forest, you may have to have something to hide behind, at one time or another. So the coils of wire were there to divide up the space. When they were first used, the actors holding the fishpoles attached to them discovered they could be made to do things, too. . . .

The wires are useful not just for hiding, but also for protecting sleeping characters. . . . In this play, you have two sleeping couples, plus Titania and Bottom asleep at various times. . . . There just wasn't room for the scenes and all the sleepers in that area, unless some part could be set off in some way. And where, for instance, can you have Oberon and Puck do their asides, commenting on the action?

Then I realised we were not using the *vertical space*. Why not have people hanging above the action? Coming in and going out from above? Why always exit at the sides? Now the simplest way to go up and down is to use the flies, the counter-weight system. So out of that idea came the trapeze bars, which are the most practical things to hang on to. And when Titania goes to sleep, she's also lifted up out of the way, but she's still in sight. So it's really a use of both vertical and horizontal space. *That* was the idea; not to use circus devices as such. It was a practical solution to the problem. The circus idea was something people talked about after they'd seen the production; it wasn't the inspiration . . .

The biggest problem was Bottom's ass's head. Originally we

thought this was the one traditional thing we couldn't avoid. There's no way of stylising it. There's no way of doing a 'token' ass's head. We thought we'd have to face up to it. So we did. We made a very elaborate pair of ears which were going to pop out of Bottom's head when he scratched it. He'd scratch one side and zzt! Then he'd scratch the other – zzzzzt! Out they'd come. We had this huge machine that was going to fit inside his cap, with the two ears on springs, controlled by buttons. It took ages to work it all out.

By the time we finished, David Waller was going the most marvelous things with his face. With his body. He *was* an ass. You didn't want to cover up his face. You didn't want to take away from what he was doing by adding furry ears. One day at rehearsal, I saw him with his funny little black rubber nose and funny cap. And that was it! He'd done it himself. We did give him some points to put on his ears – as a token – and with the little nose, it worked! And the fairies strapped some heavy wooden clogs to his feet, to make him even more clumsy and grotesque and to give him height. . . .

Snug's Lion's head mask? There again, that wasn't really designed, as such. It was Barry Stanton's idea, I think. He said, as he was supposed to be a cabinet-maker, wouldn't he start off with a cabinet as a basis for his lion's head? So we had a box with a lion's features on it, but the face is actually two doors which open so you can see Snug's face inside. . . .

SOURCE: extracts from 'Designing the Dream – From Tantras to Tunics', in *Peter Brook's [1970] Production of William Shakespeare's 'A Midsummer Night's Dream' for the Royal Shakespeare Company:* The Complete and Authorised Acting Edition (Stratford-upon-Avon, 1974, and Chicago, 1974), pp. 46–9, 51.

SELECT BIBLIOGRAPHY

EDITIONS

All the editions listed here include introductions to the play, and some also
give an outline of its stage history.

Harold F. Brooks (ed.), New Arden edition (London, 1979).
Wolfgang Clemen (ed.), Signet Shakespeare (New York, 1963).
Madeleine Doran (ed.), Pelican Shakespeare (Baltimore, 1959).
G. Blakemore Evans and others (eds.), The Riverside Shakespeare (Boston,
1974).
Horace Howard Furness (ed.), New Variorum edition (New York, 1895,
rep. 1963)
Stanley Wells (ed.), New Penguin Shakespeare (Harmondsworth, 1967).

BOOKS

Those books from which extracts have been reprinted above are
recommended. Publishing details can be found at the end of each extract. In
addition to the books and articles quoted in the Introduction, the following
studies in this and the next section will be valuable for further study.

Ralph Berry, *Shakespeare's Comedies: Explorations in Form* (Princeton, 1972).
Katherine M. Briggs, *The Anatomy of Puck: An Examination of Fairy Beliefs
among Shakespeare's Contemporaries and Successors* (London, 1959).
John Russell Brown, *Shakespeare and His Comedies* (London, 1957, 1962).
James L. Calderwood, *Shakespearean Metadrama* (Minneapolis, 1971).
Jackson I. Cope, *The Theater and the Dream: From Metaphor to Form in
Renaissance Drama* (Baltimore and London, 1973).
Franklin Murray Dickey, *Not Wisely But Too Well* (San Marino, Calif.,
1957), esp. Ch. 4.
Bertrand Evans, *Shakespeare's Comedies* (London, 1960, 1967).
A. C. Hamilton, *The Early Shakespeare* (San Marino, Calif., 1967).
Peter G. Phialas, *Shakespeare's Romantic Comedies* (Chapel Hill, N.C., 1966).
Leo Salingar, *Shakespeare and the Traditions of Comedy* (Cambridge, 1974).

Derek A. Traversi, *An Approach to Shakespeare,* 3rd edn revised and enlarged (London, 1968).
Roger Warren, 'A Midsummer Night's Dream': Text and Performance (London and Basingstoke, 1983).

ARTICLES

Georges A. Bonnard, 'Shakespeare's Purpose in *A Midsummer Night's Dream*', *Shakespeare Jahrbuch,* 92 (1956), pp. 268–79.
Peter F. Fisher, 'The Argument of *A Midsummer Night's Dream*', *Shakespeare Quarterly,* VIII (1957), pp. 307–310.
Ronald F. Miller, '*A Midsummer Night's Dream*: The Fairies, Bottom, and the Mystery of Things', *Shakespeare Quarterly,* XXVI (1975), pp. 254–68.
Kenneth Muir, 'Pyramus and Thisbe: A Study in Shakespeare's Method', *Shakespeare Quarterly,* V (1954), pp. 141–53.
J. W. Robinson, 'Palpable Hot Ice: Dramatic Burlesque in *A Midsummer Night's Dream*', *Studies in Philology,* 61 (1964), pp. 192–204.
Paul N. Siegel, '*A Midsummer Night's Dream* and the Wedding Guests', *Shakespeare Quarterly,* IV (1953), 139–44.

NOTES ON CONTRIBUTORS

PART ONE

BJØRNSTJERNE BJØRNSON (1832–1910): Norwegian novelist, dramatist and theatre manager.

G. K. CHESTERTON (1874–1936): essayist, novelist, poet and critic.

SAMUEL TAYLOR COLERIDGE (1772–1834): poet, critic, and one of the leaders of the Romantic movement in England.

BENEDETTO CROCE (1866–1952): Italian philosopher and literary critic.

JOHN DOWNES (c. 1640–1710): the prompter to D'Avenant's company for more than forty years.

JOHN DRYDEN (1631–1700): Poet Laureate, dramatist and pioneer of formal literary criticism in England.

GEORG GOTTFRIED GERVINUS (1805–1871): German historian and critic, Professor at the University of Heidelberg.

HARLEY GRANVILLE BARKER – later GRANVILLE-BARKER (1877–1946): actor, director, dramatist and analyst of Shakespeare. He was responsible for establishing Shaw as a popular playwright, for outlining (in 1904) a plan for a national theatre, and for revolutionising the production of Shakespeare.

HENRY HALLAM (1777–1859): historian and man of letters.

JAMES ORCHARD HALLIWELL-PHILLIPPS (1820–93): scholar famous for his *Outlines of the Life of Shakespeare* (1881, and reprinted).

WILLIAM HAZLITT (1778–1830): critic, essayist and political writer.

SAMUEL JOHNSON (1709–84): poet, lexicographer, critic, moralist, and one of the first editors of Shakespeare: the greatest English writer of the eighteenth century.

RICHARD LEVERIDGE (c. 1670–1758): bass singer and composer.

HENRY MORLEY (1822–94): Professor of English at University College, London, from 1865. He was influential in the development of English as an academic study, in the publication of cheap editions of the English classics, and in adult education.

WILHELM OECHELHÄUSER (1820–1902): businessman, industrialist and politician; principal founder of the German Shakespeare Society (1864). He published expurgated stage-adaptations of the plays (27 volumes, 1870–78), a collection of Introductions to the plays (1885), and *Shakespeareana* (1894).

SAMUEL PEPYS (1633–1703): diarist. At one time Clerk of the Acts, later Surveyor-General of the Victualling Office, and from 1673 Secretary to the Commissioners of the Admiralty. He was also a J.P., Member of Parliament, and President of the Royal Society.

SIR ARTHUR QUILLER-COUCH (1863–1944): critic, novelist, short-story writer, and the first King Edward VII Professor of English Literature in the University of Cambridge. Subsequently co-editor of 'The New Shakespeare'.

EDWARD SHARPHAM (1576–1608): dramatist.

GEORGE BERNARD SHAW (1856–1950): Irish dramatist, controversialist, critic and wit.

FRANK SIDGWICK (1879–1939): best known for editing several collections of ballads, *Early English Lyrics* (with E. K. Chambers), *Everyman, Tom Brown's Schooldays, The Poetry of George Wither*, and for writing poems and a novel of his own.

ENID WELSFORD (1892 – 1981): formerly Fellow of Newnham College, Cambridge, and University Lecturer in English; author of *The Court Masque* (1927) and *The Fool, His Social and Literary History* (1935).

H. WOELFFEL: unknown apart from the essay excerpted herein.

PARTS TWO AND THREE

CESAR L. BARBER: Professor of English at the State University of New York, Buffalo: author of *Shakespeare's Festive Comedy*, one of the most influential of modern studies, and of works on Marlowe and Milton.

ANNE BARTON (formerly Anne Righter): Professor of English Literature in the University of Cambridge since 1984. Her publications include *Shakespeare and the Idea of the Play,* the New Penguin edition of *The Tempest,* editorial contributions to *The Riverside Shakespeare,* and a study of *The Way of the World.*

JOHN RUSSELL BROWN: formerly Professor of English, University of Sussex; in 1982 he was appointed first Director of the new Drama Center, University of New York at Stony Brook. His many publications on Shakespeare include *Free Shakespeare, Shakespeare's Dramatic Style,* and *Discovering Shakespeare: A New Guide to the Plays.*

ROBERT W. DENT: Professor of English in the University of California, Los Angeles; author of *John Webster's Borrowing.* From 1959 to 1965 he was Bibliographer of the Shakespeare Society of America.

STEPHEN FENDER: Professor of American Studies, University of Sussex.

G. K. HUNTER: Professor of English, Yale University, and Honorary Professor of the University of Warwick. His publications include studies of Lyly, Webster, Peele, two works on Shakespeare's late comedies, and *Othello.* He is 'English' editor of the *Modern Language Review.*

SALLY JACOBS: designer of sets and costumes for many productions in Britain and the United States, several for the Royal Shakespeare Company. Since 1970 she has been Lecturer in Theater Design, Californian Institute of the Arts, Los Angeles.

FRANK KERMODE: King Edward VII Professor of English Literature, University of Cambridge, 1974–82. His publications include *Romantic Image, John Donne, The Sense of an Ending, Continuities, Shakespeare, Spenser, Donne,* and *Renaissance Essays.*

G. WILSON KNIGHT: Emeritus Professor of English Literature, University of Leeds, famous for several books on the interpretation of Shakespeare: (*The Wheel of Fire, The Imperial Theme, The Shakespearian Tempest, The Crown of Life, The Mutual Flame, The Sovereign Flower*) as well as for books on Milton, Pope, Byron, Ibsen, John Cowper Powys, and British Drama.

JAN KOTT: poet, dramatist, critic and Professor of Literature at the University of Warsaw. *Shakespeare Our Contemporary* has had a strong influence on several recent productions of the plays.

MINOR WHITE LATHAM (1881–1968). Nine years before *The Elizabethan Fairies,* Dr. Latham published *A Course in Dramatic Composition* (also with Columbia University Press).

ALEXANDER LEGGATT: Associate Professor of English at University College, University of Toronto.

BENEDICT NIGHTINGALE: Drama critic of *The Guardian*, later of the *New Statesman* and *Harper's Bazaar and Queen*.

GEORGE C. D. ODELL (1866–1949): at the time of his death Professor Emeritus of Dramatic Literature at Columbia University, famous for his *Annals of the New York Stage* (15 volumes) and *Shakespeare from Betterton to Irving*.

PAUL A. OLSON: Foundation Professor of English and Director of the Tri-University Project, University of Nebraska.

NOEL PURDON: formerly teaching at Cambridge and Bristol Universities, he is currently Senior Lecturer in Drama, Flinders University, South Australia.

WILLIAM ROSSKY: Professor of English, Temple University, Philadelphia, author of articles on William Faulkner and Mark Twain.

ERNEST SCHANZER (died 1976): he taught Literature at the universities of Toronto, Liverpool and Munich. His publications include *Shakespeare's Appian* and *The Problem Plays of Shakespeare*.

ROBERT SPEAIGHT: actor, director, lecturer and author of four novels, biographies of Thomas à Becket, Hilaire Belloc, and William Poel, critical works on Shakespeare and George Eliot, and theatre history.

ANDREW D. WEINER: Associate Professor of English, University of Wisconsin. Author of *Sir Philip Sidney and the Politics of Protestantism,* and articles on Sir Thomas More, Sidney, Spenser, and Milton.

HARCOURT WILLIAMS (1880–1957): actor, producer at the Old Vic, 1929–33.

DAVID P. YOUNG: Assistant Professor of English, Oberlin College, Ohio. Author of *The Heart's Forest: A Study of Shakespeare's Pastoral Plays*, and *Sweating It Out* (poems).

INDEX